Manso

Garcas

COLOMBIA   YE

ECUADOR

PERU

BRAZIL

AMAZON

BOLIVIA

CORUMBÁ   (STORY AREA)

PARAGUAY

PACIFIC

CHILE

ARGENTINA

URUGUAY

ATLANTIC

The
MATTO
GROSSO
of
BRAZIL

TIGRERO!

TIGRERO!

by SASHA SIEMEL

PRENTICE-HALL - New York

First Printing.... October, 1953
Second Printing.. October, 1953
Third Printing... October, 1953
Fourth Printing.November, 1953

Library of Congress Catalog Card No. 53-9629

Printed in the United States of America

Acknowledgment

All my life I have been a man of action rather than words; and it is not easy for me to put action into words. I wish to render my grateful thanks to those who have helped me, including many members of The Adventurers Club of New York and the Explorers Club; and in particular, I wish to acknowledge with sincere appreciation the help of Theon Wright, Past-President of The Adventurers Club, who has assisted me in the assembling and the preparation of this material and in the editing of the book.

S. S.

Foreword

Sasha Siemel is unique, not only as a hunter but as a man.
He is unique as a hunter because he is the only living white
man who has fought fierce jungle jaguars with a spear. When
it is realized that these jaguars—or *tigres*, as they are called in
the Matto Grosso of Brazil—weigh twice as much as an average man, and can disembowel an ox with a single sweep of
their razor-sharp claws, the feat becomes rather startling.

His uniqueness as a man lies, I think, on an entirely
different foundation, although somewhat interrelated with his
talents as a hunter. I first met this white hunter of the Matto
Grosso about twenty years ago. He was sitting on the edge of
a bed in a New York hotel room, explaining for my edification
how he killed *tigres* with a spear.

I had been asked to do a story on the "Tiger Man" from
the Brazilian jungles, and I remember wondering whether this
was an advance pitch for a circus act. Sasha Siemel looked
more like a professor of ornithology just back from a bird-
banding expedition than a tiger-fighter. He was of medium
height, less than six feet tall, and weighing perhaps a hundred
and eighty pounds. He wore a full beard, which gave his rather
gentle countenance a Christ-like appearance.

Just to get the conversation started, I asked him why he
used a spear instead of a gun to hunt *tigres*. His reply was
more startling than his appearance.

"It is safer," he said. "Particularly in high marsh grass."

If a man with a gun misses his first shot, he explained,
he seldom gets another shot at the *tigre*, which moves with
extraordinary agility. If it leaps in the direction of the hunter,
it will probably rip through him with one cut of its claws. If
it turns in another direction, it will usually be lost in the grass
before he can fire again. On the other hand, a hunter with a
spear can continue to fight as long as he can stand up.

I mention this because it reflects something of Sasha Siemel, the man. The reason is logical, and entirely accurate— except that few men have the personal fortitude to stand up to a charging *tigre*. Sasha Siemel is one of those few.

In later years, during evenings at The Adventurers Club of New York (which, incidentally, awarded its "Adventurers Medal" to Sasha Siemel) I began to know this strange, quiet man and to understand his unique character. He had spent more than thirty years in the jungles of Brazil; and yet he told stories of hair-raising experiences in a soft-voiced, mild-mannered way that made them seem almost routine. And perhaps they were, to Sasha.

Many men of an adventurous nature unfortunately are also exhibitionists. They sally forth into the wilderness, risking their lives for trophies—such as the heads of animals, or even of humans—which they can haul back to civilization as visible evidence to support their bragging among their friends.

Sasha Siemel is not of this kind. He has been a lone hunter, who has lived and fought alone. Oddly enough, about the only real fear he has ever experienced has been the fear of dying alone. A sudden twisted foot, or a fatal error of judgment deep in the jungle with only his dogs and the vultures as witnesses, and Sasha Siemel might have been only a small rack of nameless bones, forgotten in the wilderness.

One of the truest tributes to Sasha Siemel was paid by a fellow-hunter, who had been with him in the Matto Grosso.

"What I admire most about this man," he later told friends, "is not that he can spear a jaguar. As he says, the Indians can do that. But he never refused a challenge; and he was willing to match himself against any living creature—man or animal. This is the high road to adventure."

Theon Wright

Chapter 1

I first heard of Joaquim Guató from my friend Dom
Carlos Roderigues, the one-eyed thief-taker of Passo Fundo
who had spent many years in the Matto Grosso. "Joaquim
is an old man now," Dom Carlos told me. "Most of the time
he sleeps in his hut, drunk with *cachaça*. But he is able to go
into the jungle alone even at his age, and kill the *tigre* with
his spear. This is something that no white man, as far as I
know, has ever done; and if you learn to do it you will quench
your thirst for outdoing all mankind!"

The old man chuckled, and wiped his mouth with the
back of his hand. For a few seconds he stared at me with
his single glittering eye, as if he were enjoying a secret bit of
humor.

I had come down to Dom Carlos' place in the early
evening, while the sun still made a sea of blood over the
shaggy tablelands of western Rio Grande do Sul. Beyond
this glowing rim of earth, a thousand miles inland, stretched
the dark, forbidding plateau of the Matto Grosso, a land of
treacherous forests and swamps and the shadows of death;
but at the moment I was not thinking of the "Green Hell"
of Brazil or its Indian hunters. I had come to ask Dom Carlos
how I should act to avoid killing a man.

Dom Carlos was in a way the unofficial sheriff of Passo
Fundo, but I had come to see him not because of his con-
nection with the law, such as it was, but because he was my
friend and a man of kind and humane judgment. He lived
in a low-roofed house on the outskirts of town, set back in a
small grove of *lapacho* trees and surrounded by a mud-walled

yard filled with green trees and flowers. He was sitting alone in the *patio* of his house, squatting on a stool and scratching his hunting dog, when I walked into the yard. His lean, leathery face crinkled in a good-natured smile, and he waved a crooked stick he used for a cane. The reflected shadows of the setting sun made a reddish halo of his bristling white hair.

As soon as I sat down and explained the reason for my visit, he launched into a general discourse having little to do with my problem.

"In Brazil we have a philosophy," he said, staring at me with his solitary eye (the other having been gouged out by a bandit who did not live to brag about the affair). "We never interfere unnecessarily in the affairs of another. Never provoke a quarrel. If you are attacked or insulted—" he leaned over and scratched the ears of his dog, which looked up appreciatively, "kill your enemy, just as you would kill Lobo here if he attacked you. Whoever attacks or insults you is diseased."

He looked affectionately at the subject of this morbid illustration, and Lobo returned the gaze with docile admiration and a couple of thumps of his tail.

"Mind you," Dom Carlos continued, pressing into my knee a finger like a gnarled twig, "if you should kill Favelle, Lobo and I would follow you and, God being willing, I would add your ears to my string."

The reference to the ears was not without point. Dom Carlos was a professional thief-taker—an occupation peculiar to that wild region where there was little written law and no one to enforce such laws as were written. His business was catching thieves and murderers, for which he was paid privately by the victim or, in the case of a murder, by interested relatives. He had the finest collection of ears in the Rio Grande do Sul—all cut from the heads of bandits he had overtaken. The ears had been dried in the sun, and were of every size, shape and color; and he had hung them on a string over his door as testimony that wrongdoers seldom eluded him.

"Then your advice," I said, "is to avoid Favelle?"

"Not at all," he said. "You must do what your will and

your conscience dictate. If you should have to kill him—" he shrugged his thin, straight shoulders and spread his hands, "I would have to track you because his friends would pay me to do that. Without my services, there would be no law in this part of the Rio Grande do Sul."

This Favelle was a thin, pallid little French-Brazilian, with a small man's dislike for anyone bigger than himself. I had no particular wish to kill him, or even harm him; but he had developed a hatred of my brother Ernst and myself that bordered on madness. It was one of those small feuds, built on trivial things, which can fill a man's mind.

"I cannot very well avoid the little weasel, since we work at the same place," I said. "And I do not intend to run from him."

"No, you will not dodge him," Dom Carlos said. "And Lobo and I will have the nasty job of trailing our friends and bringing back their ears." He grinned at me, his lone eye full of understanding. "You are cursed with a thirst for the impossible, Senhor Siemel. You cannot pass a challenge. Perhaps it would be best for you to go immediately into the Matto Grosso, as you and your brother have planned . . . There you will find many things to challenge you, including animals as well as men."

It was at this point that he told me of Joaquim Guató.

"There is an old Indian whom you probably can find on the Rio São Laurenço. I will give you directions for finding him when you go there. His name is Joaquim and he is known by the surname Guató, from the tribe to which he belongs. He is a great *tigrero*, and he knows the art of killing the *tigre* with a spear."

The *tigre* is the South American jaguar. I had heard of these Indian spear-hunters, and I knew that for the most part they do not hunt alone, but in packs. When they trap an animal in high grass or in a tree, they attack with spears. There were rare stories of lone hunters, known as *tigreros*, who went into the jungle alone on the trail of marauding *tigres* who kill not only cattle but humans; but there was some doubt as to whether any of these hunters really existed, and I knew of no one who actually had seen them hunt.

"You will find in this Joaquim Guató a man who knows the jungle," Dom Carlos went on, still scratching his dog. "He knows it as a wife knows her husband. The singing waters of the stream, the whisper of the marshes . . . even the trees talk to him. He has killed thirty-five *tigres* singlehanded, with his spear. He knows by the moisture on the rim of an animal's footprint how many hours have elapsed since it passed by. He can tell by the way the jungle cat switches its tail exactly what it intends to do—whether it will charge or slink away.

"In the jungle," he said, warming perceptibly to his subject, "an animal is often quite as good as a man, and sometimes better. Only the most cunning hunters survive, because even your gun is of little use if you do not understand the hidden meanings of things. I myself am handy with a weapon —" he made a swooping movement with his free right hand, and it came up with his .44 pistol in the palm, the barrel angled carelessly at the ground. This was a trick he had learned from a visitor from Texas, and he was childishly proud of the accomplishment. "But I would scarcely trust my life to my ability with a gun. You are quite strong, my young friend— which is why Favelle dislikes you—but some full-grown *tigres* are more than nine feet in length and weigh up to four hundred pounds. Their claws can slash open your chest with a single stroke. They are a great deal stronger than you and more deadly. For instance, you are quite willing to be fair in your judgment when it comes to killing Favelle or not killing him. You would not kill him unnecessarily. Yet this *tigre* has no such fine sense of fairness. It would kill you without hesitation, and perhaps eat you as well. This judicial quality is a mistake on your part, for which you might easily pay with your life. I think perhaps the best thing for you and your brother to do would be to go into the great jungle, and find my friend, Joaquim Guató. He will show you some things that are not yet written in the books of civilized man."

The old man stopped scratching the dog's neck and sat staring at me in silence with his one gleaming eye, the useless one contracting in an exaggerated squint, as if to give his good eye the advantage of uninterrupted vision. I had noted this muscular mannerism before; it meant that Dom Carlos was about to divest himself of a profound judgment.

He resumed scratching Lobo's neck.

"Quite a few years ago, when I was a young man, I had the opportunity of watching Joaquim Guató destroy a *tigre*. It was necessary from my point of view that he kill the beast, because I was flat on the ground with a twisted foot and would have been the next morsel on the *tigre's* menu. I was then a rider for a great ranch east of the Xarayes marshes, lying midway between the Rio Araguaya and the Upper Paraguay. This country is the wildest you will find anywhere, and the big spotted cats roam along the fringes of the jungle, destroying hundreds of cattle each year.

"Joaquim and I had gone out with two dogs before dawn to track a *tigre* that had been especially troublesome. Shortly after it was light one of the dogs picked up the spoor on the edge of a small lagoon. It was a big one, weighing perhaps three hundred and fifty pounds from the size and depth of the track. It was only an hour or so ahead, and seemed to be moving in a leisurely way. It was noon, however, before the dogs had the fellow cornered on a small, circular island, surrounded by a dark mire of rotten water and mud, with only a few tufts of grass and broken boughs showing above the treacherous surface. We were afoot—having left our horses at the edge of the marsh. I was carrying my rifle, and Joaquim, who was approaching the little island ahead of me, was carrying only his heavy spear. The staff of this weapon was about six feet long, with a two-foot iron blade fixed to the end.

"Joaquim made a sweeping movement of his hand, as if to warn me to stay back. However, I was anxious to get a shot at the cat. The exhaustion of hours of riding through the marsh trails had dropped from me as quickly as a fever passes. In the excitement of bringing the big cat to bay, I had no sense of caution. I began to run off to the right of Joaquim. An instant later my foot caught on a hidden vine and I sprawled full-length in the mud. My gun went down with me and I found myself sucking foul marsh water into my lungs. I was half buried in the slime, but managed to push my way forward to a rise of land a few feet ahead. By the time I had pulled myself out of the mire, I was able also to understand my situation. I had lost my gun and had no other weapon. The *tigre*, which had been crouching at the foot of a huge fig tree, rising straight up from the island, had now moved forward a few feet and was observing me with apparent curiosity. The dogs were clamoring at the edge of the island, barking insanely, and the cat was flicking his tail back and forth in a slow arc, and now and then reaching out with a quick slap at one of the dogs, much as it might bat at a mosquito. I tried to climb to my feet to look for my gun when I felt a stab of pain in my foot. I realized with a spasm of the most ghastly fear that I could not rise. My ankle was either broken or twisted.

"At this point I tried to call out to Joaquim, but I was so choked with water and mud—and perhaps my throat was so paralyzed with fear—that I could hardly make a noise. I lay face forward, looking at the *tigre*. Then I saw Joaquim, a few feet beyond the *tigre*. He had gained the island while I was splashing and clawing toward the small hummock where I lay. However, even in my dazed and terrified state of mind, I realized that if he diverted the beast, he would have almost no chance of retreat backwards into the swamp. I lifted my hand and tried to shout, probably making no more than a gurgle which was hardly audible in the din of the dogs' yapping.

"Joaquim, holding his spear in his left hand, reached down with his right hand and seemed to have grabbed a fistful of mud and grass. He threw this at the *tigre* and hit him squarely in the face.

"If you ever wish to see outraged dignity, raised to such a maddened pitch that it becomes awesome, just toss a handful of mud into the face of a *tigre*, my son. The beast turned, and from where I lay, I could see the red glow of its fiery throat. The sunlight, slanting through the branches of the fig tree, lighted the black spots on the brown hide, and it

providing Favelle also did not force the issue. If he did . . . I would not dodge a meeting.

The old man's face wreathed in a generous smile.

"Probably you will kill him," he said. "But go with God!"

I left him squatting on his stool, petting his dog. The dim radiance of a lantern, which he had hung over the door, cast a glow upon the aura of his bristling hair, giving him the appearance of a gnome.

As I walked homeward along the road lighted only by the cavern of stars, it struck me that nothing actually had been solved . . . but somehow Dom Carlos had added to my understanding. The feud with Favelle diminished in importance, and in its place I found myself thinking of a mysterious country lying beyond the rim of the northern hills. As I headed up the road toward the little one-room shack where Ernst and I lived, I worked out plans in my mind as to how we could wind up our affairs quickly and start for the diamond fields. The fire of interest that Ernst had stirred in my mind the night I arrived in Passo Fundo had been reawakened by the old thief-taker's words.

Somewhere, deep in the lands beyond the Uruguay and the Paraná, there was an old man, wrinkled and brown as an autumn leaf, perhaps stretched asleep on a dirty mat in his hut of thatched acuri leaves, drunk with Brazilian rum. In the morning he would arise and set off alone into the jungle, armed with a spear . . . I had the notion I might find this old Indian hunter, and go into the jungle with him.

Chapter 2

Ernst was sitting on the edge of his cot when I shoved open the door of our shack. It was a small place, built of mud packed against interlaced sticks, with the usual thatched roof; and behind was a lean-to which we used for a tool shed. Ernst was clicking the mechanism of a Smith & Wesson .44 pistol, squinting through the barrel.

He laid aside the gun as I entered the room.

"What did the old man have to say?" he asked. "Did you explain that I shall kill Favelle at the first opportunity?"

He scowled slightly, and resumed working on the gun. Ernst was heavily built, with a great breadth of shoulders, but shorter by two inches than I. His blond beard and curly hair gave him an air of recklessness. At first I did not speak, taking time to throw off my coat. I had learned to gauge my brother's moods by his eyes; and at this moment they were bright with reckless impatience.

Although Ernst was older than I, I think I realized then that it was I who must bear the responsibility of a decision. I believe it was more because of Ernst—his quick, irresolute temper and uncertain moods—that Dom Carlos was urging us, in his oblique way, to leave Passo Fundo. The old man liked us both, but Ernst was more of a source of anxiety to him.

This would be the third time in two years that I would be closing the doors behind me. The first time was on a cold, rainy day when I landed at Pôrto Alegre, on the southern tip of Brazil, and headed into the wilderness along a road that finally brought me to Passo Fundo. I had a letter in the pocket of my greatcoat to a German settler in Rio Grande do Sul, with whom I hoped to find work; and I also had the vague notion that I would find Ernst somewhere in the inland regions of Brazil. Three years before I had left my brother in a construction camp in southern Argentina.

My thoughts on that day were not about Ernst, however; nor about the German settler. I was thinking, hopelessly and miserably, of Elsa. I remember stopping for a moment on a rise of land, where the road curved over a hill leaving Pôrto Alegre behind; and I looked back, like Lot's wife, at the shabby cluster of shacks and a few warehouses on the dock. The little freighter that brought me up from Buenos Aires, docking the night before, lay against the jetty, barely visible in the rain. I thought bitterly that the cold mist, blotting out the ship and the headlands behind Pôrto Alegre, was also blotting out the world behind me.

This was only a few days after I had left Buenos Aires because I thought that was the only way I could remove the torment I had created in the lives of Elsa, whom I loved, and her husband Hans, who was my best friend. At first I had thought of shooting myself; but at twenty-four there is a great resistance to death. So, instead of putting a bullet through my head, I took a freighter up the coast, intending to travel into Brazil's inland wilderness.

For many days I made my way into the interior, hardly thinking of what I intended to do. I found the farm of the German settler, to whom I had a letter attesting that Alexander Siemel was honest and hard-working, with some skill in mechanics; but the broken fences and the little cluster of weary-looking huts seemed so dismal and uninviting that I did not even stop, but continued to a little village beyond.

This place was more wretched, if possible, than the farm; and one night at the local "hotel," with its population of bugs and vermin, cured me of wanting to become a resident. I continued my journey inland, stopping at farms where I often earned enough mending tools and machines to pay for my food in the towns; and in this way I finally arrived at the farm of a Polish family, engaged in the building of a new government road into Passo Fundo. The old Polish farmer, whose name was Ladislaus, was quite friendly toward me, and during the weeks I stayed there he talked of the virtue of taking up government land and becoming a farmer.

The man's wife had somehow wormed out of me the story of my love for Elsa; and perhaps they felt it was the healing salve for all wounds of the soul to work with the soil. At any rate, I obtained a grant of some two hundred hectares of land; and with the encouragement of the old man, I tried to farm.

Ten months of back-breaking and wholly unrewarding effort convinced me that I was not a farmer by instinct. Meanwhile, a letter from home brought the news that Ernst was still in the Matto Grosso; and so I sold my land and headed for the nearest town, which was Passo Fundo. This was the second time I had turned my back on life behind me; but this time I had a plan. I hoped to earn enough money in town as a mechanic to travel to the Matto Grosso and find Ernst.

On the outskirts of the town, of perhaps two thousand people, I came upon a German engineer, pacing among crates of machinery in a small construction yard. A dead cigar was clamped between his teeth, and he was chewing furiously upon this. I asked him if there was work for a mechanic, and gave him my name.

"Siemel, eh?" He spit out part of the chewed cigar. "No, there is no work in this damned place—they have sent only half the machinery!" He glowered at me, as if I were in some way responsible. "What name did you say?"

"Siemel," I repeated. "Alexander Siemel."

"Siemel, eh?" He grunted and spat again. "Yah—there is another fellow by that name in town. A big ox of a man, with a yellow beard. He asked for work, too—but I think maybe he is too sick to work."

"It must be Ernst—my brother!" I exclaimed. "Did you say he was sick?"

The German nodded.

"Sick or lazy—I don't know which." He pointed down

the road. "His place is down the road, but you'll probably find him in the *cantina*."

I hastened down the road, following his directions, and found the shack. No one was home, but a neighbor directed me to the *cantina* in town, on the *plaza*, where he said Senhor Siemel might be found.

I left my haversack at a small "hotel"—a square, flat-roofed building that looked more like a high-walled jail than a place for paying guests. The front door hung askew, due to a bad hinge. I had found a thin little man with a sallow face and a pair of spectacles poised on his sharp nose, sitting behind a counter in the small lobby. He gave me directions for finding the *cantina*. As I approached the place, I could hear singing and a few shrill shouts. I went up to the door and pushed it open. Noise and smoke filled the room, and for several seconds I looked around, trying to pick out Ernst among the patrons. For no particular reason I found myself looking at a sharp-faced little man who was sitting at a table, facing the door and staring at me with nasty, insolent eyes.

Then I saw Ernst. He was sitting at the same table, his face turned partly away. My brother was singing a Russian ballad and hammering rhythmically on the table with a bottle. Apparently he was attracted by the gaze of the little man at the table because he turned and looked at me. For a few seconds his brows contracted in a frown. Then his blue eyes lighted with recognition, and he jumped to his feet.

"Alex, my boy!" His great voice boomed across the room, and he started toward me, his wide shoulders swaying as he slid through the crowded tables. He reached me in a few strides, and gripped my hands. Even though he might be ill, his fist had not lost its strength.

Something in Ernst's manner surprised me. Perhaps it was the extreme exuberance of his greeting. He seemed to be forcing himself to good spirits, and I knew instantly he was not well. As we stood surveying each other, the sharp-faced little man with the nasty eyes, who had been at Ernst's table, came toward us, holding a bottle.

"Senhor Siemel!" he shouted, brandishing the bottle.

"Do me the honor to introduce me to your friend! We will drink a toast!"

Ernst turned to the fellow, and smiled—rather uneasily, it seemed to me. He held the man back with his hand.

"In a second, Ricardo—in a second!"

Anger, like a deep shudder, welled into my brain. It is sometimes difficult to say why one gets angry. Perhaps it was the man's offensive, almost patronizing familiarity with Ernst, coupled with my worried realization that my brother was sick. I could have choked the fellow with my hands. Ernst, sensing my anger, quickly swung himself between us.

The little man drew himself up with a fierceness of demeanor peculiar to Latin people, particularly small ones.

"Please be good enough to forgive us," Ernst said quickly, in Portuguese—which I did not understand well. "Gentlemen, this is my brother!"

He bowed slightly, addressing anyone who was listening. The little man, holding his bottle aloft, was caught on a point of dignity. He lowered the bottle, and also bowed. Perhaps I bowed, too. In any event, the crisis was over, and a few minutes later Ernst and I were out on the hard-packed road, walking toward the hotel where I had left my knapsack.

"Who was that little rat?" I asked, as soon as we had left the *cantina*.

"A fellow named Favelle," Ernst said. "He is a nasty little pest, but he paid for the bottle—I could not insult him."

I said nothing. Ernst walked with easy strides, talking as we moved along. My brother had always been the roving member of our family, and I can remember how I had worshiped his daring and sense of freedom when we were boys in Latvia, where we were born. When he left home to go to South America, a dozen years before this, I had been a boy of twelve; but I secretly made up my mind to run away and join him. Later we learned that Ernst had joined the Argentine Navy; and when I was sixteen, I made plans to run away on a freighter. I did this, with the connivance of a young man who was in love with my sister Selma; but it was nearly two years before I reached South America. Meanwhile I spent a year and a half in the United States, first in New York and later in Chicago, and when I found Ernst at last, in a construction camp in Argentina where they were building a railroad, I was a young man, fairly hardened to the business of making my way in life.

Ernst and I had separated, he going north to the diamond fields of Brazil, while I returned to Buenos Aires, where I met Hans and later, his wife Elsa. I had not seen him since that day, and had received only one letter; and therefore we had much to talk about.

He told me of the diamond fields, where he had travelled as a repairman, earning his living with odd repair jobs in the diamond camps.

"The wealth is fantastic, Alex!" he said, his blue eyes lighting with the old recklessness. "It is lying in the streams—virgin treasures, my boy! And ours for the effort of picking them from the gravel!"

"Why did you come back here, Ernst?" I asked curiously.

He slapped his leg with a big hand, and laughed.

"I wished to have a little wine with my diamonds. After I arrived here, my horse died, and I could not go back until I had enough money to buy another horse." He looked at me fondly. "Now we will go back together!"

"You have been living here since you left the Matto Grosso?"

"Of course. I work at the silver shop of Herr Schmidt. Tomorrow I will get a job there for you, and together we will earn enough to buy two horses and a mule. Then we will return to the diamond fields together."

He leaned back on the cot, and sighed. "Ah, Alex—it is good to see you again! My young brother!"

He seemed to grow pensive for a moment, his mood changing rapidly.

"Ernst, who is this fellow Favelle who spoke to us?" I asked. "Do you owe him anything?"

"No—he buys drinks with his money, that is all. I dislike him, of course—" Ernst looked at me, smiling good-naturedly.

"Forget him, Alex! He was offensive—and you lost your temper! It is nothing to think about."

I looked at my brother curiously. I had seen the time when he would have knocked the little pipsqueak Favelle across the nearest table with a side blow of his hand. But there was something different about him . . . a lack of sureness, which he tried to conceal with heartiness.

"Why do you associate with such people?" I asked.

Ernst grunted, and stared at his big hands.

"One cannot live alone, Alex. There are many worse than he—and besides, he is not my friend. I merely drank with him."

I said nothing further about Favelle. Meanwhile I recounted my own experiences briefly, including my travels up from Buenos Aires; and I explained that I had located him through the German contractor.

"I know him," Ernst said. "He is suffering from the disappointments due to the continuous non-arrival of materials."

"He said you were ill, Ernst. Is that so?"

"Nothing serious," he said, with a shrug. "I have an old wound in my shoulder—" He pulled open his shirt and showed me an irregular scar. "A present from a damned *caboclo!* I shall meet him again some day!"

I felt a vague hint of something; and I could not help wondering whether Ernst's departure from the Matto Grosso may have had something to do with the wound in his shoulder. It came home to me that there were things in the pattern of Ernst's life that I did not understand—and perhaps that he did not want me to understand.

I had been studying Ernst's face as we talked. His features were drawn. There was an outward appearance of the same commanding geniality I had known, but there was a difference that showed in his eyes. It struck me that he was sick in mind as well as body.

I realized that he was watching me, a slight smile hovering at the corners of his mouth.

"You, too, have changed, Alex," he said.

I must have looked startled, and his smile broadened.

"You have grown older, eh? What makes you so serious and severe? Is it religion, or a woman?"

I felt my face flush, and I suddenly thought of Elsa. It struck me with some surprise that this was the first time in many weeks I had thought of her.

"I was in love," I said. "It is over now."

Ernst's laugh boomed out. Then he said, with surprising gentleness:

"Love is never over, Alex. It merely changes—the way we change our clothes with the seasons." There was a dryness in his voice that made me wonder whether Ernst had ever been in love. He was made for it—and I was sure, after my affair with Elsa, that I was not. "Tell me about it, Alex."

I was not anxious to revive this bitter memory; nevertheless, I told him the story. I had met this friend, Hans, at the printing shop of *Caras y Caretas*, a weekly in Buenos Aires, where I worked at a cutting machine. We boxed and wrestled at a local athletic club, and I grew to like him. Later I visited his home where I met his wife, a simple, beautiful German girl. With painful detail, I recounted my love affair.

"Did your friend know about this?" Ernst asked curiously.

I nodded. "He offered to leave—to give her a divorce. That was when I left Buenos Aires."

"You were right to leave," Ernst said. "The girl was not for you."

"What do you mean, Ernst?" I demanded. "I am still in love with her—although I shall never see her again!"

Ernst looked at me with a trace of a smile.

"Perhaps you are in love, Alex. I'll confess I don't quite understand you. You may have been in love with the idea of love—as I have been. At any rate, let's talk about the diamond fields. That's where we are going!"

We talked until the sky outside began to brighten; I listened to Ernst's stories of his travels through the Matto Grosso the way a starved dog looks at food. We made plans to work together in Passo Fundo until we had earned enough money to buy two horses and a mule. Meanwhile I would

21

perfect my knowledge of the mechanic's trade, at which Ernst was already quite proficient, and we would travel as roving repairmen.

"That was my business before, when I travelled among the camps," Ernst said. "My friend Dom Carlos Roderigues says that any fool can dig a diamond, and he will pass it on to the storekeeper, or a gambler or a woman. But a man who lives by a trade will keep what he earns."

The next day I moved my few belongings into Ernst's shack. By mid-afternoon I had arranged to go to work in the silversmith shop, owned by a German-Brazilian, Herr Albert Schmidt. My first job was to assist in turning a huge angle, or roller, which flattened the silver into thin sheets. Herr Schmidt had called two other men to the turn-bar, and together we heaved on it. I did not see the face of the man next to me, being intent on following the old German's instructions. Perhaps in my zeal to make a good impression, I put more effort into the work than was necessary. At any rate, I heard a low voice at my side say contemptuously:

"So you choose to ignore your friends of the *cantina*, Senhor Siemel! And now you make a great effort to show the boss how strong you are! Possibly in your country draught animals do not talk, eh?"

The remark was so plainly offensive that I turned in surprise. I am not an unusually big man—slightly under six feet, and my weight then was less than two hundred pounds. Then I recognized the man. It was Favelle.

Chapter 3

During my first half year in Passo Fundo I learned much that was useful, including the art of repairing guns, which was one of Herr Schmidt's sidelines; and I also learned a great deal about the character of Brazilians. Ernst and I seldom visited the *cantina*, but we mingled in the evenings with the men who worked at the silversmith shop, and I learned to like and understand these people—with the exception of Favelle.

He did not actually bother us, but there was a constant feeling of friction. I finally concluded that he was particularly annoyed at Ernst's failure to join him at the *cantina*—a habit which Ernst had dropped, now that we were together and working toward a common goal. Then suddenly two events occurred, which changed our position in Passo Fundo, particularly our relations with Favelle.

One afternoon Ernst informed me with an unusual burst of enthusiasm that a Paraguayan "strong man" had come to town to exhibit his strength. He was to give an exhibition at the public square that evening, and immediately after work that day Ernst and I wandered down to the plaza to see the event.

Workmen were erecting a wooden platform in the square, and hundreds of townspeople were clustered around, discussing the new arrival. In Brazil, crowds do not assemble *en masse*; they collect. Each person strolls individually about, smoking a cigarette and displaying amusement at what goes on. Once the show begins, they grow excited, and work themselves up to a pitch of enthusiasm, but they never seem to lose the character of being individuals, rather than a crowd.

Ernst and I pressed close to the platform to get a glimpse of the "strong man," who was standing nearby, looking tolerantly at the admiring crowd. His name, we found out, was Senhor Marcelo Caceres. He wore a spotted *tigre* skin slung over his shoulders like a cape, fastened at the waist with a broad, black belt. He also wore black tights, which showed the bulging muscles of his thighs and calves. He was brown and powerfully built, and his features were heavy, with a huge jaw, thick lips and a hooked nose, which seemed to draw his brows into a perpetual scowl. Nevertheless, he grinned in response to the admiration of the crowd.

"Marcelo is the strongest man alive!" a short, baldish man with a black coat and derby hat was informing the people clustered around the stand. "Even the animals in the jungle fear him. The jaguar will slink away at his approach."

He waved the stub of an unlighted cigar, which he had chewed down to the band, and Marcelo bowed in acknowledgment.

"Lie upon the stage, my little one!" the bald man—evidently his manager—commanded. "Show these good people your superhuman power."

Marcelo flung off his cape and jumped to the platform, stretching out on his back. The little man motioned to a huge Negro, who appeared carrying an anvil. This was laid on the platform and finally placed on Marcelo's chest. Then the Negro laid an iron bar, perhaps an inch thick, on top of the anvil.

"You look pretty strong, *senhor*," he said, turning suddenly to me. "Would you like to try to break that bar, using a hammer and a chisel?"

At his signal, I jumped to the stage. Ernst was grinning broadly, enjoying the affair. Suddenly, as I looked down at my brother, I saw Favelle standing near him. His mouth was drawn to one side in a crooked smile. He put a cigarette in his mouth, and then waved carelessly at me.

"You are in excellent company, Senhor Siemel!" he

24

called out, loud enough to be heard by those standing near. "One ox against another, eh?"

I saw Ernst swing toward Favelle. I was afraid something would be started, but at that moment the little manager tugged at my sleeve. He explained my task: I was to hit the head of the chisel, which the Negro held point down against the bar, and see if I could break the bar. The bar was resting on the anvil, which was still lying upon Marcelo's chest.

"If I hit it hard enough to split it, the blow will kill him," I protested.

"Not Marcelo," the little man said, obviously tickled at this unrehearsed support for his drama. "And do not spare your strength. Hit as hard as you can."

"And hit straight!" Favelle called from below. "Even an ox must have some skill!"

I looked again at Ernst's face, and I knew it would take little more to snap his restraint. I motioned to him with my hand, then walked to the edge of the stage.

"Perhaps you would like to exhibit your strength, Senhor Favelle," I said. "I didn't ask for this work, and if you can lift the hammer, come on up!"

I realized instantly it was the wrong thing to say. Favelle's face had worked itself into an actual contortion. His thin mouth began to tremble, and his dark eyes became bright with hatred. He put his hand to his mouth, drew out his cigarette and snapped it angrily against the side of the stage. Then he turned and walked back into the crowd. I saw Ernst turn also, but he did not follow.

I went back to the strong man, and picked up the hammer. While I was fairly accurate with a double-jack, having worked on the railroad in the Argentine, there was always a chance of a miss. Nevertheless, I swung the hammer over my shoulder and brought it down as hard as I could. Marcelo hardly grunted. At the third stroke, the bar snapped into two pieces, which fell clanging from the anvil. Marcelo arose, picking up the anvil under his arm, and grinned at the wildly cheering crowd.

After that we all got into the spirit of the show. I sat on

a chair which Marcelo gripped by a rung with his teeth, and he lifted me into the air. An automobile was driven over a ramp laid upon his chest. By nightfall, I had had an opportunity to observe all of Marcelo's accomplishments, and to estimate his quickness. Then I went over to the little manager, who by this time was very affable.

"Perhaps we could arrange a match—and you could draw a good crowd," I said.

"What kind of a match?" the little man asked, suddenly very suspicious.

"Wrestling," I said. "I am fairly good at it."

"How much do you expect—if you are alive to collect the money?"

"Winner take all," I said. Ernst was standing by, and he gripped my hand.

"Don't be a damned fool, Alex!" he exclaimed. "He will break you in two!"

"Then he will take all the gate receipts," I said. I looked at the manager. "How about it?"

Marcelo had come up and was listening with a good-natured smile.

"I am not a murderer," he said.

"Either meet me—or admit you are afraid," I said. Marcelo's smile disappeared, and he scowled.

"Marcelo is afraid of no one!" the little manager snapped. "Your blood is upon your own head."

Ernst was quite worried, but I was not. I had watched Marcelo, and I knew he was extremely muscle-bound. He could probably crack my spine if he got a grip on me, but I knew I fast enough to avoid him; and I was sure he was not a wrestler.

It was arranged that the match would be at the local theater, a barn-like building with a high wooden front, on Saturday night. The building was just off the square, and by sundown Saturday a crowd had collected. Bookmakers were taking bets, with the heaviest wagering on the Paraguayan strong man. Women were not permitted to attend the match, but they lingered around the square to catch a glimpse of the powerful Marcelo, who strode back and forth in front of the theater in his *tigre* skin cloak waving genially to the crowd and advising customers to come in and see the annihilation of the "blond braggart from the North."

Before the bout, Ernst and I visited Dom Carlos Roderigues at the old thief-taker's suggestion. "I wish to take all precautions against a disturbance," he said. "I shall place myself with the ticket-sellers until all funds are taken in and accounted for. Then I shall possess these funds until the match is decided. That will spare me the inconvenience of having to track anyone into a neighboring and perhaps unfriendly country in order to repossess the funds."

He turned to Ernst.

"There is bad feeling between you and Senhor Favelle," he said. "I have observed it. I shall sit with you at the match, and I trust unpleasantness will be avoided."

"Let Favelle watch out for himself," Ernst growled. "I have listened to that rat squeak long enough!"

As I stood in the ring, waiting for the match to start, I saw Favelle sitting near the ringside, with a group of men around him. They glanced at me now and then, and I noticed Favelle, with his thin, one-sided smile, seemed to be giving instructions. They were all smoking, and the dense clouds partly obscured their faces.

During the first round, Marcelo came at me in repeated rushes, his head sunk in his shoulders, charging like a bull. It was no trick to sidestep him, swing him off balance, and let his own momentum and weight send him tumbling to the canvas. Each time he arose with more effort, and finally I managed to get behind him and throw him to the mat with a waist-lock. He bridged his body, holding his shoulders off the canvas with the huge strength of his neck muscles, and the round ended in a draw.

In the second round I began to breathe with difficulty. I found myself choking from the smoke, which billowed up in clouds from the corner where Favelle and his cronies sat. Once I looked down and saw his twisted smile; but the smoke was so dense I could hardly see him. I began to cough frequently.

By this time I had an arm-lock on Marcelo. He was growing less enthusiastic by the minute and exerted all his efforts
trying to keep his shoulders off the mat, rather than attempt-
ing to attack me. However, I suddenly released the hold and
asked for time. I walked to the edge of the ring, and looked
down at Favelle.

"You are smoking more than necessary," I said. "It is
impossible to breathe. These people came to see a match, and
I hope you and your friends will avoid making it impossible
for us to go on."

Favelle, with an exaggerated sweep of his hand, dropped
his cigarette and stepped on it. The others did likewise.
Within a few minutes, Marcelo—in spite of frantic pleadings
from his manager, reminding the strong man that this was on
a "winner-take-all" basis—was so weary he could no longer
resist the constant pressure on his shoulders. I had little
trouble finally pinning him down.

As I passed down the steps of the stage platform, after the
bout, I saw Favelle among his cronies. I was hot and angry,
and still coughing. I walked over to him. His face was white,
and I knew instantly that he had bet against me, and lost.

"When you wish to blow smoke in my face, Senhor
Favelle," I said, "I would suggest you do it to me personally.
As it was, you and your friends caused the gentleman from
Paraguay to choke as much as I with your dirty trick!"

Without waiting for his reply, I walked back toward the
side door that led backstage. I felt someone touch me, and
saw that it was Dom Carlos, with Ernst close behind.

"You are to come immediately, without changing your
clothes," he said. "I have the money and your clothes, and a
cart outside." Ernst tossed me a cape, which I put around my
shoulders. He already had my clothes in a bag. In a few
minutes we were rattling along the road to our shack. Dom
Carlos said little on the way home, except that there was
"bad feeling" in the crowd.

"You were foolish to accost Senhor Favelle, unless you
are ready to kill him," Dom Carlos told me later, when we
were sitting smoking in the single room of our house. "Until

now you have kept your head, but tonight you completely lost it."

"Why?" I asked, irritated at the old man's remark. "I merely warned him."

"In this country you do not warn people uselessly," Dom Carlos said, with soft patience in his voice. "Favelle is not a fool. He does not like you and he knows you do not like him. What can you add to that by 'warning' him, as you call it? You did not warn him—you insulted him. He lost money, and he is angry because you not only caused him to lose it by beating this man from Paraguay, but because you also caused everyone else to be aware that he had lost his money. Now he blames you both for the loss of his money, and for the loss of his pride. He will never forgive you."

I shrugged, rather impatiently, I suppose.

"It is nothing to me," I said. "If he makes trouble, he will pay for it—not I."

Dom Carlos shook his head, somewhat regretfully, it seemed to me.

"You have not learned the lesson, my boy," he said. I looked at Ernst, whose face was slightly puzzled. He shook his head, and Dom Carlos went on: "Our temperament is unlike that of you cold-blooded men from the North. We would rather die avenged, than live humiliated or insulted. You will do Favelle a greater favor if you kill him, than if you continue to remain superior to him in this way."

Several months after this incident, which enriched Ernst's and my coffers to the extent of several hundred *milreis*, the second—and perhaps decisive—chapter occurred in the rising feud with Favelle.

Dom Carlos told Ernst and me that a Turkish wrestler, Leon Beduino, was on his way to São Paulo, and would stop over at Passo Fundo in the hope of picking up a few *milreis* in a local fight.

"Do not so far forget yourself as to challenge this man," Dom Carlos told me. "He is not a muscle-bound strong man. He snapped an Englishman's neck in a bout in the South. I may even arrest him for murder."

Beduino was one of the "terrible Turks" who came to North America in the early part of the century, and created havoc in American wrestling circles until Mahmoud, their greatest wrestler, was defeated by Frank Gotch in 1911. This Beduino had come to South America where he travelled among frontier towns, taking on local challengers.

The *plaza* was packed on Sunday night when Beduino arrived. He rode a donkey into the square, and dismounted. The Turk was a bronzed ape of a man, weighing about two hundred and fifty pounds, with a small, round head and tremendous curved moustaches. His thick lips were shaped in a fixed smile, which gave his face a malignant expression. I disliked him immediately.

He bowed, and made a preliminary speech—a challenge to any local man to wrestle him. I pushed up close to look more carefully at him. It was unusual, I knew, for anyone to wrestle and box professionally, since the two require development of different muscular processes. One requires tremendous back and shoulder muscles, which prevent quick reflexes and timing needed for hitting power.

I remember Dom Carlos' warning, but I also felt that I had judged the Turk accurately. He was probably a better wrestler than I, but a poorer boxer.

"Senhor Beduino!" I said. "Perhaps I can accommodate you—on one condition."

He stared at me, his little pig-like eyes sizing me up physically.

"What is this proposition?" he asked suspiciously.

"If I agree to wrestle you tomorrow night, will you box ten rounds with me the following night?"

He considered this a few seconds, and licked his lips uncertainly. Then he nodded.

"It is agreed," he said.

Dom Carlos expressed disgust for my brash action, yet I think he was secretly pleased. "He is thicker than the strong man, but probably quicker," he said to me later. "If you are cunning, you can stay two rounds with him. You cannot, of course, expect to win."

I nodded. "But I can beat him boxing," I said. "And I do not think he can pin me in two rounds of wrestling."

There was a great crowd on hand for the first match, and Dom Carlos, bustling about with the professional activity of a half-dozen policemen, found time to tell me that a great many had come armed with guns.

"Why?" I asked.

The old thief-taker shrugged. "Many are Favelle's friends," he said. "Perhaps he has a plan to create a diversion. In any event, I have asked many of your friends to bring their guns, also. I cannot stop Favelle's shooting, but I can see that matters are equal."

Dom Carlos let the lid of his good eye drop in an exaggerated wink. I could not decide whether he was joking, or had deliberately invited a riot.

If Favelle had a "plan," it resulted in saving me perhaps from severe injury, and possibly from being maimed or killed. The bout had not progressed more than a minute or so before I knew the Turk was the most formidable wrestler I had ever met. I had all I could do to evade his crushing grip, and once he caught me with one mighty swing of his arm around my waist, I felt as if a python had encircled me. I managed to slip free as he strove to pin my arm back with his other hand, and dove for the ropes. Under the rules, he had to wait until I came out.

Suddenly, as we were maneuvering for holds, head to head, I felt my jaw batted to one side and an agonizing pain shot through the left side of my head. The Turk had bitten clear through my ear. I had noticed his full set of gold teeth, and I think he sharpened them for the match. I drove my fist instinctively into his flabby stomach, and he gasped. I felt the blood running down my neck from the bite in my ear.

"Try that again and I'll turn this into a fight now," I said through my teeth.

He growled something, his face twisted into a ferocious scowl, and lunged at me. As we came together, I heard him mutter that if he could get his hands on my throat he would "risk a lynching." By this time I realized I was fighting for

31

my life. The Turk was more powerful than Marcelo, and experienced at every trick in wrestling. I slipped desperately from his grip and he came at me again like a maddened animal.

At this point, I heard a shrill voice—Favelle's, as I found out later—scream:

"*Viva Turco! Kill the gringo bastard!*"

Favelle fired his gun into the air and instantly Dom Carlos was on his chair. He also fired at the roof. A few more shots added to the din. The shooting halted Beduino in his charge. He turned toward the crowd, and before I realized what was happening, he slipped through the ropes and was lumbering up the aisle. By the time I oriented myself to the situation, Beduino had disappeared and Dom Carlos was in command. He stood on the chair, waving his gun and calling for order. He was a dangerous and formidable man, whose reputation commanded great respect in that country.

The shooting stopped and the clamor subsided. The manager of the theater stepped out on the stage, wiping his face, then waving his hands and rolling his eyes wildly as he implored the audience to respect the dignity of his theater. "There will be no boxing tomorrow!" he shouted, but it was drowned out by the crowd, which by now had a thirst for action.

Dom Carlos followed me to the dressing room, where we found the Turk busily climbing into his clothes. His fierceness had evaporated; he simply begged to be let out of the entire bargain.

"I am a professional performer," he said. "I am not a boxer, *senhor!* You will excuse me—I am leaving this place at once!"

Dom Carlos assured him there would be no gunplay the next night. Beduino finally consented to the bout if he was promised half the gate in advance. I agreed to this. By this time I had become so enraged at his tactics that I wanted personally to administer a lesson—and I knew he was no boxer.

The bout was hardly to be classed as boxing. Beduino

knew nothing about boxing skill, and at first moved around the ring pawing at me in an unwieldy fashion, trying to push me rather than to hit me. I had intended to give him a lesson and the crowd a good show, but the roar of the crowd seemed to arouse in him some kind of fury or excitement.

After taking a few sharp jabs in the face, he began suddenly to gnaw at the thongs of his gloves. I realized I would be in serious danger if he got the gloves loose and his powerful hands were free to grip me. I began to aim at his neck with the hope of straightening him up so I could hit him flush on the jaw, but my gloves bounced off the ripples of muscle as if the man's neck were solid rubber.

He had ripped one glove almost free, and raised his head to glare at me. I hit him on the side of the jaw with every ounce of strength I had, and he tumbled forward on his face. It was lucky he did, because I think I almost broke my hand with that punch. It was weeks before it was well enough to shake hands.

That ended the bout. Dom Carlos came quickly to the side of the stage, elated at the results but obviously anxious that there be no disturbance. I had not seen Favelle at the ringside, and mentioned this to Dom Carlos.

"He was there—in the rear this time. He did not wish to have you accost him again. Nevertheless, I must warn you against this man," the old thief-taker continued earnestly. "His mind is bitter, and when a man like Favelle grows bitter, his mind will work continuously. He will plan something. Such a man must regain his esteem at all costs, and that makes him dangerous."

Ernst and I bought a mule with the earnings from the Beduino bout, and with rather malignant humor, we named it "Beduino" in honor of my recent foe. We also purchased tools, and we had a second mule, in addition to Beduino, and a horse. We needed only one more mule to be equipped for the journey to the diamond fields. Beduino, the mule, became my personal mount, and for the next few years was with me on all my travels.

My bouts with Marcelo and Beduino had increased my

popularity in Passo Fundo, particularly with the men who worked in Herr Schmidt's shop. The victories were accepted as triumphs for the town, and Brazilians are quick and generous in their native pride. With Favelle, however, the effect was exactly the opposite. Although he became outwardly formal toward Ernst and myself, he seldom missed an opportunity for a venomous remark or a thinly veiled insult. He had even forgotten his score against Ernst, and concentrated his hatred almost wholly upon me.

One day at the noon meal, served in the dining room behind Herr Schmidt's shop, I accidentally took Favelle's seat at the table. It was a natural mistake, and in almost any other case the man whose seat had been taken would find himself another for that meal. Favelle came behind me, however, and I was not even aware he was there until I heard his cold voice:

"Move over, *filho da puta!* That is my seat!"

The expression he used is fighting language in almost any tongue. It is roughly the equivalent of the American "son of a bitch." I knew instantly that everyone else in the room expected me to take up the challenge. Dom Carlos' words suddenly acquired a real meaning . . . Favelle could not hope to stand up in a fight; and he would rather die than be inferior.

There was dead silence after Favelle's remark, and as I swung around I could see that his face was a ghastly color, and he was trembling. I bowed slightly, excused myself, and changed seats. Ernst had turned toward Favelle, and I knew by the expression on his face that he would be after the little man and perhaps strangle him if a fight broke out.

Nothing further was said, as I sat down. That evening I went down to Dom Carlos' place, and it was then that he told me about Joaquim Guató.

Ernst hated the idea of leaving in the face of Favelle's open challenge—as I did; but he finally agreed that we would leave. "I would like to stamp on his face in the dust as I would on a snake," he muttered. "But—very well, Alex. We will leave."

Two days later we arose several hours before dawn. We had packed our tools the night before in four large *bruacas*—square leather bags which can be mounted on a pack-saddle; and these were strapped on the mules. Our plan was for Ernst to take his own horse and two mules, and ride three days' journey to the north, crossing the Rio Uruguay, and await me. I would follow on my mule Beduino, when I had completed the unfinished work at Herr Schmidt's shop.

Ernst finished loading the mules, and tested the cinches of his horse. Then for several minutes he stood before the fire we had built for light, smoking a final cigarette. A dark *poncho*, thrown over his shoulders, made him seem even bulkier than he was, in the light of the fire. Finally he tossed his cigarette into the fire.

"I will cross the Uruguay tomorrow night or early the next day," he said. "By then you should be leaving. I will ride to Clevelandia, and meet you there three days later." He paused a minute, then said: "Take care of yourself, Sasha. I shall wait until you come."

Ernst seldom used the Russian diminutive of my name, since most people called me "Alex"; and I knew he was deeply moved. Both of us realized that in the next few hours the decision would be made . . . whether we would flee into the jungle as fugitives, or travel our own way as journeymen mechanics.

It seemed to me, as I watched my brother standing there as motionless as a figure chiseled in stone, that Fate had taken charge of our lives. We were not going because of our own choice, but because of events out of our control. I have seldom experienced such a feeling of inevitability. Years later I had the same feeling when I faced a *tigre* in the jungle, knowing the issue was life or death, and yet feeling as if the results had already been written.

Ernst sensed my mood, and smiled, slapping me on the shoulder. He put his foot into the stirrup and swung up quickly on his horse. He waved casually, and trotted off into the darkness. I saw his shadowy bulk dissolve in the thickets and then listened for several minutes to the clank of the cowbell around the neck of the lead horse, fading into the distance.

For a little while I felt lonely, sitting before the fire in the darkness before dawn. But soon my cheerfulness returned. We were at last on our way, and it seemed to me that Ernst's departure was the last obstacle. Had I given sufficient thought to Favelle and the nature of his hatred, my feeling might have been different. Years later I learned from Joaquim Guató a simple bit of jungle wisdom: When you are confronted by an animal, do not waste your time planning what you will do until you have first figured out what the animal is going to do.

Early in the morning I set out for Herr Schmidt's shop. I wanted to get to work early and finish the jobs we had left as soon as possible. As I swung down the pathway from our shack into the road, I saw Dom Carlos a short distance up the road, sitting on his dun mule. He wore a great white *sombrero*, which he affected after the manner of the man from Texas who had taught him to draw his gun quickly.

As I passed, he raised his hat, giving me the benefit of a sort of grinning smile.

"Good morning, *senhor!*" he said. "I heard a horse and mules pass in the night—which is very good. I trust you have your own mule in readiness, *senhor*. Lobo began to howl this morning. He is a smart hound, that one—he already senses a good run!"

Chapter 4

*Shortly after work began at Herr Schmidt's shop, I ap-*proached him to advise him that my brother had departed, and that I would be leaving as soon as our work at the shop was finished.

"Your brother has gone!" the German exclaimed. Favelle was standing nearby, and I saw him turn sharply toward us.

"He left this morning," I said, looking directly at Favelle. "We are bound for the Matto Grosso. I will, of course, remain a few days until I have completed our affairs—my brother's as well as my own."

The shop was not large, and the men working at benches near the windows turned and looked at me. A few came over to hear more details of our departure.

Favelle stood beside the big mangle in the corner, away from the others, one arm resting languidly upon the big turning bar. His mouth was tight . . . the same expression I had noticed the night of my fight with Marcelo, when Favelle had lost his bets.

Herr Schmidt coughed and apparently feeling that some comment was called for, began quite formally to make a speech.

"It is with great regret that we bid you good-by, Senhor Siemel," he said. His rather prominent eyes swerved uncertainly to where Favelle was standing, and I realized that he was embarrassed at Favelle's attitude, which was not friendly. "You have been excellent workmen, and have conducted yourselves in a manner that has brought honor to our place of business. I believe I speak for all of us—" he hesitated, looking almost pleadingly at Favelle, "when I tell you that our good wishes go with you."

On a sudden impulse, I walked over to Favelle and held out my hand.

"I should hate to leave feeling that any bad wishes were following me," I said. "Senhor Favelle, will you shake hands?"

Favelle bowed with exaggerated formality, and took my hand.

"With pleasure, *senhor*," he said. "This is a great loss to the community. May I express the hope that the loss will be confined to your persons?" He bowed again, and turned toward Herr Schmidt. I had noticed that Favelle had a habit of balancing on his toes when he was under an emotional strain, probably to give himself the appearance of greater height. "You will excuse me if I go and check my tools."

The insult was so open I could not ignore it. At the same instant, anger struck me like a physical blow. It was the sensation of almost uncontrollable fury that possessed me the night I met Ernst in the *cantina*.

Herr Schmidt bustled up and placed himself between us.

"Favelle!" His omission of the *senhor* was a sign that he was greatly upset, since Brazilians seldom forget formality. "You have no occasion for such a remark!"

"He has been using my file!" Favelle snapped. "It is on his bench now. I merely wish to assure myself that it is here when he has left."

I turned toward my work bench, almost sick with anger. I knew if I continued to look at Favelle, I would hit him, and in my state of mind I believe I could have killed him with one blow of my fist. Favelle was trembling as I turned away; he seemed to be goading himself. All at once I remembered Dom Carlos' remark, as I passed him earlier in the day, that Lobo had "begun to howl."

Herr Schmidt, trying desperately to minimize the affair, followed me to my bench with one hand on my shoulder, chattering almost incoherently about the great affection he had for Ernst and myself. I had reached a point where my patience was all but exhausted; and I merely shrugged and went about my work. Herr Schmidt stood there uncertainly, his protruding eyes roving from me to Favelle. Apparently he was torn between a desire to express his feelings toward me and fearful that any demonstration might provoke Favelle further. It seemed ironic that it was Favelle—not myself— whom he wished to soothe.

At the noonday meal in the common dining room, where Herr Schmidt always presided, he rose and lifting a glass of wine proposed a toast to Ernst and myself.

"To our departing comrades! They have been a great credit to our shop, and to our town!"

Favelle was on his feet in a second.

"To our Russian friends!" he said, loudly. "May they go far!"

I leaned back against the hard back-rail of the long bench at which we sat. It seemed to me that I would not be able to last the day without a settlement with Favelle, and if it had to come, it might as well happen now.

Everyone was applauding, however, apparently unaware of the sarcasm in Favelle's toast. Favelle also applauded, louder than the rest. Afterwards, however, he subsided and sat in sullen silence for the remainder of the meal, saying nothing further.

I worked intensively during the afternoon, and by evening had completed everything except a silver stirrup mounting. I ate my supper alone, after the others had left, to avoid any further trouble with Favelle. By this time my own thoughts had become obsessed with a gnawing notion that perhaps I should not try to avoid the issue with Favelle. I wondered whether I was evading the man. During my years alone in Buenos Aires I had become something of an amateur philosopher. I read Hegel and Schopenhauer, and also Goethe; and from this mental discipline I learned to study men's motives and passions objectively—including my own. It was inevitable that I should question my own motives in this matter.

Was I in reality escaping from something? Obviously, I

was not evading a physical encounter with Favelle for any reasons of personal safety. As I had told Dom Carlos, I could have broken the man with my two hands. Was there some power that Favelle possessed—perhaps that of ridicule —that I was afraid to face? Was I actually afraid to encounter Favelle in a battle of wits?

These thoughts drummed through my mind as I returned to the shop, and as a matter of habit picked a file from the rack. These tools were considered the common possession of all the workers; and at night with only one or two at the shop, there was never any question of priority or preference. In this case, I was alone in the shop.

I began to work on the silver stirrup frame, which required delicate welding. It is necessary to concentrate on such work, since the melting point of the solder is only slightly below that of the silver itself. The owner was probably some *gaucho* from an outlying ranch, and this was part of an ornate saddle, his most prized possession. He would never know who did the job; yet the honor of Herr Schmidt's establishment required that it be done perfectly. I was intent upon this work, and was not aware that anyone had entered the place until I turned, at a small sound, and saw Favelle standing a few feet away.

He was balancing on the balls of his feet, and I knew from the way his body swayed that he was drunk. I said nothing, but turned back to my work. A few seconds later I heard the door open—my senses were sharpened this time by the presence of Favelle—and I heard Herr Schmidt's voice.

"Senhor Favelle," he said quietly, "come here—I wish to speak with you."

I heard Favelle's footsteps. Then I heard Herr Schmidt ask in a whisper:

"Why have you come to the shop tonight?"

Favelle replied in a sharp, strident voice, obviously intended for my ears, "I have come to defend my tools."

I looked at the file in my hand. For the first time I noticed that I had picked the file usually used by Favelle. I carefully laid down the stirrup frame, which I had completed welding. Then I rose from my seat and turned toward Favelle and Herr Schmidt.

Favelle's face was visibly pale, even in the dim light of the shop. His mouth was pulled to one side in a sort of crooked smile, and his lips were quivering, as if his face were no longer under muscular control. I actually felt pity for the man; he was no more the master of his actions than a small boat whirled violently through rapids.

As I turned, Favelle snatched a heavy soldering iron from a bench. He faced me with this in his hand, and I mentally agreed with Dom Carlos that Favelle was no coward.

I walked directly toward him and on past him to the coat rack. Herr Schmidt had stepped aside, his jaw slack and his mouth partly open, but he said nothing as I strode by him. I snatched my coat and hat from the hook where I had hung them, and turned directly toward Herr Schmidt.

"Good-by, senhor," I said. "There are one or two small things which anyone can finish. You have paid me, and there is nothing more you owe me."

I opened the door and walked out into the night. I had determined that I would do nothing to provoke or even permit a fight in the silversmith shop. Once outside, I walked quickly around to the open space beside Herr Schmidt's shop. There was a lapacho tree a few feet from the road; and I crouched there in a shadow made by the rising moon. I was facing the rear of the shop, and could see anyone leaving. A small dormitory building was set diagonally from the corner of the shop, and I knew Favelle must pass near me to reach this building.

I am not quite sure what was in my mind. Lying in ambush is not a habit with me, and I do not think I intended to kill Favelle. But I meant to settle our quarrel, once and for all. I had reached a point where only this thought burned in my mind. I was numb to everything else, like an animal stalking its prey.

It was June, and the night was cold. After a while I drew my leather jacket closer around me; but my eyes never left the corner of the house. The moon, rising stealthily behind me, made a white scar across the side of the building; and there was a dim glow in the single window facing me; but otherwise the place was dark.

I heard Herr Schmidt's voice once, apparently bidding Favelle a gruff "good night." A door creaked and the light went out inside the shop. Then Favelle stepped from the corner of the house, and I rose and started toward him, calling: "Favelle!"

He turned toward me and suddenly screamed:
"*Bandido!*"

I ran toward him. I did not want Herr Schmidt coming out to investigate the noise of a disturbance. As I ran I saw that Favelle was tugging at his waistband. I knew he sometimes carried a gun—not for use, but for a swaggering effect. I almost dove the last few feet, reaching for his hand, but he stepped back, and was holding the gun loosely in his hand.

"Put away the gun, Ricardo!" I said sharply, and reached for the gun barrel. Favelle did not utter a word. His lips were drawn back in a kind of snarl, and his eyes gleamed like bright black beads in his white face. I realized the man was mad.

He lurched toward me, lifting the gun, but did not fire it. Whether he caught his finger on the trigger guard, or was too frozen with insane rage to shoot, I could not tell; but I knew my only chance was to get the gun away from him. As he came toward me, I reached down and knocked the pistol to one side, at the same time grabbing his wrist.

This seemed to touch a spring in him. From the swaying, almost awkward advance toward me, he suddenly was after me as I tore the gun loose, clawing and scratching at my face with one hand, and tearing savagely at my other hand, which now held the gun by the barrel. I had a ghastly feeling that I was dealing with a man who had completely lost his reason. Favelle was making a sobbing, gasping noise, almost like a gurgle at times.

At that moment I heard Herr Schmidt's voice, calling

querulously from the far side of the shop building, where he had his quarters:

"Senhor Favelle—is it something?"

I was afraid to prolong the fight. Favelle was ramming his head against me, clawing for the gun; and I suddenly realized that he was trying to bite me. I was strong enough to hold him off with my right arm, but it was like holding off a mad dog. I had to end it some way; and so I raised the gun barrel and brought the butt down like a club on his head. It struck with a queer, hollow sound, and Favelle dropped to the ground without another cry.

I knew it was a hard blow. I leaned over and pushed his shoulder, and he rolled over. His face, very white in the pallid light of the moon, looked sightlessly at me. There was not a sign of life in him.

Somewhere in the back I heard a door slam; and I knew Herr Schmidt would come bustling out if he did not get an answer to his call. I did not have the slightest qualm over what had happened; yet I did not want to be caught in this situation. I stood erect again, breathing heavily, and as I did so a figure rose from a clump of shrubbery a few feet away. I recognized the white *sombrero* of Dom Carlos.

"So you have done this crazy thing," he said in a low voice, coming toward me. "I cannot understand why you did not leave town decently, as I suggested. Then this would not have happened."

He looked down at the still figure on the ground, and even touched the body with his toe.

"He called me a thief," I said. "I could not leave without demanding an explanation from him."

"There is no explanation for a thief!" Dom Carlos snapped, stooping over to examine Favelle's face more closely. "Either you are or you are not—and I take it you are not."

"Of course I am not," I said angrily. "I meant to impress that upon this stupid fool."

"You have impressed him," Dom Carlos said, looking up and down the road. His single eye seemed to cover the entire area in one sweeping glance. "I shall have to examine this man thoroughly to see how much life you have left in him. Meanwhile, go to the graveyard—do not stop at your house, because the mule is no longer there."

I nodded, and started to mutter my gratitude, but Dom Carlos waved me off with a flourish of his hand.

"Be on your way," he said. "Three hours is not long— and in your case, it is getting shorter. Herr Schmidt will have his trousers on in a few seconds, and I cannot very well tell him you have run away if you are still here."

He hunched down to examine Favelle's head, which showed an ugly stain now covering the side of his face. I said nothing more, but started up the road to the graveyard, which was a half-mile north of the silversmith shop. I found my mule Beduino, his lead rope fastened to a shrub, irreverently munching a clump of grass that grew upon the last resting place of some former citizen of Passo Fundo. Within a few minutes I had mounted and we were off at a trot along the road Ernst had taken that morning.

The road was little more than a wide trail, which followed the rolling hills toward the summit of a low range which lay between Passo Fundo and the Uruguay. Beyond this crest the land fell away in a succession of tumbling hills. There was not a light nor any sign of human life; and the steadily plodding hoofs of the mule provided the only sound. Now and then I looked back upon the dark, empty road, wondering when I would see the outlines of pursuers break through the vague shadows of the scattered clumps of moonlit trees. However, Dom Carlos had promised me three hours' start, and I felt sure he would keep his word.

I rode steadily for perhaps four hours; then I stopped for a brief rest. The feeling of being hunted did not at first occur to me. It was after some hours of steady riding before I began to understand that I was in truth a fugitive, fleeing for my life. This is a sensation that is unique; nothing in a man's previous experience prepares him for it. It is not fear, because fear exists actively only when danger is faced. It is a deeper feeling, growing gradually in the lower layers of the senses;

and it is an enduring feeling. The need for escape grows until it dominates a hunted man's thoughts.

My situation, of course, was fairly simple: I merely had to keep on going as fast as I could, until I reached the river. My sole chance lay in keeping ahead of the old thief-taker and his dog; because Lobo would follow my tracks unerringly, and leaving the road to hide was out of the question.

When the moon sank toward the fringe of the hills to my left, I turned into a small ravine where I hobbled the mule, unrolled my *poncho* and lay down for a short rest before dawn. At daybreak I was up again, refreshed by the cold morning wind.

As the sun unravelled the morning mists along the flat hills over which the road passed, I could observe the character of the country. We were less than thirty kilometers from Passo Fundo, yet all trace of civilization seemed to have been left behind. The trees thinned out as I rode up across the lower foothills. There were rustling sounds in the thickets along the trail, perhaps the noise of tiny animals; and now and then the screeching blast of a macaw broke upon the silence.

The trail was not hard to follow. Dom Carlos himself had outlined to Ernst and me the route which would take us most quickly to the Uruguay. Now and then I passed a small hut where some hardy settler, with more courage than good sense, was struggling in the unequal fight against the soil; but the farms were small and widely spaced, and I had little fear that news of my flight from Passo Fundo could have reached these places ahead of me.

Late in the first day I saw a rider on a barren hill a mile or so to the left, and I turned hastily off the trail so that the mule and I might be hidden in the thickets. After several minutes I realized that if it were Dom Carlos, the dog Lobo would lead the way to my place of hiding. So I started forward again, hurrying faster to make up the loss of precious time.

Passo Fundo lies about a hundred kilometers south of the Uruguay; and early in the second day I rode down through tangled thickets to the rim of a bank of red cliffs, and saw the muddy waters of the river below me. The Uruguay was one of three great rivers that must be crossed on the way to the Matto Grosso; the Iguassú and the Paraná being the other two. The brown current churns wildly down from the uplands of Santa Catherina, flows out into the broad valley that lies between Uruguay and Argentina, and then empties into the great Plata River Basin, fed by one fourth of the inland waters of South America.

There was a moment of elation as I looked down upon this river—not that I had evaded pursuit, since I was not yet across the river; but because it seemed to me this was a great landmark in my journey into the wild lands beyond.

For the first time in two days the feeling of being hunted —of constant watchfulness on the road behind me—gave way to eagerness. Beyond the Uruguay was a new country, and beyond that, perhaps a thousand miles inland, was the "Great Jungle" and the diamond fields of the Matto Grosso.

I had seen no sign of Dom Carlos, and I think I must have dismissed to a great extent the notion that he was following me—or that I had killed Favelle. I certainly would have seen Dom Carlos on my trail somewhere along the road; and if he was not following, it must be that the blow of the pistol butt was not fatal to Favelle.

The trail descended sharply from the rim of the cliffs into a ravine, which wound down to the river bank. I followed this, letting Beduino, steady and sure-footed, have his head. The day was bright and clear, and I could see glimpses of the glittering water as I turned through the tortuous corners of the steep trail. At the bottom we emerged upon a flat, open space and turned toward a ferrying point at the foot of the trail.

The ferry was an unwieldy affair, consisting of three dugouts held together by a platform which served as a deck. A wire, strung between the two banks which were about a quarter of a mile apart, was passed through a pulley to guide the ferry; and motive power was provided by a ferry-tender who walked from one end of the craft to the other, pushing against the wire with a forked stick which he twisted slightly, to give it purchase.

I had crossed to the north bank of the river, and started along the road which led into the haven of Santa Catherina, when I heard a shot from the other side. I looked back and saw a figure sitting on a mule on the rim of the red cliffs. He raised a white *sombrero*; and with that unquenchable vanity over his adeptness at drawing a pistol, he pulled his gun from his holster and fired into the air.

Dom Carlos had reckoned well on the three hours' start he promised me. He had arrived at the ferrying point thirty minutes behind me; and although something in his curious code required that he follow me all the way to the river, I doubt that he had pushed his mule very fast. He was an expert with a pistol, and had he arrived a few minutes earlier, he could have shot me easily from the top of the red cliffs.

Chapter 5

The road to Clevelandia, where I was to meet Ernst, wound upward from the river, through deep gorges and pine forests toward the village, nestled deep in the Santa Catherina hills. The place was named in honor of the American President Grover Cleveland, in a burst of national gratitude after he had settled a boundary dispute between Brazil and Argentina in favor of Brazil. It was a typical town, smaller than Passo Fundo with a population of perhaps six hundred souls; but like most towns of southern Brazil, it was built around the small town square, or *plaza*.

There were a few men loitering in the square when I arrived, jogging into town on my mule, Beduino; but it was *siesta* hour and most of the townspeople were asleep. I found Ernst in the *cantina* on the square, sitting alone.

"You have had trouble?" he said, when he looked at my face. I nodded.

Ernst listened while I told my story, then he asked: "Are you sure the blow killed him?"

"It must have killed him," I said. "Otherwise Dom Carlos would not have followed me to the river."

"He is a shrewd fellow," Ernst said. "Perhaps he wanted to be sure you were well out of the province. He had no stomach for chasing you."

Years later I learned how keen Ernst's judgment of the old thief-taker had been. When Dom Carlos left Passo Fundo, three hours after I left, Favelle was unconscious, but still alive. The old man had ridden two days on my trail just to take the precaution of seeing that I left the province. This, of course, I did not know at the time. I believed I had killed Favelle, and perhaps was a wanted man.

I asked Ernst if he had made any plans for us to continue our journey.

"We should remain for two or three days," he said. "I have arranged for certain repair jobs with the man at the village corral. There is a small wagon-shop where some tools are in need of repairing. These people live with their broken tools until someone comes along who can mend them."

A man sitting at a nearby table had risen and was coming toward us. I recognized him; he was Pedro Ramos from Passo Fundo. He had left the place hurriedly several weeks before, after a knife fight in which his opponent died of his wounds. This Ramos was a thin, agile man, swarthy and dark-eyed with black hair that flowed over a low forehead. He had a narrow, rat-like face, and swaggered slightly as he approached with a glass in one hand.

Ernst caught my glance and looked up. He stopped speaking and leaned back, his great body suddenly relaxed in a kind of suspended animation that I knew, from previous experience, might be a prelude to quick and violent action.

"Good day, *senhors!*" the man said, coming to a stop and teetering a bit. His manner was formally courteous, after the fashion of most Brazilians. "Will you drink with me in honor of our fortunate meeting here?"

I tried to match his courtesy, but I fear I failed to act convincingly. Bowing slightly, without rising, I thanked him but declined.

"My brother and I are engaged, as you can see, in a discussion," I said. "Later, perhaps."

The little man stiffened.

"You have arrived only lately," he said to me. "You left Passo Fundo suddenly, *senhor?*" He grinned rather wolfishly; and I felt an unclean association with the man. After all, we were both fugitives.

"My plans are entirely personal, Senhor Ramos," I said. "I do not recall having asked you to explain why you left Passo Fundo."

This was a mistake; I knew it the instant I spoke. It placed both of us on practically the same footing, and men of the character of Pedro Ramos are quick to spot such a flaw. I felt that I had exposed myself unnecessarily to suspicion.

The man stopped teetering; his dark eyes brightened. He raised his eyebrows in an exaggerated expression of inquiry.

"Do not take offense, *senhor!*" he exclaimed. "Everyone knows why I left Passo Fundo. I killed Sancho Ramirez, as you know—in a fair fight—"

Ernst rose. His eyes were blazing and I knew he would take my quarrel as his own if I did not stop him. Hastily, I said to Pedro Ramos:

"No offense, *senhor*—none at all! My brother and I have things to talk about. Perhaps we shall see you later."

Ramos bowed, again with exaggerated formality, and withdrew to his table. Later, as Ernst and I talked, I observed him leaning across the table, whispering to his comrades. Apparently we were the subject of their discussion, since they looked at us frequently.

Ernst and I unrolled our *ponchos* that night in the tool shed, where the owner of the wagon-shop, a cheerful, middle-aged German, cleared a place for us. There was only one small hotel in town, above the *cantina;* and it was so filthy we had decided not to stay there. We spread saddle blankets on the hard-packed *adobe* floor of the tool shed, using our saddles for pillows and *ponchos* for covering, and were quite comfortable.

We sat cross-legged on our blankets for perhaps a couple of hours, and talked over our plans.

"There is no use deceiving ourselves," I said. "I am a fugitive—and if you continue with me, you also will be a fugitive. We must decide now what to do."

Ernst, always a mystery of emotional mobility, rocked the little shed with his booming laugh. He seemed greatly amused.

"Alex, where we are going there are a thousand fugitives! You would be hard put to find anyone who is not fleeing from something—at least a wife, or a wife's husband. Three days from now we shall be on our way—and I doubt if the people of Clevelandia will know where we are going, or care."

"What about our friend Pedro Ramos?" I asked.

"Alex, why are you forever making enemies of these little men? You ask for trouble. Pedro wanted to swagger a little—so why not let him? It would have impressed his comrades. No doubt he has acquired a reputation here as a bad man, and if you had slapped him on the shoulder and greeted him as a man to be respected, he would have been your fast friend."

Ernst's remarks, well-intentioned as they were, struck me unfavorably. I said nothing more; but after I had rolled up in my *poncho*, tucking the cold canvas around my neck against the chill of a Brazilian winter night, I remained awake, considering the strange situation in which I found myself.

The unexpected meeting with Pedro Ramos had driven home to me the change in my status. He could not have known, of course, what had happened in Passo Fundo. And yet, with that cunning peculiar to people who live by their wits in wild places, he had immediately detected something unusual in my sudden appearance in Clevelandia. In a short time some traveller would arrive and the facts would be known. I could not avoid the grim truth: I was a wanted man. Even though Dom Carlos had no desire to follow me, there were others who might be attracted by the idea of a reward. Perhaps Pedro Ramos would send word back to some friend! I knew there were friends of Ricardo Favelle who would urge my capture, and perhaps offer a reward.

I had no regret over what had happened; Favelle had forced the issue, and I had had no choice. There are times— few enough, God knows!—when a man knows without question the rightness of his position. I was certain I was not wrong in killing Favelle—if I had killed him—yet now I found myself a hunted man. In the eyes of others I was no different from Pedro Ramos, who had killed a man and fled.

These thoughts weighed upon me; I felt at a lower ebb

of despondency than at any time since I had left Buenos Aires. It seemed to me the world had closed behind me.

It was natural that my thoughts, in the darkness of that mud-walled hut in the little village in the hills of Santa Catherina, should have drifted southward—to Buenos Aires, and to Elsa. It was more than two years since I had seen her; yet, by closing my eyes, I could picture her face clearly, in all its loveliness. I could even remember the soft sound of her voice on that last dismal night when she told me that Hans knew of our love, and had suggested that she get a divorce.

"I could not do that, Alex," she had told me, pleadingly. "I cannot leave him—even though there were no child, I still could not leave him. You should have seen him, Alex . . . he was so terribly hurt!" And then, after I had pointed out— rather meanly, I suppose—that I, too, was hurt, she had said: "I love you, Alex—but you are a wanderer. I do not criticize you for it—I love you for it. But you are a bird on the wing. I may want to roam, as a matter of excitement; but I will want my home and children more. In a few years you would hate me for that. If I went with you, it would be just one experience for me—but with you, it is your life."

Many times I had turned Elsa's words over in my mind; and as the months had passed, the hurt grew less. I began to understand the meaning of what she said. But now it came to me in a different sense. Here I was, in truth, leaving everything behind me for the lonely life of a wanderer.

It was my life—whether I liked it or not! Ernst might be right: the Matto Grosso, full of fugitives, would find room for me. But where else would there be room? I would be barred from any large city; and always the past would pursue me . . . the threat of exposure by someone who had known me in Passo Fundo as "the man who murdered Ricardo Favelle!"

Early in the morning, in the scant light before dawn, I rose and dressed; and for perhaps half an hour I stood outside the shed, looking northward at the ragged edge of the forest, forming an impenetrable wall against the lightening sky. In later years I was to know something of the strange world that lay behind that wall . . . the damp, rotting jungle marshes, hot and steaming under the pitiless rays of the tropical sun; the insects, some of them deadly, which plague you night and day; the great spaces of high yellow grass, dotted with patches of *capão*; the animals, prowling as silently as ghosts in the night; the parched plains of the west, without water or shelter, where men died in the hopeless agony of thirst; the mining camps, filled with offscourings of coastal ports, half-caste natives and hard-bitten, leathery *garimpeiros*, the "sour-doughs" of Brazil's backlands. But on this night I saw only the black forest, and listened to the faint rustle of leaves quivering in the cold wind that comes with the dawn.

I heard the door open and Ernst stood beside me. He was cheerful as usual in the morning; and he quickly set about selecting tools for the work we were to do that day.

That morning we worked in the wagon-shop; and at noon we walked down to the *cantina*. It was *siesta* hour, and a number of men were lounging in front of the *cantina*, some sprawled asleep on the hard-packed ground, hats covering their faces; and others leaning against the side of the building engaged in desultory discussions among themselves.

Pedro Ramos was standing near the door of the *cantina* as I walked up with Ernst; and something in his manner made me ready for trouble. He was whittling on a rope of plug tobacco, cutting off shavings for his pipe with a long pointed knife. This is a favorite trick of a certain type of knife-fighter; while pretending to be cutting the tobacco, they suddenly turn the point of the knife toward an intended victim and stab him before the man has a chance to defend himself.

I stopped deliberately in front of him. He looked up with bright, insolent eyes, but did not move aside to let me pass. I knew from his attitude that he did not intend to move.

"Yesterday you asked certain questions about my departure from Passo Fundo," I said. "I do not have to reply to such questions from anyone who chooses to ask them—but in this case I will tell you. Four nights ago Favelle and I had an argument at Herr Schmidt's place. He drew his gun and I

53

took it away and killed him with it. Do you have anything to say about this?"

My voice was probably sharp and challenging. A faint smile crossed Pedro Ramos' face, and he looked down at the plug of tobacco he was whittling. Then he said softly:

"We both have a reputation now, eh, Senhor Siemel?"

The pride of certain men of this type is often fantastic. I knew Pedro Ramos was thinking that if he should kill me, he would acquire the reputation of a great killer of men—having disposed of his victim in Passo Fundo, and of myself. In the curious code of that country his prestige would rise enormously. There was no doubt in my mind that I could knock the knife point aside and break his arm if he tried to stab me. But I did not want to fight the man; I was not a killer by any kind of instinct, and I chose the better course. I laughed at him.

This was so surprising that Pedro Ramos dropped both hands and stared at me. I pushed past him and walked into the *cantina*. The men standing around quickly made room for Ernst and myself.

Later in the day Ernst spoke to me about it.

"You were wise to avoid trouble, Alex," he said. "Yet I cannot help feeling that this is not a place for us to remain. You have made another enemy, and tomorrow he will be plotting some kind of answer."

The affair with Pedro Ramos had sickened me of Clevelandia, and any other place that might remind me of Passo Fundo and the world behind us. I had controlled my temper with Pedro, just as I had with Favelle—and as to the latter, it had not helped me in the end. Something of Dom Carlos' sage philosophy was creeping into my thoughts: "Never provoke a quarrel . . . but if you are attacked or insulted, kill your enemy, just as you would kill Lobo if he attacked you!"

Ernst and I agreed that we would complete such work as we had promised to do, and leave the next day for the north. Shortly after dawn the following morning we were riding across the green hills toward the plains of Paraná and the Matto Grosso which lay beyond.

Originally we had planned to travel as directly as possible toward the Matto Grosso, and the diamond fields, which cover a vast region stretching westward from Goyaz to the Bolivian border. Goyaz, east of the Matto Grosso, is nearly a thousand miles north of Clevelandia. Except for a few towns and the small, narrow-gauge railroad that runs directly across Brazil from São Paulo on the coast to Pôrto Esperança on the Rio Paraguay, there was nothing but wilderness between us and our destination.

Two things prevented us from carrying out our plan of travelling directly to the diamond fields. The first was the nature of the country, which was wild and desolate, and only sparsely settled; and in many areas without any established routes except for the trails which the native mail-carriers followed. These mystifying couriers seemed to be able to traverse treacherous forests and swamps with comparative immunity from the primitive tribes of Indians, including some of the most savage to be found anywhere in South America. They would plunge into little-known trails and turn up with fair regularity at outlying settlements. Few white men, however, would venture over these trails, and Ernst and I certainly were not equipped to cross the treacherous morass of the Paraná marsh alone with any hope of reaching our destination.

The second thing that delayed us was the germ of an idea that had been growing in my mind since my talk with Dom Carlos. It was the story of that old Indian who went into the jungle, armed only with a bow and arrow and a spear, and conquered jungle jaguars in singlehanded combat. I could not be sure how much of the story was true—how much Dom Carlos had told me in the hope of getting me out of Passo Fundo. Nevertheless, I found the flame of that desire constantly fanned, and I knew that sooner or later I must head for the São Laurenço, which lay between us and the diamond fields. To reach it, I would have to detour westward from the travelled route; and I secretly hoped that when the time arrived for this decision, I could persuade Ernst to come with me.

If we should go into the jungle looking for Joaquim Guató, I knew it would delay our arrival at the diamond fields perhaps a year, and therefore I hesitated to bring up the matter. I knew Ernst thought mostly of the fortune that lay hidden in streams in the high plateaus of the Matto Grosso. Once the fortune was found, he would be impatient to head for the coast again.

For my part, I was more fascinated by Dom Carlos' story of the tough old Indian who could stand against the fury of a maddened jaguar. There was a strong chance that the Indian would have died by this time; yet I could not abandon the idea until I had proved to my own satisfaction that it was impossible. If there was such a man alive, I wanted to find him. I wanted to see for myself whether such a thing was possible . . . because if the story were true, then it was a greater challenge than I had ever faced, even in my fights with Marcelo and Beduino.

So, without disclosing to Ernst exactly what was in my mind, I encouraged him to follow a route that would lead us toward the São Lourenço.

Chapter 6

We followed a meandering course across the pine-covered hills of Santa Catherina and beyond the Rio Iguassú, which divides Santa Catherina province from Paraná. Our route was not fixed; we travelled from town to town, remaining in the larger villages, such as Guarapuava, north of the Rio Iguassú, for many days and even for weeks, depending on the number of guns and other things that needed to be repaired.

At each town we had only to count noses to know how many guns must be mended; because in these places there was usually one gun for each male inhabitant, and all were in need of repair. Brazilians are not overly careful with their weapons; and we usually stayed until we had fixed all the guns in the town. There were weapons of every make and model, and Ernst and I soon became expert in repairing almost any kind of firearm.

Our travels took us westward along the Iguassú through two hundred and fifty miles of solid forest. We camped one day above one of the Iguassú waterfalls known as the *Garganta do Diablo*, or the "Devil's Throat," where a cataract higher than Niagara plunges into a cauldron deep in the jungle. This magnificent spectacle was to be seen only by birds and animals of the forest, and a few Indians and stray travellers like ourselves. Yet, to me, it rivalled Niagara, which I had seen in my travels in the United States; and it was more dramatic because of its isolation.

From the Iguassú we pushed westward across the Rio Paraná into Paraguay; and then toward the badlands of the *campo cerrado*. Here the hot winds blew up from Paraguay like a breath of pestilence, scorching the earth and those few unlucky humans destined to live or travel there. Villages were few and far apart, and the inhabitants were a dismal collection of ragged men and women and dirty children. In some of the larger places there were a few guns to be mended, but little money to pay for the work.

For several weeks we travelled through the plantations of eastern Paraguay, where the fields were worked by slaves whose lot is as miserable as that of any laborer in South America. This is the land of the maté, or Brazilian tea. Where the land had not been cleared for planting, it was coated with thick forest; indeed, the jungles along the Iguassú and west in Paraguay are more dense than any in the Matto Grosso.

It was in this country that Marcelo Caceres, the powerful Paraguayan whom I had fought in Passo Fundo, had been born. His tremendous neck muscles were the result of a strange kind of pack-carrying peculiar to this region. The field laborers carried great bundles of maté weighing from three to five hundred pounds. The bundle is slung over the back and carried by a wide band suspended from the forehead. The strain on the muscles of the neck required to carry this kind of burden strengthens the muscles until the neck ceases to exist, and becomes a mass of muscular tissue thicker than the head.

After we crossed the border from Paraguay into Brazil, and were at last in the Matto Grosso, I felt that we were getting close to our destination. Until now, the diamond fields had been like a dream, the end of a rainbow. It seemed that it would be only a short time before Ernst and I would ride out into our promised land. Actually, it was to be nearly three years before we rode into the diamond country.

The region we had entered bore little resemblance to the jungles. There were great patches of trees along the rivers, but as we rode northward we soon came out upon an expanse of sterile plains that supported little plant life and almost no animal life.

We were now on the campo cerrado, the bleak wasteland that stretches five hundred miles from the plains of Paraguay to the rock-crusted highlands of Goyaz. The hard, unyielding soil produces little for the scant population, and even the birds and beasts of the jungle do not venture very far into this region. The plains are rutted and broken with dry river beds, and covered with a mottled sprinkling of gray trees, stunted and gnarled, and dotting the earth like ghosts. They provide a mocking reminder of the pleasant pine forests to the south and a bitter foretaste of the damp jungle beyond.

The entire area seems to be useless for any human or natural purpose. It is as if Nature made a ghastly mistake, becoming confused as to whether the place was to be a jungle or the plains, and ending with a bleak mixture of both. Even the hardiest animals shun this sterile and often waterless waste, leaving the land to vultures, tarantulas and ticks. The latter are by far the deadliest inhabitants.

They are known as *garapata do chão* (ground ticks), and the area, which falls roughly on the Tropic of Capricorn, is known to Brazilians as the "*garapata* belt." The *garapata*, which lives in the dust of mud-walled houses, makes the hammock more necessary than the gun in the *campo cerrado* —and it was not long before Ernst and I learned this bitter lesson. It was actually through the agency of a tiny *garapata*— unintentional on the tick's part, to be sure—that we met Apparicio, and through him I was led ultimately to Joaquim Guató.

Ernst had become irritable and impatient to get north to the cooler country of the Rio das Garcas. He was less adaptable to this barren country than I, since he liked the livelier life of cities and even towns far better than the lonely trails. He cursed the *garapata* and the human inhabitants alike, and the miserable monotony of the landscape stifled his love of action and change.

We rode north, beyond Campo Grande and the narrow-gauge railroad which winds inland from São Paulo to Pôrto Esperança. Several days' ride beyond Campo Grande we came upon a settlement of perhaps two hundred souls. We were tired and dirty and saddle-weary. As we rode into the small square, or *plaza*, flanked with a cluster of mud-walled houses, topped with thatched *acuri* leaves, an elderly, dark-skinned man came out to meet us. He was evidently a man of some distinction in the place, since the women and children trailed respectfully behind him. The man lifted his hand in greeting.

"I have the honor of being the mayor of this place," he said, gravely and without the pomposity his words might have conveyed in another setting. "Do I also have the honor of greeting the two Russian engineers, who are famous for repairing guns and mending the sick?"

I was surprised, and, like anyone, I was pleased that he should know of us in such a remote place. We had been travelling within a few hundred miles of this region for half a year, and were known in most of the larger towns further south; but I hardly expected to be greeted in this small hamlet. The reference to "mending the sick" had to do with the medicine kit we always carried, and for which we made no charge.

I nodded; and Ernst, who had observed a shallow river running through the village behind the "church," which consisted of four poles, with sides partly covered with intertwined sticks and *acuri* leaves and a thatched roof, immediately asked that he be directed to the watering place, where we could unpack the animals.

The old man glanced at my brother, and said rather abruptly: "Behind the church." Ernst, hardly noticing that he had offended the old man, started off, leading the mules, and waved to me to follow. I dismounted, however, and approached the old fellow.

"Perhaps you have a small place we could rent for a few days," I said. "We will pay you, and we will be glad to repair as many guns as we can during the time we stay here."

The old patriarch bowed, and said it would be "an honor" to furnish us accommodations on his *rancho*. He evidently referred to the scrabble of small huts and lean-to shacks clustered near the church.

"First, may I ask your indulgence in an important matter," he said. "I have a guest in my house who is ill of a festering of his legs."

I signalled Ernst to ride on down to the river and unload the animals. I would join him later. Then I followed the old man, who told me his name was Eusebio. His house was larger than the other huts, but dark and foul-smelling inside. At the rear, lying in a hammock, was a long, thin man in a white shirt. His bony legs, protruding from the shirt, had been wrapped in strips of dirty cloth and leaves. One glance told me the man was in great pain, and very sick. He looked at me as I came up to the hammock, and managed a wry sort of grin. Then he said, in very good Portuguese:

"Good afternoon, *senhor*. I am glad you have come."

"What is the trouble?" I asked.

"I have been bitten by these cursed ticks." His thin, wide mouth twitched from time to time with pain as he spoke; and his dark eyes, glittering with fever, did not waver as he looked at me. "I am from the Rio Grande do Sul," he continued. "We do not have such miserable insects in that country."

I nodded; but I also became wary. His reference to the Rio Grande do Sul might make it extremely possible that he knew of Ernst and myself and our reasons for leaving Passo Fundo.

"You are from Rio Grande do Sul?" I asked. "What part, if I may ask?"

He grimaced.

"From the western part. I am a cowman—from Allegrete. Do you have to know where I come from in order to do something about these damned bites? I will pay you for your medicine."

I smiled, and touched the man's shoulder. He was tall—above the average height of a Brazilian—and his face, naturally thin, was gaunt from the wasting effect of the poison in his system. His eyes were bright and feverish, but his wide mouth showed traces of good humor in spite of the constant pain. I was sure that if he knew of our reason for leaving Passo Fundo, he would have betrayed the knowledge.

"Please do not be offended," I said. "I did not mean to

be rude. I also come from the Rio Grande do Sul—from the town of Passo Fundo."

There was no recognition in his eyes; and so I concluded there was nothing to worry about. I said I must get my medicine kit, and returned to my mule, unstrapping it from the saddle. Dom Eusebio trailed along beside me, watching anxiously as I opened the kit and took out cotton, peroxide of hydrogen—the universal disinfectant in those days—and zinc ointment. The man in the hammock watched from the narrow slits of his eyes while I examined the wounds.

The bite of the *garapata do chão* is dangerous, but the greatest peril lies in the infection which may set in, usually from scratching it. In this case the infections had grown deep, and both legs were badly swollen and almost gangrenous. I was not sure whether it would be possible to arrest the infection, and I turned to look at the sick man. Although his teeth were clenched from the agony of my examination—each wound must have been like a pit of acid in his flesh—he managed again to grin.

"Your legs are badly infected," I told him. "I shall have to clean each wound separately. It will be very painful."

"There is only a small difference between being boiled in water or oil," he said. "As long as you leave the legs with me, I shall be satisfied."

I had observed the man's face, and was impressed by what I saw. He was deeply tanned, as most cowmen are; and his cheeks had a drawn look that comes from continual suffering, yet there was intelligence and friendliness in his face—two qualities that were rare in that remote region. I had an instant liking for him.

He endured the dressing of the wounds stoically, now and then giving vent to a grunt or a sigh. When I had finished, he began puffing on an ill-smelling cigar, watching me while we talked. I learned that his name was Apparicio, and he had been travelling for many months in the country to the north.

"You are travelling south?" I asked.

He shrugged.

"Wherever I can find work. I was to meet a man from Descalvados, but I have not found him. The only thing I am sure of is that I do not intend to remain here. I will go as God wills it—on my horse, or into the ground."

He explained that he had stopped a few days at the little settlement to earn his food, and while rising from his hammock one morning had carelessly stepped on the dirt floor with his bare feet. Before he was aware of his mistake, several ticks had fastened on his legs. The *garapata* can be brushed off easily, but they leave a bite which soon begins to smart.

"I scratched the bites," he said, still puffing on the cigar. He was relaxed to some extent after the cleansing of the wounds, which must have relieved the painful pressure of the swellings. "Perhaps this was foolish, but in my own country, we scratch such bites. This was several weeks ago. I have stayed here since, hoping my legs would get better, but instead they have gotten worse."

I cautioned him against letting dirt get into the wounds, which I had covered with zinc ointment and bandages. Then I went out to join Ernst. Dom Eusebio followed me, offering the hospitality his *rancho* afforded—which was little more than a mud hut and a little food—if I would remain until the sick man was on his way to recovery.

I said my brother and I would consider remaining a few days. There were perhaps a hundred guns in the village that would need repair, and we would be able to replenish our supplies of food and stores of cartridges, and perhaps pick up a few *milreis*.

Ernst was agreeable to the idea of staying, after I explained the old man's offer.

"What difference does it make where we stop?" he said, with a vague bitterness. "Before the wet season comes again, we should be on the Rio das Garcas looking for diamonds. Meanwhile, one place is as good as another."

I did not disclose my real reason for wanting to remain. In addition to the fact that I should remain with Apparicio until his wounds began to heal—which is a responsibility of anyone practicing medicine, whether he is a trained physician, or merely an itinerant "medicine man" like myself—I had found out some facts from the sick man.

He told me he had travelled beyond Coxim to the São Laurenço River. I wished to talk with him further about these places; and in particular I wanted to find out what he knew of Dom Carlos' legendary Indian hunter.

The following morning I went over to Dom Eusebio's house, and examined Apparicio's legs. The swellings had become less inflamed, and his fever had lessened. While I was inspecting the wounds, Dom Eusebio came into the hut, his black face wrinkled in a frown.

"The local sheriff has expressed a wish to see your papers," he said. "It is a stupid formality—you have them, of course?"

I looked sharply at the old man. The request startled me, because it was not usual in such places; and it had not even occurred to me there would be a sheriff in such a remote place.

"I have them, of course," I said. "What does he wish to see them for? Is it customary to make inquiries of travellers in this place? Perhaps this sheriff prefers to repair the guns of this town in his own way, in which case my brother and I will be glad to continue on our way."

Dom Eusebio's frown became more perplexed.

"Do not take offense, *senhor!* I will tell the *caboclo* to mind his own affairs." The word *caboclo* is used in Brazil to designate a half-caste whose ancestry is so uncertain that the amount of Negro blood in his veins is not known. Dom Eusebio shuffled out, evidently to put the "sheriff" in his place.

Apparicio had listened to this exchange, and was watching me with an amused smile.

"I would not worry about the old fool," he said. "In the first place, he is not a sheriff—only a deputy, who gets a few *milreis* for representing the law in this miserable community. He feels he must be official when a stranger arrives. Also, he is jealous of the mayor."

While I was dressing Apparicio's legs, he talked casually of the country to the north, and spoke enthusiastically of the people.

"They are the kind who mind their own affairs," he said; and I glanced up, wondering whether any significance was to be attached to his words. Apparicio was staring thoughtfully at the ceiling, and I followed the direction of his glance. He was concentrating upon the activities of a spider that was trying to loop a strand of web around a dangling bit of *acuri* leaf. The spider had run out to the end of the strand, from which he swung in a slight arc. The faint breath of air in the room had created a pendulum motion, but he was improving upon this with a cunning example of instinctive engineering. He would retract his body an inch or so on the strand, then run out to the end, giving the swing of the strand additional momentum; and finally this increased to the point where the spider finally touched the end of the palm leaf, and hung there.

We laughed at the same instant, and I caught a look of understanding in Apparicio's eyes. I felt a stronger liking for Apparicio, since he seemed to appreciate this heroic persistence in the tiny desert creature.

"The spider eats the pesty flies," the cowboy said, with a grin. "Therefore it is my friend."

After I returned to the hut where Ernst and I established ourselves, I thought over the request of the sheriff, and decided there was no reason for concern. However, Apparicio had evidently caught some significance in the exchange of words between Dom Eusebio and myself. Ernst had laid out his tools, and was working on several guns on a bench which he had made by laying two boards on a couple of stools.

"There has been a request by the sheriff to look at our papers," I finally said.

Ernst looked up from his work.

"For what reason?"

"I do not know. Dom Eusebio brought me word, and said he would settle the matter. It does not seem likely that word would have reached the sheriff after so many months."

Ernst shrugged indifferently.

"What can the sheriff do? This is another province. In this country everyone has a past . . . and therefore no one has a past."

"That is what Apparicio said," I remarked. Ernst looked sharply at me.

"You have discussed this with him?"

"No, certainly not," I said, wondering at Ernst's tone. "We discussed the country north of here. He has been in much of it."

While I worked, I found myself thinking again of the request of the sheriff for our papers. It was not the request itself which disturbed me; I doubted that it was anything more than officiousness. But it was the suddenly renewed sensation of being hunted. I had not thought about this since the first days of our flight from Passo Fundo, and I did not like it.

A few days later I broached to Ernst a thought that had been on my mind.

"This Apparicio should be well within a week or so," I said. "He knows the country north of here. Why should we not hire him as a helper?"

Ernst looked at me.

"Do we need a helper?"

"Perhaps not . . . But his wages would not amount to much. He would be worth his keep. And he has been in the jungle, also."

Ernst smiled; and suddenly I knew that he had been aware all along of my undisclosed desire to find the old Indian hunter, Joaquim Guató.

"Very well," Ernst said. "If you wish to hire him, Alex, we shall have him along. Have you spoken to him?"

I said I had not. The next day, however, as I was bandaging Apparicio's legs, which had already begun to show improvement, I spoke to him about the São Laurenço country. He had travelled north of Corumbá, to Amolar, where the Rio São Laurenço branches off the Paraguay to the northeast, and along this river to São Laurenço *pantanal*, a strip of marshland with tall grass and patches of *capão*. This was the great *tigre* ground of that area.

Somewhere within the triangle, formed by Corumbá, São Laurenço, and Coxim, I felt I would find the old Indian, if he were still alive.

"I worked for a while at Descalvados," Apparicio said. "This is west of the Rio Paraguaya. I know the country well enough to find my way. However, unless one likes the jungle, it is hardly worth the effort to go through it. There is a road from Corumbá north to Lake Gaiba, west of the Paraguaya, and it crosses over to Amolar. Beyond that is Descalvados and to the east is Cuyabá. This is the diamond country where you and your brother wish to go."

"Have you heard of an old Indian who kills the *tigre* with a spear?" I asked.

"I have heard of the story," Apparicio said. "I have not seen these hunters, but I have heard of that one who works on the *rancho* Fazenda Alegre, near São Laurenço. He kills the jungle animals, which destroy the cattle and even attack the people who work on the ranch."

"Does he hunt alone?" I asked.

"Indians do not usually hunt alone," Apparicio said. "I have heard of this one who does—but who knows? There are many tales of the jungle, and few are true."

I was inwardly excited. This much was true: There was such a hunter as Dom Carlos had described! I asked Apparicio many questions with a feverish interest that must have surprised him. Then I told him about Joaquim Guató and his interest became as lively as my own. Finally I suggested that he accompany Ernst and myself northward. He agreed immediately—without even mentioning wages.

When I told Ernst that I had made an arrangement with Apparicio, he looked at me curiously, but merely nodded. It was settled that as soon as we had completed the repairing of the guns that had been brought to us— and Apparicio was well enough to travel—we would start north. This would be in two or three weeks.

A few days later Dom Eusebio came into our hut, followed by a ragged half-caste, wearing a dirty leather jacket which usually indicated some kind of local police authority.

"Your papers, *senhors*," he said, brushing past Dom Eusebio. "I must request that you present them to me."

I saw Ernst reach for a loaded revolver, and I quickly rose and took a packet containing our identification papers from a *mochila*, and passed them to the little half-caste. He looked them over with an air of gravity, and returned them to me. After they left, Ernst—who had been in a state or poorly suppressed anger—said with exasperation:

"Let us get out of this place, Alex. That man has been snooping around as if we were thieves."

"Perhaps he has some reason to suspect us," I said. "He may have some word from Passo Fundo."

Ernst scoffed at this. He pointed out that we had had no word from Passo Fundo since we left more than nine months before; and since we were fairly well known in the towns through which we passed, this would certainly indicate that we were not being pursued. Later in the day Dom Eusebio came back, full of apologetic explanations. I asked him if there were any specific reason for the action.

"It is of no consequence, *senhor*," he said. "The man merely wishes to emphasize his importance—to my detriment. He cannot read."

Ernst insisted, however, that we plan to leave as soon as possible.

"The rains will come soon in the north, and it will be another six months before we reach the Rio das Garcas. I have been through that country—it is not easy to travel during the heavy rains."

I agreed. Apparicio was almost well enough to travel, and I told Ernst we could leave within a week. We completed the jobs we had on hand, and on the day before our departure, after we had packed our tools and other belongings, and were ready to leave, I suggested that we explain to the new member of our party why we had left Passo Fundo.

Ernst was perplexed at my proposal.

"You hardly know this fellow, Alex," he said. "Besides,

it is not necessary to disclose our personal affairs to everyone who works for us. He knows nothing of us, but if he senses a reward, we will not merely have pursuit on our heels; we will have it riding with us. He may betray us at the first chance to some small-town policeman."

Ernst's reaction to my suggestion was natural; yet I felt the time had come for some sort of decision.

"We cannot always run as hunted men, Ernst," I said. "This fellow is honest, and I trust him. If we can trust no one, then we are outlaws. We will always be running. If we have to come to an issue—if we really are hunted men, then I would rather have it come this way. At least we will know what our future is going to be."

Ernst did not entirely see my reasoning; yet I felt that the burden of secret knowledge, shared only by ourselves, was a bad thing. It cut us off from the world. If we told Apparicio of the affair at Passo Fundo, frankly and without concealment, it would clear from our minds the feeling of being hunted.

And I also was quite certain Apparicio would not pass any such information to a law officer, merely to collect a reward. I had talked many hours with him, and I felt that I knew him.

That night I invited Apparicio to our hut to discuss plans; and I told him of our quarrel with Favelle and what had happened the night I left Passo Fundo.

He listened quietly until I finished; and watching the slight muscular indications of expression on the face of this tall, thin-faced man, I became completely confident that I understood his character. After I had concluded my story, he said:

"I would not worry over this matter, Senhor Alexandre. It is more than a year ago, and in this country things like that die quickly. Senhor Ernesto can assure you that little attention is paid to such things in the Matto Grosso. Every man is driven there by something—either his past or his future. Fear and greed are the two strongest passions that can drive men into this country, and these forge a great brotherhood among them.

"If the little *caboclo* has said nothing further, you can be sure that he is not looking for a reward. He is not sufficiently clever to keep silent about such a thing."

The following day the three of us headed north toward Coxim.

Chapter 7

The Great Marshes of the Paraguay River lie along the center of South America, a vast and terrifying morass of jungle and treacherous swamps. The land is half-submerged in the wet season, much of the surface covered with hidden pools, filled with a rank growth of plant life that has been boiling and steaming under the baking heat of the equatorial sun for millions of years. The marshes sprawl across the heart of the continent in an irregular pattern, following the course of the Upper Paraguay River, and spreading out over its main tributaries for almost a thousand miles.

It is a paradox of this steaming, fetid swamp that in dry seasons the very land that is flooded during the heavy rains projects like dry bones from the skin of the soil. Men and animals have died of thirst on barren ridges that six months later will be half-submerged swampland.

Along the eastern boundary of this chain of swamps is the *campo cerrado*. The bare ribs of this bleak country are interlaced with the jungle in a manner that is not unlike the bones and flesh of an animal: that is, the soft bottom lands fill in between the spine-like highlands of the dry *campo cerrado*. The change in the countryside follows a pattern: first there is a fringe of thicker trees—*muliana* and *lixeira*, the latter furnishing a powder from its dry thorny leaves that is used by Indians as emery; then a stretch of tall marsh grass leading gradually downward to the swampy lowlands where the water-fills are surrounded with huge *buriti* palms, standing sixty to seventy feet high with a massive crown of fan-like leaves; and around these are slenderer *carandá* palms and the spreading trees of the jungle—the giant "wild fig," or *banyan*, the *piuva* and the *jatobá*.

The town of Coxim lies near the confluence of the Rio Coxim and the Taquari, two rivers that form a general western boundary of the Great Marshes of the Matto Grosso. These marshes extend northwest as far as the Chapadão range, a *planalto*, or plateau, that juts like a spur from the eastern Andes; and south into Paraguay and the Gran Chaco.

Coxim itself is on the *campo cerrado*; but a few miles to the north the jungle begins to spread along the rivers and around water holes. The *campo cerrado* gradually curves north toward the high flatlands of the Planalto do Matto Grosso, and the diamond fields. I had already decided on a detour through the São Laurenço country to find out whether Dom Carlos' old Indian hunter was flesh-and-blood, or merely a product of the old bandit-chaser's imagination, but I had not mentioned this to Ernst.

I had noticed a certain restraint between Ernst and Apparicio; and a few days before we reached Coxim I decided to talk this over with Ernst. We were resting on the bank of a small stream. Apparicio had gone into the forest to shoot a couple of birds for our dinner, and Ernst, digging the heels of his boots into the soft bank, seemed moody, and almost sullen. I decided to bring into the open things that I knew had been on the minds of both of us for many days.

"You do not like Apparicio," I suddenly suggested. Ernst looked at me, and smiled with that good-natured tolerance that older brothers have for juniors.

"I have not said I do not like the fellow, Alex."

"If you wish," I continued obstinately, "we will dismiss him when we reach Coxim. We cannot travel together as enemies."

Ernst shook his head slowly. His blond beard made him seem older than he actually was; yet I had the feeling that my brother was not old enough for this world of forests and swamps and barren highlands toward which we were heading. His temper had become thin and he was easily irritated by small things.

"You and Apparicio are very much alike, Alex," he finally said. "I do not resent that. What I do resent is this damned country! I hate the loneliness—and the lonelier it becomes, the better you like it!"

I smiled; but I felt badly, because I knew it was now inevitable that Ernst and I would part. He would never consent to the journey into the jungles of the São Laurenço country.

The bonds between Ernst and myself were deep, but nothing was deep enough to make him like the hard, desolate country through which we were travelling. Ernst enjoyed stop-overs at towns, and even our stays at the big *ranchos* we had visited as repairmen. We were always welcomed warmly, and Ernst liked people. But on the long rides over the bleak wastelands, or through the jungles of the Iguassú, he had shown an aversion to loneliness in many ways. We had simply reached an inevitable parting of our paths.

Ernst's words brought a stab of regret; and at the same time I was glad of this chance to clear the air between us.

"Why don't you stay in Coxim while Apparicio and I ride north?" I suggested. "We can meet later at some town we will agree upon."

Ernst looked at me, and managed to smile. But there was an edge of bitterness in his voice, and his eyes reflected the hurt.

"You want to find that damned old Indian," he said. It was as if he had known of some secret infidelity on my part for a long time, and now he had brought it to the surface. I could not repress a smile, and Ernst suddenly laughed, and put his hand affectionately on my shoulder.

"Go ahead, Alex—look for him! I would not go into that marsh country for a thousand Indian legends! I have no stomach for such places."

We said little more. It was agreed that Ernst would remain at Coxim until he heard from us; and we would rejoin each other perhaps at Cuyabá. Apparicio and I meanwhile would continue northward through the jungle toward the São Laurenço.

When Apparicio returned, he seemed to sense that we had reached an understanding. With an instinctive knowledge of wild things, he also had a sure instinct about people. He caught my eye and smiled; and nothing further was said until we reached Coxim and I explained our plans.

Ernst had become cheerful again, once it was settled that he would stay in Coxim. It was a small town, little more than a village of perhaps fifteen hundred people. But Ernst did not require large numbers of people; he just wanted other human beings around, a place to drink and exchange gossip, and a woman now and then to create a diversion. He possessed an unfailing fatalism which, in a way, was his greatest charm. When I was a boy this had impressed me as a sort of devil-may-care cheerfulness; but his easy acceptance of life, as long as it was lively, had now emerged as weakness rather than strength in his character. What I had admired in boyish worship, I now realized made him utterly unfit for life in these wild places.

Ernst's instinctive habit of carefree indifference to what the future held as long as the present was pleasant, had also created an uncertainty in his own mind as to how well his nature fitted with life. This lack of sureness had driven him to a kind of sullen despair; and in all likelihood that was what drove him into *cantinas* where he could resolve his inner forebodings in the warmth of *cachaça* and the friendly smiles of women.

Coxim was a dusty little place, perched on a rim of low hills of the *campo cerrado*, above the Rio Coxim, where it branches from the Taquari. The blazing heat of the Brazilian sun beat down on the earth with increasing fury as we rode into the town.

There was vaguely unpleasant news in store for us, however, when we arrived in Coxim. The three of us were sitting at a table in the *cantina*, talking over our plans, when a thin man, wearing bluejeans and the inevitable sleeveless khaki jacket that was a kind of symbol of frontier law, came up to our table and planting his feet rather far apart, asked sharply:

"You are the Russian engineers from the South?"

I nodded, a bit surprised at the belligerence of his tone. "You have come up from Rio Grande do Sul—from Passo Fundo, eh?"

This time I nodded more warily, and glanced at Ernst. Apparicio was idly drumming on the table, with his customary manner of saying nothing and observing everything.

"We have been in Passo Fundo—several months ago. Why do you ask?"

The little man shrugged.

"There was a fellow through here some weeks ago. He also came from there and asked about you. Perhaps you are looking for a friend, eh?"

I shook my head.

"We were not expecting to meet anyone. However, we know many people in Passo Fundo. Did this fellow have anything to say—as to why he was inquiring about us? Perhaps I could identify him in that way."

The little Brazilian shook his head; and I realized from watching his expression that what I had taken for belligerence or perhaps suspicion was probably a natural expression on his face. We asked him to drink with us. I did not want to question him directly as to the motives of the man who had asked about us; yet I felt sure it had something to do with Favelle. From what the little Brazilian—the *delegado da policia*, or constable, as we learned—had to say, the stranger's inquiries were more than casual. He had wanted to know whether we had travelled through Coxim; and finding that we had not been there, he had said nothing further, which increased my suspicion that this concerned the affair with Favelle.

I glanced once at Apparicio, and he shook his head slightly. I understood what he was trying to tell me: that it was dangerous to ask questions in the Matto Grosso. Regardless of what the purpose might be, inquiries incurred suspicion; and therefore we quickly dropped the subject.

When we had left the *cantina*—or *bolicho*, as these places are known in the Matto Grosso, since they combine the services of a saloon, tobacco shop, small grocery store and lunch counter—I turned to Ernst:

"We must get out of here as soon as possible," I said. "I do not intend to be hunted—and if it continues, I shall become the hunter." I turned to Apparicio. "What do you make of this?"

The *gaucho* shrugged.

"It is not often that officers will go so far. Each province is broad, as you know . . . and there is enough lawlessness in the Rio Grande do Sul to occupy the law officers there. It may be the *tocaya*."

This, I knew, was the Brazilian code of revenge. It was a vicious practice, abhorred by most law-abiding Brazilians, in which those whose relatives have been killed hire a paid assassin to even the score. I turned to Ernst:

"Since we do not know this fellow, we cannot very well hunt him down. Do you wish to remain here, Ernst—there may be danger to you, also."

Ernst shrugged.

"I will stay, Alex. Go hunt up your Indian. You will find a dried old man, drunk with *cachaça*, who will boast of the deeds of his youth—which no one believes or disbelieves, since no one cares what lies an old Indian tells. If you wish to travel two hundred miles through the stinking jungles for that pleasure, you are welcome to it."

In spite of Ernst's laugh, I knew he was sorry to see us go—not because he had any fear of the *tocaya* (ambush), if that was the explanation of the stranger following us; but because it might be the last time we would see each other.

The country into which Apparicio and I planned to journey was more remote than the lonely lands over which we had travelled; and the jungle held dangers more formidable than any we had faced. There was a possibility that we might plunge into the Great Marshes, which lay to the north of Coxim, and never be heard from again.

Years later, when I learned to estimate these dangers—and knew more about the ways of travel in the jungle—I realized how foolhardy the journey could have been. At the time, however, I was more concerned with the immediate problem created by the mysterious stranger who had inquired about us.

In my own mind, I had killed Favelle. I was certain that the stranger mentioned by the *delegado da policia* was hunting me, either officially or as an agent of the friends or relatives of Favelle. There seemed to be only two possible courses open: either track down my pursuer, and settle with him—which would have been difficult, since I neither knew who he was nor where he was; or go into the jungle where it would be almost impossible for him to track me.

The latter course coincided with my own desire to find the Indian spear-hunter, Joaquim Guató. Ernst, of course, understood this; and although he maintained an attitude of cheerfulness, there was an underlying hurt. I think he felt that I preferred to travel with Apparicio into the wilderness, rather than remain with him; and to some extent he was right. Apparicio was a born woodsman, and I knew there was much I could learn from him.

"I will meet you in Cuyabá after the rains," Ernst said. "I doubt if you will get past the São Laurenço before bad weather sets in. In that case you will be stuck there until the next dry season. When you are floundering along the marsh trails, Alex, just remember that I will be quite comfortable here in Coxim."

My brother laughed; but there was a vague bitterness in his eyes, and from the glance he gave Apparicio, I knew he felt an underlying resentment that I had chosen to travel with the *gaucho* into the jungle, instead of remaining in Coxim.

Chapter 8

We rode out of Coxim toward the jungle—I on Beduino
and Apparicio on his horse, leading a mule; and again I felt a
curious sense of inevitability, as if some force stronger than
my conscious mind had taken charge of my life. It is a strange
feeling, almost a sensation; and many times I have felt that
this sense of inevitability has made the difference between
life or death for me. In the jungle men as well as animals
learn to rely on a sure instinct rather than reason—perhaps
because the vagaries of thinking serve little purpose in an
emergency, except to distract the thinker from what he must
do to keep from being killed. This is particularly true when a
man faces a charging *tigre*. Unless he can concentrate on
what he has to do, he will be killed, because the big jungle
cats do not seem to suffer from the cluttering delays of a
logical mind.

We followed a course to the northeast of Coxim, keeping to the highlands of the *campo cerrado* until we reached
the jutting fingers of the jungle. These patches, covering
bottom lands near the rivers, or water holes, are known as
capão. Sometimes they are miles across, and as the land de-
scends from the high, barren country into the lush lowlands,
there is dramatic change in the scenery.

As soon as we began to drop down toward the water holes
and streams, we would encounter high marsh grass; and the
thorny *lixeira* and *paratudo* trees of the dusty plains would
be replaced by patches of *piuva* and now and then a giant
"strangler tree"—the *banyan*, or wild fig; and slender *acuri*
palms. As we descended into the low areas, the taller trees

would appear—the *anjico* and *cedro* trees, and great *buriti* palms, towering sixty or seventy feet high, with magnificent spreads of fan-like leaves.

For several days we skirted the border of the Great Marshes of the Paraguay, which spread over a vast morass of half-submerged land stretching almost to the border of Bolivia. Much of the land east of the Great Marshes is wild cattle graze, and thousands of head of stock are scattered over inland empires the size of Rhode Island.

One evening we camped near a half-dry water hole—it was the end of the dry season, but the heavy floods had not started pouring down from the north—and Apparicio shot a swamp buck, which we hung in a tree near our camp fire. We were in the marsh-grass country, and these were the places where the prowling *tigre* roamed at night; but neither Apparicio nor I had given much thought to the possibility of one of the jungle cats invading our camp at night.

We strung our hammocks and turned in; and perhaps a couple of hours later I was awakened. The embers of our fire still glowed, faintly pink in the darkness; and overhead the clear blaze of stars in the tropical sky gave the only other light in the utter blackness of the forest. At first I could not determine what had awakened me; but I knew that something had happened—some sound in the night had penetrated my sleep.

Then I heard a distinct sound which brought the first shock of pure fright I had experienced in the jungle. It was the unmistakable sound of bones cracking. At first I had a ghastly instant when I thought it might be Apparicio; but a slight motion of his hammock a few feet from mine enabled me to make out the faint outline of his body, sitting upright in the hammock. Apparently Apparicio had been awakened by the same sound that had disturbed me.

I had hung my pistol holster at the head of my hammock, the belt looped over the branch from which the hammock was suspended; and I carefully reached over and pulled out the gun. The terrible crunching of bones went on a few feet into the darkness; and by now I realized that some animal had pulled down our swamp buck and the cracking noise I heard was the sound of the beast's teeth grinding on the carcass.

For several minutes I listened, hardly daring to breath. The beast that was devouring our swamp buck must be a *tigre*, I decided. No other animal in the jungle, not even the *jacaré*, or marsh crocodile, had jaws powerful enough to crunch the bones of a deer. My mind seemed to be locked in the grip of an almost paralyzing fear. I doubt if I could have moved if I had wanted to; and there was no particular reason for wanting to move. The steady crunching, now and then interrupted with a sucking snarl, left little doubt as to what was going on a few feet away.

Suddenly there was a silence, and I gripped the handle of my pistol. At first I thought the animal had seen either Apparicio or myself, sitting in our hammocks; but after a few seconds there was a rustling noise, and I realized the deer carcass was being dragged across the ground. A minute or so later, I heard Apparicio's low whisper:

"*Senhor*—are you awake?"

I slipped off the hammock and moved cautiously over to the fire. Apparicio came up beside me, his flashlight aimed at the place where the deer had been. We decided to alternate guard duty for the rest of the night, but neither of us slept. The next morning we saw the tracks of the midnight visitor. They were large, and we could see where the beast had dug in its claws, tearing at the deer.

The experience left a sense of apprehension of the mysterious danger of the jungle that I had not felt before. As we rode out across the marsh grasslands that morning, I had acquired a sobering respect for the wilderness through which we were travelling; and I decided that hereafter one of us would stand guard at night.

Toward evening we rode down a long slope and saw the lazy curling of smoke against the haze of gold over the green roof of the jungle. A scattering of huts lay along a river bank, and on a small knoll behind them rose a square, white house, mud-walled but as imposing as a medieval castle rising above the squalid huts at the foot of the hill. The rays of the setting sun splashed the walls with a pink tinge, giving the scene an air of unreal beauty. At the edge of the little settlement a *vaquero* was crouched over a calf, wielding a thin, sharp knife—apparently slaughtering the animal for the evening meal. Apparicio, who was haughtily proud of the skill of southern *gauchos*, looked critically at the operation. In reply to a question, the man explained this was the *rancho* of Dom Juão Cajango.

We rode on toward the big white house, and our *"Ho de casa!"* brought out a white-bearded patriarch—evidently Senhor Cajango—who greeted us cheerfully and suggested we put away our horses and come into the house for dinner, which was being put on the table. We washed at the watering trough and entered the big dining room. There were no women at the table, although a woman served us. After we had eaten a rather sparse dinner of *charqui*—jerked beef— rice and beans, the old man asked our business. I told him: I was a travelling mechanic and Apparicio was my assistant.

The old man nodded. He was strangely built, with an upper torso that was military in its straightness, almost to the point of being deformed with erectness, if such a thing is possible; and his lower half was like a pair of barrel staves, bowed from years of clamping his legs on horses. The hoop-like shape of his lower extremities, and the stiff uprightness of his upper body, coupled with his white beard which flowed over his chest in a snowy avalanche, gave him altogether a weird appearance. His inner character, as we quickly found, con- formed to his exterior in its curious contradictions. Although Dom Juão was the owner of a cattle empire that would cover half of Belgium, with at least fifty thousand heads of stock, spread from the edge of the jungle to the highlands of Goyaz, he was one of the most obdurate hagglers I have ever known. In addition to serving a table so frugal it would have made an Indian turn up his nose in scorn, allowing his household and his two sons only the skimpiest and most inedible food, he bickered for every *milrei* in a bargain, and cackled with glee every time he knocked the price down.

Our conversation soon developed into a haggling match over how much Dom Juão was willing to pay for the mechanical jobs that needed to be done around the house. He had a half-dozen sewing machines in various states of disrepair. Apparently he sent to São Paulo for a new one whenever an old one broke down, which must have cost a good deal. But when I offered to repair them at seventy *milreis* each, the old man literally clawed his beard with indignation. I suggested, with such courtesy as I could muster, that a man of his wealth, living in this remote region without repair facilities handy, might take advantage of the arrival of a repairman and pay reasonably, if not generously, for the service; but Dom Juão seemed to feel that it was a show of weakness to settle for anything more than the lowest price he could bargain for, and he bargained to the bitter end on each job.

He was curious about my camera, and asked many questions about my reasons for taking pictures in such a God-forsaken country. I told him I understood from my assistant, Apparicio, that this was *tigre* country, and I was hopeful of getting pictures of them.

"I have a *tigre* in one of the outer corrals," he said. "You are welcome to take a picture of the animal."

"A live *tigre*?" I asked.

"No, of course not. He is dead and stinks a little, but the picture will not show the smell of the beast. I will not charge you for the picture."

I hastened to explain, while absorbing this unprecedented display of generosity, that I was not interested in pictures of dead animals. I wanted to take the picture while the *tigre* was living, and, if possible, at liberty.

"Sacred Mother of God!" he exclaimed, throwing up his hands. "You cannot do it—nothing like that has ever been done! Only the bravest hunters ever see a *tigre*, and no one has taken a picture of one. It is not only foolhardy, but entirely unnecessary. The dead ones look exactly like the living ones, except that they are more limp."

There seemed no point in trying to explain my reasons for wanting to capture the jungle king alive on a film plate;

so I said nothing further. However, a few days later while I was repairing his sewing machines—we had settled on sixty *milreis* a machine—Dom João came excitedly into the room where I was at work.

"My two sons will start tomorrow on a hunting journey to the west." he said. "There is a *tigre* that has destroyed many of my cattle, and it is time to put an end to him. I am old, and I would be glad if you would go with my sons. Perhaps you can take your picture."

I quickly agreed to accompany the two boys. Dom João even offered me the use of his gun—an ancient muzzle-loader, which he said could be filled with a double-load of powder and chopped nails. I was not sure who would suffer the more from such a blast—the *tigre* or myself; but I thanked him and told him I would take my Winchester carbine.

The two boys, George and Bernardo, were familiar with handling dogs, and also knew the country; and it was only a few hours' ride the following day before we arrived in the area where the *tigre* had been reported. I was not familiar with this kind of hunting, and I watched closely. The dogs trotted along without much direction, sniffing the ground as they ran. The boys were guided entirely by the actions of the dogs. We covered perhaps an hour of riding when the lead-dog took off with a sudden deep-throated baying, and the other dogs—whining with excitement—followed the lead-dog.

For a few minutes I tried to keep up with the chase on my horse, but soon the thickets became so heavy, and strangling tentacles of rope-weed so troublesome, that I climbed off my horse, tethered it to a tree, and ran on afoot. The elder brother, George, had also dismounted, and when I caught up with him the dogs were circling around the mouth of a hole.

"*Caytetú!*" George exclaimed in a whisper, pointing to the hole. The animal to which he referred is a small wild pig, less dangerous than the wild hog, or *quexada*. Whether the dogs had originally been on the track of the *tigre* and had somehow been distracted to follow the *caytetú*, or whether we had been mistaken in the spoor they followed from the first, I did not know. But the prospect of catching the jungle pig, which is extremely tasty, aroused George and Bernardo to a pitch of excitement.

The sudden switch from hunting a *tigre* to chasing a wild hog dampened my ardor; but I helped the boys build a fire over the hole, and within a few minutes a black animal with bristling hair on its back dashed wildly through the flame and smoke, squealing in terror. George and I shot at almost the same instant, and the pig rolled over.

That night I sat before a fire, eating *caytetú* and listening to Bernardo, still at an impressionable age, recite grisly tales of *tigre* hunting he had heard from the *vaqueros* on his father's ranch.

"One night in the forest near this place," the boy said, his eyes rolling so that I feared he would frighten himself into a fit by his own story, "a *vaquero* and three Indians camped at night. Only the *vaquero* had a hammock and a mosquito net, which the *tigre* will not touch. During the night the *tigre* came into the camp, and the *vaquero* was frightened, but he remained in his hammock with the net drawn over him. All night he heard the terrible screams of the Indians and the cracking of bones as the *tigre* ate them. In the morning the entire camp was red with blood, and only the *vaquero* was alive."

I listened to the boy's bone-chilling stories, wondering what slivers of truth might lie in them. I had heard that *tigres* seldom attack at night when there are humans around, unless they are hungry; but who can know in advance whether a *tigre* is hungry? As the night waned, I arranged with George to stand guard—Bernardo being too young for such a responsibility. George took the first watch and I the second; and an hour before daybreak I aroused the sleeping boys. We started out at dawn, and were less than a half-hour out of camp, when the lead-dog broke into a deep-throated bay.

George spurred his horse toward the spot, and we found the wide prints of *tigre* paws in a muddy patch of ground.

I knelt down and saw holes driven an inch into the ground by the tremendous claws.

"The beast was preparing to leap," George said to me, in a low voice. "Otherwise the claw marks would not show at all."

The sight of that huge track brought the first real tremor of excitement. Until now, a *tigre* had been an imaginary animal as far as I was concerned. I knew they were large brutes, comparable to Bengal tigers, which I had seen in a zoo; and I knew they could kill cattle, and even humans. But this was my first real contact with a flesh-and-blood *tigre*—and this one was roving through the same forest where I was, perhaps not too far away!

I had little time for imaginings, as the dogs bounded through the light brush and were quickly lost from view. I followed George, keeping my course chiefly by sound. I could not help wondering whether the big cat might have decided to climb a tree, and perhaps wait for his pursuers to ride under the branch where he crouched. It occurred to me, also, as I spurred my horse after George, that I actually knew little about the habits of these beasts; and I was not sure that George and Bernardo knew much more.

As the dogs drew closer, their insane yelps increased. I began to feel a sudden feverish excitement, which I later learned comes invariably on a *tigre* hunt, even to experienced hunters. I had my gun in my hand, ready to shoot; but I was particularly anxious to get a picture of the living *tigre*, and I had passed the camera case to Bernardo when we started out in the morning.

Suddenly the barking of the dogs became wild and snarling. George jumped off his horse, and I followed suit. We broke through the brush, and a few feet beyond I saw one of the dogs, lying on his side, his stomach torn out with a great slash; and its bark had become an agonized scream. I aimed at the dog's head, and fired.

George turned at the sound of the shot, and scowled at me. He apparently thought I had fired in haste or excitement. Then he saw the dog, and his face became deathly pale. I started to speak to George when I suddenly saw him pointing into the deep forest just ahead. I followed his glance and suddenly I saw something that I shall never forget—even though I have seen hundreds of similar sights since that day.

Crouched on a limb, perhaps twenty feet from the ground, was the big spotted cat—the emperor of the jungle! At first I glimpsed only a flash of yellow and black. Then I saw the outline of the body, lying on a thick branch. It was a beautiful animal, its yellow hide covered with black patches. The huge head was turned toward us. The face, framed in the fork of the branch, seemed calm and almost indolent. The round, intelligent eyes surveyed us with a sort of disdainful curiosity. Later I learned that the *tigre* has accustomed itself to being hunted by the only animals in the jungle who might collectively be called its match—the wild *peccarí*; and because the *peccarí*, who fear nothing, will attack the big cats, the *tigre* has learned to retire to a tree and there patiently await the exhaustion of the wild hogs' early enthusiasm.

Once the hogs have turned away, the *tigre* will select a straggler and leap—and usually that advantage is sufficient to reduce the *peccarí* pack by one.

In this case, the big cat apparently assumed that we were like the *peccarí*, and was merely waiting us out.

I found myself staring at the pointed face, the unblinking eyes and the black triangle of its nose; and thinking: "At last I am face to face with this king of the jungle!" I suppose there is something hypnotic in such an experience; at any rate I realized I was trembling physically, but otherwise not moving. It was not panic; although it may have been in part fear. In any event, I was seized with the most concentrated sensation of inner excitement. It was almost with an effort that I forced myself to realize that the *tigre* might leap at any moment, and I must be ready to shoot. I needed no experience as a hunter or exercise of the imagination to know that it could slash life from the dogs and ourselves with a few sweeps of those flashing paws.

I turned toward George, who was standing a few feet away, to see if he was ready to shoot; and I was startled to find him staring at the *tigre* with a wild expression. I suddenly realized the boy was thoroughly frightened.

This had a calming effect on me, because I must now rely entirely on my own judgment to direct the attack.

"Find Bernardo!" I whispered across the few feet that separated us. "Tell him to bring my camera. I will see that the *tigre* does not get away."

George stared unbelievingly at me for an instant; then he turned, and I could hear the sound of his retreating footfalls. I kept my eyes on the cat, which seemed utterly oblivious to the snarling of the dogs beneath him. His tail continued to switch back and forth, and now and then he turned in a leisurely way to gaze across the clearing.

It was perhaps a half-hour later that I heard the crackling of brush, and the two boys plunged out of the thicket. I think George was surprised to see me still there; he said nothing as I motioned for Bernardo to hand me the camera. I passed my gun to him.

"Be ready to shoot if he jumps," I said.

Bernardo was as terrified as George had been, but he gamely clutched the gun. Dom João had assured me both boys could shoot, and I was sure one of them would hit the *tigre* before it could reach me. What I did not understand, of course, was the unpredictable nature of the big cats. I have seen them fret for half an hour at the snarling of dogs, batting at them now and then with a big paw, and then suddenly turn and slink off; and under identical circumstances, I have seen them suddenly charge into the pack of dogs.

I managed to cut away a few branches to get a better view of the beast, still crouched on the branch and hardly moving, except for the reptilian rhythm of its tail. I set the focus of my camera and snapped the shutter.

The slight noise had occurred when the dogs were for a moment silent; and the click of the shutter evidently attracted the cat. The huge head swung toward me, and I quickly handed the camera to Bernardo.

"Give me the rifle!" I whispered urgently. I felt the stock in my hand, and at that instant the cat bunched itself and leaped effortlessly to the ground. It was a graceful, flowing movement; and as it thudded lightly on the soft soil the dogs scattered back. At that moment Bernardo screamed.

The dogs had returned to the worrying attack, leaping at the spotted flanks; but the *tigre* paid little attention to them. Its eyes were now directed at Bernardo, balefully regarding the boy, who had pressed his fist against his mouth, as if to stifle another cry, and was staring wide-eyed at the animal.

I brought up my gun just as the *tigre* charged, and had a glimpse of the enormous cavern of its mouth. I fired almost point blank into the great pink throat, and then I saw one huge paw flailing through the air. Bernardo went down under the impact, as I instinctively fired again, this time at the side of the animal's head. At the same instant I caught a glimpse of George on the other side, also firing at the head. The big animal seemed to crumple into a ball from the impact of the two shots.

Bernardo was on his knees, one hand covering his face, and I could see a long rip along the side of the boy's shirt. At first I thought the *tigre's* razor claws must have clawed the boy's side, but apparently the *tigre's* paws had contracted from the effect of the first shot. Bernardo was stunned by the blow of the big padded paw, but otherwise he was unhurt.

The *tigre* was dead. After George and I had assured ourselves of this, we helped Bernardo to his feet. The boy was white and trembling a little at first, but he soon became calmer, and I think perhaps slightly ashamed of his frightened scream.

"You were brave," I told him. "Had you tried to run, it is possible neither George nor I could have gotten a shot at him."

The boy was badly shaken, but he managed to help us skin the animal. In spite of the close call Bernardo had from the unpredictable charge, I felt a vague sympathy for the big jungle cat. In the half-hour I had watched it, crouched in complete dignity above the yapping dogs, the animal seemed to have acquired a personality; and perhaps it would not be exaggerating to say that I actually had begun to feel friendly toward it. Now it lay on the ground, limp in death. I could not help wondering, as I examined the powerful shoulder muscles, what shadowy reactions of curiosity, or perhaps of amazement, may have passed through the dim recesses of the animal's brain as it sat there and watched my strange antics. It had made no overt move until it heard the camera click; and it had not charged until Bernardo screamed.

There is little room, of course, for sentimentality with a charging *tigre*. Yet I felt no elation at killing the animal. And since that day, shooting a *tigre* has never given me any feeling of pleasure. They are dangerous, damaging animals; and some become murderous killers and have to be destroyed in order to protect cattle. This is particularly true of female cats, who will attack a man to protect their young—and once they have sensed the simplicity of killing an unarmed and helpless human, they become roving murderers. The *tigre* of the Matto Grosso is the size of an average Bengal tiger, and the power of their scythe-like paws is indescribable to anyone who has not seen the devastating effect of one sweeping slash that can disembowel an ox. No human could hope to survive a charging *tigre*, unless he had a gun or a spear.

In spite of their ferocity, I have never experienced a feeling of hatred for them. I have killed nearly three hundred during my thirty-odd years in the jungle—and over thirty of these with a spear—yet something in the calm, almost regal disdain of that first *tigre*, the slightly aloof curiosity with which it watched me click the camera, has made it impossible for me ever to regard this lonely lord of the jungle with anything but the deepest respect.

Chapter 9

For the next two weeks Apparicio and I remained on Dom Juão's *rancho* completing the repair jobs I had agreed upon. I grew to like the old ruffian in spite of his unquenchable thirst for getting the best of a bargain. He had listened to his sons' account of the *tigre* kill, and of my picture-taking exploit, which they magnified into an act of unparalleled courage; and as a result he called me *"Barba Vermelho"*—the "Red Beard," which to him was an accolade of friendship.

I was eager to push on toward the São Laurenço, however; and as soon as the work on the sewing machines and a few other broken items had been finished, Apparicio and I prepared to leave. Our departure was enlivened by the expected wrangling over the sums I had been promised. The old man stood at the gate of the *casa*, his thin but vigorous torso stiffly upright upon his ridicuously bowed legs, and his white beard blowing out like a cataract in the wind, as he tried to beat me down from my price even as I was leaving.

Finally, in apparent anger, he tore a fistful of bills from his pocket, brandished them in my face, and screamed:

"Take them, *bandido!* It is all I have—and you have robbed me!"

"How much?" I asked, without touching the bills.

"Three hundred and twenty *milreis* . . . all I have!"

His black eyes glittered as I shook my head.

"Six machines at sixty *milreis* each," I said. "That is three-sixty. We agreed on forty *milreis* for the other jobs."

Actually we had agreed on a hundred, but I was in a hurry to leave; and I had deliberately overcharged the old fellow in anticipation of the argument that was sure to come.

He pulled out a few more bills and stuffed them into my hands. I counted them carefully before accepting them.

"Take them, and be damned to you—Red Beard!" As I mounted, the old man began to cackle furiously. "I beat you at the end—it should have been four-forty!"

I laughed and waved to him.

"It should have been five hundred, old man! You are a hundred *milreis* richer!"

He laughed gleefully, and followed my horse, walking beside it, as I moved down to the gate. Apparicio had already gone ahead with our mule, and I was to meet him late in the afternoon. Dom Juão bellowed hoarse instructions after me as I rode off; he had already told me how to reach the next *rancho*. His two sons, who were fast friends since the picture-taking episode on the *tigre* hunt, followed me a short distance on foot and urged me to return again.

The parting with Dom Juão had left an underlying regret with me. The old man was like a strange cocoon, inside of which there were all manner of odd characteristics . . . some pleasant, some weird, but all interesting. I had seen little of the distaff side of his family, although a few times I had seen his wife, who remained in the rear of the house. But he lived almost apart from the women of the household, nursing his crusty opinions of life; and even his sons were permitted to invade his solitary living habits only by appointment, as it were. I never saw him again, and I never saw anyone quite like him.

Apparicio had made a night camp when I arrived by the river bank where we were to meet. He had packed early to get a good day's travel with the pack-mule, knowing that I could travel faster and overtake him. Mules are better travellers than horses in the wild country, and they are more tractable, providing there is a lead-horse, known as a *madrinha*, for them to follow. But they also are slower.

We had, by now, been on the trail nearly two months since we left Ernst in Coxim. There was no possible way, of course, to communicate with him in this remote country.

Postal service is entirely a private matter in the outlying *ranchos* and settlements; a *vaquero* is dispatched with a wagon, or sometimes by boat, every month or so to take out mail and bring in postal packages and supplies from the nearest town, which might be Coxim or Bahus. It is many days before he returns. The main postal routes are to the west, through Corumbá and Pôrto Esperança.

We were, in fact, on the backbone of the continent, as far as the Amazon Basin is concerned. To the east was the southern tip of the Araguay, the southernmost river that flows out of the great mouth of the Amazon, more than fifteen hundred miles to the north. About 500 miles to the west was the Paraguay, and south was the Paraná. Thus we were on a triple watershed, from the sides of which flowed waters that would arrive in the Atlantic Ocean more than four thousand miles apart.

My knowledge of the wilderness—the birds and animals, and the habits of life in the jungle—had increased greatly through the eyes and ears of Apparicio. I had seen one of the oldest inhabitants of South America—the *tatu bolita*, or "ball armadillo," whose ancestry goes back fifty million years —roll into a ball that only a jaguar can bite through; I had seen the racoon-like *coati*, with its white face and sharp nose, and great tail that stands upright like a column of fur—also with an ancestry some fifteen or twenty million years old; I had watched the tiny marmoset, that can be held in the hand and looks like a miniature black-face minstrel show comedian, play out its droll antics on a tree branch; and I had heard the raucous screech of the "howler monkey," its piercing din drowning out all other jungle noises.

Perhaps the most spectacular of all the Matto Grosso's wild life are the birds, many of them—such as the bobolink and the buff-breasted sandpiper—immigrants from North America. They vary in shape, size and color—from the crested *hoatzin*, known as the "stinkbird" and probably the oldest feathered denizen of South America, to the ungainly *toucan*, with a large beak like a banana and called *tucano* by the natives.

As we rode deeper into the marshes, I became aware for the first time of the primordial rankness of the jungle. This land, filled with black lagoons and soft, sponge-like earth that was rotten from the millions of years it had been partly submerged, was like a throwback to an era that is long gone from most of the earth's surface.

It required little exercise of the imagination to see through the dim recesses of the great colonnades of trees the shadowy shapes of prehistoric monsters. This was a land so ancient that it seemed that nothing of this age on earth could survive. The sun burned with unrelenting, almost savage intensity, and it seemed to suck up the moisture from the ground, only to pour it back again in torrential rains.

Apparicio had a sense of trail-finding that bordered on the supernatural. He would lead us through half-sunken areas where I was sure each step would send us plunging into a bottomless morass. The stench of rotting things was everywhere, like a puff of wind from the caves of the dead; and at night as I lay in my hammock, listening to the chug of the *jacaré* slithering into a nearby creek, I wondered how human beings could have the temerity to invade such a place.

The drone of insects, rising in hot swarms from the almost tepid waters of the black marsh-pools, was a constant overtone that never left us during the day; and at night it was replaced by the whining of mosquitoes, so thick at times that I could feel them beating against my hand if I laid it against the side of my net.

We lived as much as possible off the natural fare of the jungle, shooting small game and now and then snagging fish from the streams. In some strange, almost sinister way, the jungle absorbs those who invade it; and I found that eating and sleeping in the dark, murky recesses of the Great Marshes was like being born into a new world. I became absorbed in the many noises, as we plodded through the marsh-trails, and particularly in the varied and brilliant birds.

Few birds fly over the *campo cerrado*, but in the jungle swamplands they abound, and their cawing and screaming and shrill notes fill the air with such a constant din that it soon becomes like an overtone; and more distinct noises, such as the teeth clashing of the *peccarí* or the distant bawling of a howler monkey can be distinguished easily.

There was a growing delight in being able to absorb and understand these jungle noises. Nothing is more breathtaking than the sudden whirr of a ruby-throated hummingbird, which migrates thousands of miles from North America to the marshes of the Matto Grosso. This tiny, ecstatically beautiful little creature, whose wings can beat as fast as fifty to sixty strokes to the second, moves like a streak of light—yellow and gold and blue—and with such speed that it is virtually immune from harm. The hummingbird has even developed a pugnaciousness quite out of keeping with its size; and it is not unusual to watch one of them attack a much larger bird and drive it away from food. I have heard Indians describe hummingbirds that have taken complete possession of a tree, driving off all other birds and even the smaller monkeys with their dive-bombing tactics.

Apparicio watched my growing interest in the strange life under these green palaces, and many times interjected an explanation of some jungle antic, even without my asking. There is a strange bond that grows between men in the jungle, where nothing else is human; it is a sense of perception that is like the instinct of animals.

On one occasion Apparicio sat on his horse and howled with laughter at my astonishment when I fired my rifle at a *coati*—or *coatimundi*, as they are often called—and at least twenty dropped to the ground at my shot. I could not believe what I saw: one shot fired at a single target, and I had hit twenty!

Actually, the little *coati*, a distant relative of the North American possum, instinctively "plays dead" when any danger appears. Since its nose is the tenderest part of its anatomy, it puts its paws over its snout and rolls over on the ground, lying absolutely still. These *coati* had been scuttling around a tree when I shot, and the entire pack instantly rolled over in suspended animation. When I recovered from my amazement, Apparicio explained that it was nature, not my superb marksmanship, that caused the debacle.

As Apparicio and I journeyed deeper into the jungle, we found many signs of *tigre*. Along the banks of streams there would be prints of enormous paws; but Apparicio, with practiced perception, would point to indications that they were old footprints.

"Only in wet ground can you tell how many hours it is since they have passed by," he told me. "On dry ground there is no print. Therefore a dry footprint is many days old."

Within four days we reached the next *rancho*, to which Dom Juão had directed us. The *casa* was on a sandy stretch of land near a stream, partly obscured by banana trees. The owner, Dom Feliciano Alvarez, to whom I had been given a message of introduction by Dom Juão, greeted us warmly.

"Whoever is a friend of that old pirate is my friend!" he exclaimed; and I knew that he also had a fair appraisal of the lord of Bananal. At the Rancho Uyeré, as it was called, we met a sick, tired old farmer named Manoel Ribeiro. This acquaintance was brief and ended tragically when the old man was shot from ambush by a servant, a thick-set, bull-necked man from São Paulo. I gained a new respect for Apparicio's judgment of men in this incident; he had immediately tabbed the servant, known as Paulista, as a murderer when we first met him.

"*Paulista, nem fiado, nem a vista!*" he had said; which means loosely, "Do not trust a man from São Paulo!"

After we left Dom Feliciano's Rancho Uyeré, we stopped at the farm of his neighbor, a tall, spare Brazilian named Zorico, who had three wives. At Zorico's place we were told that a *vaquero* would leave in a few days with the mail; and I sent a letter to Ernst at Coxim suggesting he meet us in a few weeks at Cuyabá.

From the long waterless stretches where we frequently had to dig water holes near the base of an *acuri* palm to get water for our animals and ourselves, we veered to the northwest toward the swamps, intending to cut through the heart of the jungle toward the Pantanal do São Laurenço.

At the house of a sugar planter, Senhor Chico Pinto, on the southeastern rim of the *Pantanal*, I asked a question that had been in my mind since we started our journey into the São Laurenço country: Did he know of an old Indian hunter called Joaquim Guató, who killed *tigres* with a spear?

"Joaquim?" The planter pondered; then he nodded. "There is such a fellow . . . at least he is called Joaquim. The name 'Guató' is that of the tribe of Indians to which he belongs. He works now and then for me, but in the hot seasons when the *tigre* preys upon cattle, he works as a hunter for the big Rancho Fazenda Alegre which extends north of the river almost to Cuyabá. He roams far into the jungle, but I have not seen him hunt with a gun. I doubt if he owns one."

I asked him for directions for finding the old man, and he laughed.

"Forgive me—but you may as well ask the location of the wind! He is worthless, this old fellow, but he travels far. I have given him a hut to sleep in a few kilometers to the west. If he is around, you will find him there."

"How long has he worked for you, Senhor Pinto?" I asked. It seemed to me unreal that I should at last have come upon the track of this *tigrero*, whose name was a legend in the Rio Grande do Sul, and yet was regarded as a "worthless old Indian" in this country.

Senhor Pinto said he had been around for many years; in fact, he could not remember when he was not around.

"He is without fear when he is hunting," he said. "I think word of his ability with the *zagaya* has spread among the *tigres* themselves. They grow fewer year by year."

The zagaya, I knew, was an Indian spear. My heart must have beat faster, and I could hardly keep the excitement from my voice as I pursued my inquiry. The planter, sensing my excitement and having the Brazilian's talent for romantic exaggeration, accommodated me with more exploits of the old Indian, until I was unable to distinguish between his legitimate enthusiasm and his desire to satisfy my imagination with fiction, which is a form of courtesy peculiar to Brazilians.

"Many years ago—perhaps twenty or thirty, he came to this place. He was known to have killed at least a score of the fiercest *tigres*. He hunts with dogs, but otherwise he is alone. In the tall marsh grass, he alone can destroy the *tigres*, because a gun is worthless where the target cannot be seen."

I asked more questions: Was it a common thing among the Indians to hunt only with a spear? Senhor Pinto shook his head.

"Indians hunt with the *zagaya* and with bows and arrows, but not alone! They hunt in packs. There have been one or two perhaps who have hunted alone—but in this region there is only Joaquim. And of course, no Brazilian has the skill or the swift action of the native hunter. When the beast is charging, only one mistake can be made . . . and after that there is no further contest. The hunter will be dead."

He said this calmly, yet with a keen perception of the dramatic effect on his audience. I glanced at Apparicio, who was sitting with us in the little square room of the planter's home that served as a "guest room." It was a bare, mud-walled house, with open spaces of perhaps two feet between the top of the wall and the eaves of the *acuri*-thatched roof.

Outside, the sibilant noises of the jungle made a nocturnal overture to Senhor Pinto's story. I shook my shoulders to awaken my sense of reality. It seemed to me, in a wild instant of fancy, that I might expect to see the triangular face of a *tigre* in the black space between the eaves and the wall, perhaps gently inquiring as to the whereabouts of the Indian, Joaquim Guató, who had killed his brother.

That night, when Apparicio and I had retired to a hut to which the sugar planter directed us—we had agreed to remain until I could examine his milling machinery—I determined to find the old Indian. Either I would confirm Dom Carlos' story, or I would put it to rest. It did not seem possible that an Indian hunter could kill a *tigre* with only a spear. One, perhaps . . . but not twenty!

Several days later, following Senhor Pinto's directions, Apparicio and I made a short trip west to the river. We found the hut where the planter had directed us; and as we rode up, it had every appearance of being uninhabited. The eaves were propped with sticks, to keep the roof from collapsing. Mud had been plastered on the intertwining sticks and leaves that formed the walls, but much of this had peeled off. The door, hung with leather hinges, was partly open, and the place looked altogether dilapidated and deserted.

I bellowed *"Ho de casa!"* as a matter of form—although the place could not by any stretch of imagination be called a *casa*. To my surprise, a brown head was thrust through the opening, blinking in the sunlight.

"Is this the house of Joaquim Guató?" I asked.

The owner of the head came out. He was pure Indian, dried and brown. His age was indeterminate—perhaps sixty—although his skin was still smooth and supple. He wore a pair of faded blue pants, known as *mescla*, and a dirty khaki shirt, with sleeves torn off at the elbows. He had no shoes.

He nodded, and it was obvious that he was drunk. I felt a rather sick shock of disappointment; apparently I had journeyed this far "through the stinking jungle" to find exactly what Ernst said I would find . . . a drunken old Indian!

Apparicio and I dismounted, tied our horses and went up to the door. The old Indian was holding the sides of the door, as if to support himself. He was in a state bordering on stupefaction, but he finally got sufficient control of himself to motion for us to come inside.

The place was indescribably filthy. It was evident the old man lived alone; two people could not have survived the stench of the hut. A patched hammock swung in one corner of the small room, and a jug lying on its side under the hammock furnished adequate evidence of the reason for the old man's condition.

"You are the great *tigrero* of whom I have heard?" I asked, politely.

The old fellow's black eyes gleamed. A flicker of intelligence showed in his expression, but his face quickly sagged. He slumped down on his hammock and stared vacuously at us. I walked around the hut, examining a small primitive arsenal of bows and arrows. In the corner was a heavy-shafted spear, with a broad iron blade fitted to the shaft. The iron had been hammered roughly to a cutting edge, but it was not sharp.

The old Indian managed to stand up, wobbling slightly, and came over to where I was examining the spear.

"You are from the *rancho* of my master, Senhor Chico Pinto?"

I told him we were; and I added that his fame as a hunter was known far to the south, in the Rio Grande do Sul, and that I had come to talk with him. The old man's eyes glistened, and soon became wet with tears. I thought for a moment the effect of my speech and the jug of *canha* might cause him to break into a fit of sobbing. But he straightened his rounded shoulders, and looked directly at me. The Guató Indians are notoriously stoop-shouldered, and Joaquim was no exception.

"What word do you bring from the master?" the old Indian asked. "There are *tigres* far below, along the river, but near the *casa* only the *suçuarana.*"

The *suçuarana* is the Brazilian word for a puma, the North American cougar, much smaller and less dangerous than the *tigre.* Joaquim suddenly stepped out of the door, and shouted, "Dragão!"

Within a few seconds a rusty-colored mongrel loped up. The old man leaned down, at considerable risk of losing his balance completely, and fondled the ears of the dog, which rubbed furiously against the Indian's legs.

"The best hunter on the São Lourenço!" he exclaimed, and knelt down and actually kissed the dog. He had suddenly become maudlin, and I was disgusted; but Apparicio, gravely watching the scene, turned and shook his head as if to say: "Do not form your judgment too quickly about this old man."

The Indian finally straightened, his brown cheeks glistening with tears.

"They tried to buy my dog!" he shouted, raising his hand. "I would not sell Dragão for a hundred *milreis*—two hundred!" He looked at me sharply, as if he had suddenly divined the reason for my presence. "You wish to hunt with Dragão and myself, *senhor?* If so, we shall go in the morning."

The old man retired to his hut, and Apparicio and I mounted and rode back to the sugar farm. I had little hope that he would recover from his drunkenness in a week, let alone a day. But the following morning, an hour before dawn, there was a rattle at the door of my hut. I opened the door, and Joaquim stood there. He was naked to the waist, and his bluejeans were tucked in oversize boots. His face was calm and his eyes clear.

"Dragão and I are ready, *senhor.* We shall leave at your convenience." He dissolved, like a shadow in the darkness, as mysteriously as he had come.

Chapter 10

I have seldom seen a hunt begin with less preliminary fanfare. Usually the hunters sit importantly on their horses just before starting off, drinking a final stirrup cup of coffee or a hot gulp of *maté*. Then they move off solemnly in single file into the brush. There was no such ceremony in this case. When I emerged from my hut, the Indian merely appeared out of the darkness and said: "We walk!" and we were off.

I had not bothered to awaken Apparicio, and after the first half-hour I was glad he was not there to witness my exertions. Joaquim dove immediately into the metallic foliage that ringed our camp, damp with morning dew; and I followed. The dog was in the lead. I had packed my camera in its leather case, and carried my Winchester. Otherwise I was unencumbered, and might have been off on a morning stroll. But I soon discovered it was no stroll.

I had expected to keep up with the old man easily. Joaquim looked like a gnome as he ambled along with his oversize boots; but as he passed his own hut, a couple of kilometers from the planter's house, he stopped to kick off the boots and toss them through the door. Then, much to my surprise, he continued barefoot.

We followed a narrow ridge, sloping downward toward the river. The lower ground soon became dense with foliage, and beyond, near the river, I saw the beginnings of a forest. Tall *anjico* trees rose like gray parapets in the silver mist of morning, the tops tinted with gold as the rays of the sun began to slant across the rim of the low hills behind us. Soon this became a dark green, and then violent purple, as if the trees were chameleons changing colors as the sun drove the shadows deeper into the forest.

We plunged through heavier undergrowth into a forest, and now the trees seemed to rise above us like cathedral domes, towering over our heads in a massive layer of leaves. The *cedros* and *anjicos* ascended far above the more spreading *figueiras* and *lapachos*. The sky was now tinted with red and growing more azure overhead, and the whole effect was one of breathtaking splendor—except that I could not enjoy it fully due to the pace the old Indian was setting. The forest was actually in layers: the lofty battlements of the *cedros* and *anjicos* ascending above us into the sky; then the spreading domes of the wild figs and other heavier trees below; and waist-high on the ground a lush carpet of thick brushwood and ferns, which seemed far less dense where the heavy foliage above shut out most of the sunlight.

Joaquim, relieved of his oversize footgear, fairly flitted through the shadowy glades, and at times all I could see were glimpses of his brown back and bobbing head. Suddenly he stopped and held up his hand. Then he pointed to a depression in the soft ground beside a mud-hole.

"*Suçuarana!*" he exclaimed.

I had learned to discern the track of a *suçuarana* in my travels further south. They are smaller than the footprints of a jaguar, and shaped differently. The edges of the footprint were wet, but showed no dew, indicating the animal had passed within a few hours.

The sight of the track gave a quick impulse to my interest in the hunt; and perhaps the moment of rest also helped. In a few seconds we were off again. Dragão had been sniffing at the bushes beyond the mud-hole, and all at once he gave a whining yelp and jumped into the brush with Joaquim following.

The old Indian moved like a wraith through the shadowy glades, weaving among the trunks of trees that rose like ancient colonnades, colored by the golden shafts of the early sun. While I regarded myself as a good walker on a hunt, I was soon puffing like a winded horse, and had all I could do to keep up. Now and then I lost sight of him, and depended on the cracking of a small branch or the whine of the dog to keep my direction. Joaquim, I decided, must have steel springs in that tough old body.

We continued at this pace for perhaps another half-hour. I was still aware of the magnificence of the forest through which we were moving, but I had little time to reflect upon it, my mind being taken up entirely with the problem of keeping up with the Indian and his dog.

Once Joaquim stopped to wait for me; and pointing ahead to where the reddish flash of Dragão could be seen moving from one side of the track to the other, he indicated he must keep up with his dog.

I nodded and adjusted my camera case. Under no circumstances would I have suggested that Joaquim delay for me; and during the next hour I went through sheer agony, sucking air into my tortured lungs until I seemed to be breathing fire, as I ploughed through the thickets and brambles after my ghostly guide.

We finally came up to Dragão, standing stiff-legged at the foot of a huge *lapacho* tree; and since the foliage had thinned during the dry season it was not difficult to see the outline of the puma on a branch.

A puma seldom attacks a human; in fact, although they are the scourge of small animals on the plains and in the jungle, ranging from Canada to Patagonia, they shy away from man. However, any animal will attack when it is at bay, and the snarling Dragão at the foot of the tree left the puma little choice.

I unstrapped my camera. If possible, I wanted a good shot to add to my collection. Dragão, snapping impatiently, turned his head now and then as if to inquire into the cause of the delay. Joaquim had moved quietly to one side, and was holding his spear. His whole body was relaxed, and yet somehow alert. I understood Chico Pinto's words: "He is without fear when he is hunting." There was a look of concentration on the old Indian's face which—as I later learned —was the real clue to his greatness as a hunter. He was completely absorbed in the animal in the tree; and yet he missed nothing around him, including the clicking of my camera shutter. He had the ability to see and hear everything, yet nothing disturbed him from the primary job of watching the puma.

I got my picture. Joaquim seemed to know I had taken it; and he immediately pointed to my rifle. I understood I was to take the shot. I quickly raised my Winchester, and suddenly, without warning, the puma launched itself in a perfect arc and landed on a branch only a few feet from the ground. Dragão had now raised his voice into a crescendo of canine challenge. I aimed my gun and fired. The cat leaped at the same instant, and my shot caught it in the chest.

It landed on the ground, dying but still fighting, and then leaped toward me. As the puma jumped, both Joaquim and Dragão went into action. Joaquim's spear carved a straight, sure slash through the air at the throat of the leaping animal; and at the same instant Dragão went for its throat.

The spear, dog and puma met in mid-air. The point of the spear slashed through Dragão's neck and drove into the side of the puma, directly behind the shoulder. The puma was dead when it hit the ground, and Dragão was dying.

I shot once more, to be sure the cat was killed. Then I saw Joaquim slowly lower the shaft of his spear, still driven into the body of the puma. Without a word or cry, he kneeled down and took the head of the dying dog in his arms. For an instant I was sick at the sight of the stricken expression on the old Indian's face. Then, realizing that nothing could be done, I walked over to where my camera lay beside its case, and put it away.

Joaquim remained on the ground for several minutes, cradling the head of the dog and crooning some Indian words. He looked up at me once, his dark eyes black with grief. Then he bowed again over the head of his dog, who was now dead. I picked up my gear and started for the sugar farm, leaving the old Indian to his sorrow.

The next morning Joaquim came to my hut. With him

on leash were two dogs, one brown with a deep chest, narrow waist and short hair. The other was lighter and larger.

"It will be the second moon before I hunt again," the old Indian said. His voice was firm and there was no trace of the bitter grief I had witnessed in the forest the day before. "You are one who will hunt, and either of these dogs is a master-dog. But the larger one is mute on the chase, and you will need to know him better to hunt with him. Neither is Dragão, but there was only one such dog."

I nodded. Something in the simplicity of this old man struck me so deeply that I did not want to speak. I crouched down and felt under the chest of the smaller dog. The bones were strong and the muscles like hard rubber.

"I shall take the smaller one," I said, gravely; then I stepped into the hut and took down my Winchester.

"It is the finest gun I have owned," I said. "You do not require a rifle, my friend. Nevertheless, take it."

Joaquim nodded.

"The small dog is Valente," he said. "He is a master-dog."

Later Senhor Pinto said to me: "You have won his friendship, Senhor Siemel. I could not buy that dog. I tried to buy the other one—Dragão—and he cursed me for a week."

Joaquim was true to his word; he did not hunt again during the time I was at the sugar farm. And I made no effort to persuade him. Something in the primitive clash of forces—human and animal—that I had seen in the jungle was engraved as indelibly on my mind as the chalice of a Holy Order to a young priest. I had watched that half-naked figure, lithe as a cat and as steady as stone, slash the life out of a jungle animal in mid-air with a single stroke of his spear. The tragedy of the affair had been that Dragão was another like him, concentrating wholly upon his target. They were victims of a rare tragedy of jungle perfection.

The vivid dream of Dom Carlos' legend had at last become a fact. I had not seen the old Indian meet a *tigre*— and the difference between a jaguar and a puma is, of course, considerable. But I knew it was within the power and skill of Joaquim to kill a *tigre* with a spear, just as Dom Carlos had told me; and I intended one day to follow this vision to its end.

Within a few weeks I finished the work on Senhor Pinto's sugar milling machinery; and knowing that Ernst might already be at Cuyabá, I spoke to Apparicio about heading north again.

The tall *gaucho* looked at me sharply, his eyes dark and inquisitive; and he smiled rather slowly.

"You are quite certain it is well for me to join you and Senhor Ernesto?" he asked. Something in his words caught my attention.

"Of course it is all right, Apparicio," I said. "Unless you have other plans . . ."

I had noted that Apparicio was quite attentive to the presence of Senhorita Carvalho, the pretty daughter of Senhor Pinto's widowed housekeeper; and I thought perhaps the long ride through the wilderness might pall upon him, particularly if he were pursued by the vision of this dark-eyed girl, already showing the ample proportions of womanhood even though she was only halfway through her teens.

The *gaucho's* swarthy face grew a shade darker, and I could not at first detect whether it was anger or embarrassment. Then he said, "In Brazil we have a saying, Senhor Alexandre . . . 'Pick not the apple that is too green to fall, nor that which has fallen to the ground; the ripest apple is that which is ready to fall.' "

I grinned at my friend.

"You do not think Senhorita Mariinha is ready to fall, Apparicio?"

"She is but fifteen," he said gravely. "Another year and she will be ripe. Then—who knows? Perhaps I shall be riding here again."

Apparicio and I said good-by to Senhor Pinto and his family and rode north again, this time with Valente added to our party. Winter had already set in; and the cold *pampero* winds, howling up from Argentina, were sweeping across the Brazilian jungles toward the headwaters of the Amazon.

While the Matto Grosso is never cold, in the way that temperate zones know coldness, it can become uncomfortable at night. At times the thermometer may drop as much as fifty points in a few hours; and on the marshlands the rotting fish in the wake of receding floods leave a constant breath of foulness in the air, adding to the general discomfort and unpleasantness.

These marshes, which were to be my home for the next two decades, are a vast sponge-like webbing, spread over the fingers of a gnarled hand, formed by five twisting tributaries of the Paraguay. These rivers stretch northeast toward the Planalto of the Matto Grosso. The highlands above Cuyabá drain southward into the Paraguay and north into the Araguay and the Amazon Basin; and in places it is less than twenty miles from the headwaters of one system of rivers to the headwaters of the other.

When the rains come in the hot season, the lower country is flooded. Thousands of animals and quite a few humans drown each year; and yet in the same pools the fierce flesh-eating *piranha* that can strip the flesh from a man's bones in a matter of minutes, will die on the ground a few months later, as the autumn sun draws the water from the steaming soil and leaves it parched and bare. This alternating process has been going on for millions of years, creating one of the most impenetrable and least economically useful areas in the world for the encroachments of civilization.

Apparicio and I followed the course of the Rio São Laurenço down through the *pantanal* until we reached the point where the Rio Cuyabá branches off to the north; and then we followed the fringe of the great Xarayes marsh toward the uplands again. The ground was hard and dry in most places, since it was winter and the floods had already receded; and the stench of dead things drew great flocks of *urubú* in ghoulish convoys through the leaden skies, wheeling and settling upon the naked trees, or rising from some decaying carcass in the marsh grass in such clusters that they seemed to blacken the sky against the faded sun.

As the hot summer months began, we finally rode out of

the low hills and down upon the town of Cuyabá. This was the capital of Matto Grosso State, although there were only about twenty thousand inhabitants at that time; and its only distinguishing features were two magnificent rows of royal palms and a white church. Below these palms, which stood like white-coated sentries, was the *plaza*, with its rows of large buildings flanking the cathedral. Cuyabá was much like any other town in the Matto Grosso—a drab, dusty collection of one-story mud huts sprawling among the foothills along the banks of the river. The town was a meeting place for the hard-bitten *garimpeiros* from the diamond creeks, who rode in after long months of back-breaking labor to trade a few glittering stones for transient days and nights of pleasure in Cuyabá's *bolichos*.

We camped outside town, having arrived in the evening; and the next day we rode into town to look for Ernst. We found him in one of the *bolichos* on the *plaza*. He was sitting at a table, with a bottle beside him; and as we entered, he rose with a wave of his arm.

He was the same man outwardly, with the same bristling blond beard, massive chest and powerful arms; but as I looked keenly at his eyes, while we shook hands, I realized there was a difference. Ernst was sick again—in his mind, rather than his body.

Before we had exchanged many words, however, he told me something which drove thoughts of his sickness out of my own mind.

"You recall the little man who had been inquiring about us at Coxim, Alex?"

I looked sharply at him; the words sent a slight shock through me.

"Did you find out who he was?"

Ernst nodded grimly.

"I not only found out who he was, Alex—I saw him! In Corumbá. It was Ricardo Favelle!"

Chapter 11

Ernst's words startled me more than I could have imagined. At first I felt a certain relief that I had not killed the man—much as he deserved killing—quickly followed by a rising anger. It was perhaps more a feeling of outrage than anger: Ernst's news reopened an old sore, that had scarcely healed; and I now knew that if I should meet Favelle again, I would kill him.

"Did you talk with him?" I asked.

Ernst shook his head.

"I learned that he had been inquiring about you and me. I saw him at a *cantina* with a group. My business was with him alone . . . I wanted to find out more about him, if possible—his reason for being up here in this country.

"Later I went back to the *cantina* to look for him, but he had left. I did not see him again."

"Did you learn of his plans?"

Again Ernst shook his head; and I realized that this placed us in a very unfortunate position, since we would now have to be on guard against Favelle. The French-Brazilian's strange code of honor, which required that a physical insult to his person be revenged by death, would not necessarily require that he forewarn the intended victim of his revenge. Whereas Ernst or I would feel it necessary to approach him, and in a sense put him on his guard, Favelle would have no such qualms. He would shoot from ambush if necessary, and feel that his honor had been fully vindicated.

I turned to Apparicio.

"What do you advise?"

He shrugged. His thin mobile features revealed that fine sense of romanticism and realism which is mixed in such effective proportions in people of Latin blood. It is a combination of sentimental perception, practical understanding and a sense of personal values which one seldom finds in Germans, for instance, or any other Northern people.

"You have only two choices," he said, finally. "You must kill him or run away from him. Since you do not know where he is, you cannot very well kill him . . . so, for the present, I think we should go into the diamond fields. If he should follow you there, it will be much easier to find him."

I considered this, and then suggested to Ernst:

"Why should we not wait here until the wet season is over? Favelle may be in the *garimpos* even now, looking for us among the diamond diggers; or he may be in the South. Whichever is the case, he will probably stay where he is until the end of the rains. We will not need to be on the lookout for him until then . . . and after that, let him be on the lookout for us!"

Ernst stroked his beard, and nodded.

"The man must be insane," he finally observed. "He provoked us in the first place . . . with no cause! Now he is pursuing us, equally for no reason."

I recalled Dom Carlos' words: "In Brazil a gun or a knife is a fair weapon, but to hit a man with your fists is to insult him beyond remedy!"

Favelle had been obsessed with a dislike of Ernst and myself, because his small man's cunning had not worked to his advantage against us. But when I struck him with the pistol, his hatred apparently had turned to a burning lust for revenge. And now he was travelling around the Matto Grosso, inquiring as to our whereabouts . . . leaving the impression, as he strutted about, that he was tracking us down!

"To hell with Favelle!" Ernst said suddenly, slapping his leg. "We shall remain here, eh, Alex? And enjoy ourselves!"

Apparicio's eyes lighted up, and he lifted his cup of *cachaça* and drank deeply.

"Good!" he said, smacking his lips. "We have been travelling a long time, Senhor Alexandre and I! It is time we enjoyed some of the gentler pleasures of life—if any are to be found in this bug-infested country!"

Ernst winked, and rubbed his fingers through his yellow beard.

"Perhaps none equal to the treasures of the Rio Grande do Sul," he said, grinning at the *gaucho.* "But some of the local pleasures are fair."

I glanced at Apparicio, thinking of little black-eyed Mariinha. The *gaucho* cocked his eye at Ernst. He had no real attachment for my brother; nevertheless, he did not dislike him, and at times even showed a friendly liking for him. But I was aware of a deep difference between Ernst and the cowman. It was very much like the difference between Ernst and myself, carried to an ultimate conclusion. Apparicio was a man of solitary rides through lonely hills; and Ernst hated this sort of thing. The same thing would apply to their attitude toward women, Ernst taking such affairs easily and carelessly, the other having fewer affairs, but being capable of feeling deeply and being deeply hurt.

I found myself mentally registering the hope that their paths would never cross in this regard.

It was settled that we would remain in Cuyabá during the hot season, while the rains were drenching the steaming jungles below; and when the dry period came, we would head for the diamond camps on the high plateaus to the north and east.

"Otherwise," I told Ernst, "I will leave you here and go south to hunt him."

Both Ernst and Apparicio were against this alternative.

"He may have gone back to Rio Grande do Sul again," Apparicio said, "in which case you will be rid of him. Unless I am greatly mistaken, he is the sort of fellow who enjoys hunting you more than he would finding you. Perhaps he made a boast to his friends in Passo Fundo, and had to make some show of carrying out his threats."

We settled in a small mud shack near the *plaza,* and within a few days were busy with our tools. Many miners came to Cuyabá for the wet season and their guns were usually in need of repair.

In the close relationship of the evenings in our shack, I learned more of the changes that had taken place in Ernst. His moods, always subject to the vagaries of his interest of the moment—whether women or whiskey—were more variable than ever.

He could not endure being alone for any length of time; and at times, when Apparicio and I sank into the solitude of our own thoughts, which is natural to men who live in lonely places, Ernst would suddenly jump up and mutter an imprecation against the abysmal boredom of the hut, and head down the road to the *cantina*.

It seemed to me that Ernst and I had grown far apart since we left Passo Fundo. The gap in our understanding, which had been widening during the long ride northward into the Matto Grosso, had reached the proportions of a chasm in the year we had been apart. It had never been my habit to talk with Apparicio about my brother; but the things that were driving Ernst and me apart from each other were bringing Apparicio and myself closer together.

Finally, when we were alone one evening in the cabin, I asked the tall *gaucho* if he understood the reason for Ernst's irritability. Apparicio shrugged, a slow smile lighting his features with the combination of sympathy and good humor which was part of his character.

"Your brother, Senhor Alexandre, is not restless because he is not doing what he wants to do, but because he does not know what he wants to do. Therefore, he is always wishing for something, yet he does not know what it is, and therefore he will never reach it."

"What about women?" I asked. "He talks with them in the *cantina*, yet he seldom sees any of them more than once."

Apparicio lifted his shoulders politely; perhaps, under any other circumstances, both of us would have been aware of the impropriety of discussing the personal affairs of my brother, who also was Apparicio's employer. But between us there was a thread of understanding, spun by the common experiences of a year of travelling together over lonely trails. Actually, I had a much closer understanding with Apparicio than I did with Ernst—although the depths of Ernst's and my feeling toward each other never lessened.

"Those are not the women for him," Apparicio finally said. "If Senhor Ernesto could find one woman . . . But he will not." He considered this gravely for a moment, then went on, with great seriousness: "Senhor Alexandre, the women of Brazil are not like women of the North. In this country women understand what part they must take in life, but they must have the respect of the man they go with . . . even if it is only by chance that they go with him. Do you understand? They must know that they are much desired . . . perhaps a little gift or something. Then they will go. Otherwise they will spit in a man's face; and perhaps their brothers will find it necessary to avenge an insult."

This I had found to be true; the women of Brazil—and in particular those of the farms and ranchos we had visited in outlying places—were generous, without the restraint of the women of the North. But they required a certain respect, which could be demonstrated in small attentions, such as a gift; and without these romantic preliminaries, they were inaccessible.

Ernst had never bothered to understand this sensitivity of the Brazilian—that inborn sense of personal respect which is so natural to them. For example, a Brazilian actually feels pain at the embarrassment of another, and he will evade and even lie to prevent that embarrassment. This sensitivity, I realized, was part of the code of honor which made a blow of the fist an irreparable insult; and in the case of Favelle, this was coupled with the man's inherent smallness and inner hatred of anything that demonstrated that smallness. Had I been able to make Favelle feel I had respect for him—which I did not have—the feud would never have developed; but this was a kind of hypocrisy to which I could not bring myself.

We had arrived in Cuyabá a few days after Christmas; and it was almost six months later, as the rains receded from the *Planalto* and the dry, cold weather moved in from the south, that we headed out into the diamond country.

Brazilian diamond fields in many respects followed the pattern of gold-mining in North America. Diamonds had been found in Brazil a century before the great discoveries at Kimberly and Bulfontein; and Brazilian diamonds were on the world markets long before the African fields began to pour out their treasures. But because the Brazilian diamond is smaller than those of Africa and India, they have been regarded as "cheap stones." Actually, they rank karat for karat in value with the best stones found in Africa or Asia.

Brazilian stones vary in color, from pure white to pale gold, green, blue and "smoky." Many have a yellowish tinge, which may have caused traders to regard them as "cheap." There are diamonds in many parts of South America, from the upper waters of the Orinoco to the cold plains of Patagonia; but the most prolific fields have been those in the Planalto do Matto Grosso. They are found in the savannahs and creek beds in country that is so inaccessible that only the hardiest and most adventurous men find their way into these diamond fields. The diamond diggers are known as *garimpeiros*, the Brazilian equivalent of the Alaskan "sourdough."

Diamonds are found in Brazil much the same way that gold was found in California and Alaska—that is, by "panning" in the creek beds. The diamond digger uses a pan made of light, hard wood—usually *gameleira* wood. Gravel is dug from the edge of the creek and first sluiced through a box, with sieve holes bored through an iron sheet. This allows the finer sludge, or silt, to filter through into the *gameleira* pan. The digger then works this soil with his fingers, gradually pouring off the muddy silt until a layer of small, hard pebbles is left. Among these he will find the diamonds.

This method is neither thorough nor highly productive; and it requires much hard work. After a day of this kind of labor, the digger is ready for the gambling hut at night; and whatever the gamblers and prostitutes fail to pick up is usually collected by the storekeeper the next day. Few diamond miners leave the camps with anything in their pockets. The wealth of the camp is taken off by gamblers, camp followers and traders.

The average diamond camp had a population of a few hundred, or even as many as a thousand or two, depending on the richness and duration of the strike. The "permanent population" consisted chiefly of *capangeiros*, or diamond buyers, and traders—such as the storekeeper or repairmen like Ernst and myself; and the *garimpeiros*. There were also transients, for the most part offscourings of the coastal ports, who for one reason or another had retired for a limited period into the remoteness of the *Planalto*. In addition to these, there was the inevitable assortment of camp followers, including murderers, gamblers and prostitutes, who managed to pluck most of the fruits of the miners' toil.

These diamond camps were boom-towns in every sense of the word. Most of them were created by a "diamond strike" and lasted only as long as the strike. They would grow up overnight—a ragged line of mud-walled or thatched huts studding the edge of the creek bank like gray cones; and, in time, a few *bolicho* would give the place a semblance of permanence. For a few weeks there would be another dusty, brawling boom-town on Brazil's rock-crusted highlands; and then, with another strike on another creek, the camp would disappear overnight as miraculously as it had been born.

It was in such a camp—the little town of Areia, midway between the Rio das Garcas, which empties into the Araguay and finally into the mouth of the Amazon to the north, and the São Laurenço which flows southward to the Paraguay—that Ernst, Apparicio and I settled in the early spring of 1922, waiting out the end of the wet season.

There were about twenty more or less permanent shacks, made of thatched walls, interlaced with sticks and packed with mud; and the usual *acuri* roofs. Strung out between the trees that lined the creek—one of the upper tributaries of the Rio das Garcas—these mud huts, a few dirty tents and one fairly respectable mud-walled building which was the "general store" made up the "town." A small cooking pit had been dug in front of each hut or tent, and smoke from these rose each evening like dark plumes in the still air.

During the day there were intermittent gunshots—the traditional signal that a diamond has been found. At night these sounds were more sinister—although violence was not as usual as might be supposed in such an outpost of civilization, the miners having worked out an extremely simple but salutary system of personal behavior. Killing a man in an honest dispute might be readily condoned, particularly if the fight was fair; ambushing a man or stealing from him was punishable by death. This set a clear standard of conduct, and oddly enough, this rough code proved highly effective. Thievery was almost unknown in the diamond camps, and killings were confined for the most part to honest differences of opinion, or to matters of honor involving revenge, which is always understood in Brazil.

The leading citizen of Areia, when we arrived, was a leathery little man named Joaquim Reis. He was part Indian and part Brazilian, plus the usual components of other ancestral bloods. He was regarded as the "mayor" of Areia, and presided at all civic and legal functions. My first experience with his wisdom was in the justice administered to a lady who had allowed her emotions to interfere with her economic judgment. She had split her "protector's" skull with an axe.

Dom Joaquim, who had become quite friendly with Ernst and Apparicio and myself—regarding us as stable members of the community—came to our hut one morning and asked me to serve on the jury, or town council, which he had called to consider the case of the murdered citizen.

The trial was held in the general store, which was the only building having sufficient dignity for a civic affair of this sort. The defendant was a more or less middle-aged lady, who looked as if she had been beautiful at one time, but whose youthful charms had long since been scuffed off in the boisterous mining camps. She appeared rather sullen, and vaguely defiant.

Dom Joaquim conducted the trial with a precision and

116

dispatch that might easily serve as a model for court procedures.

"You killed this man?" he asked.

The woman nodded.

"Why did you kill him?"

The woman lifted a dark, bony hand and let it drop in a gesture of hopeless submission. She already knew her punishment.

"He stay with Maria," she finally said, in a dull voice. Then, in a last burst of pent-up resentment: "I kill him again if I find him again!"

Dom Joaquim waved his hand in a gesture that indicated plainly the completion of the case. A small speech is required on almost any occasion in Brazil—whether it is a parting of friends, a marriage or a murder. The little mayor explained that killing in any case was reprehensible; although there might be extenuating circumstances which would require that the law deal leniently with the accused. But when a woman killed her "protector," she violated the common code in two ways: she showed lack of gratitude toward the one who had shielded her, and she destroyed the faith of other women who might be moved to a similar act of ingratitude.

"What is your verdict?" he asked the council.

Each member in turn muttered, "A *morte!*" It seemed to be foreordained. I did not vote; although aside from me, the vote of the town council was unanimous: The lady must pay a life for a life.

The swiftness of the trial and the unusual callousness of the verdict shocked me. I stopped Dom Joaquim as we left.

"What kind of farce is that?" I asked, rather indignantly, I suppose. "You should not have asked me to serve on your council, Dom Joaquim! The woman had no chance to defend herself."

The little mayor looked at me thoughtfully, his black eyes glinting with a sort of tolerant good-nature.

"You have had little experience with matters of this sort, Senhor Siemel. It is natural that you should be surprised. However, from the standpoint of the good of the community, it is impossible that the lady should remain here. It would serve as an unfortunate example to others and might create serious trouble for other protectors. Therefore the woman will be taken under guard to Santa Rita, where the sheriff is empowered to carry out the sentence. If it should happen that the lady should lose herself on the journey to Santa Rita—" his wrinkled eyes closed in what might have been a squint or a wink, "I am sure she will find her way to some other town where she will profit, I hope, from this experience."

Dom Joaquim's tender regard for the protection of "protectors" was another example of the strange paradoxes of the "law" of the Matto Grosso. I thought of Dom Carlos and his remarkable ability to mix humanity with the practical requirements of the law. After all, the lady who killed her "protector" was receiving only the measure of mercy that I had gotten from the old thief-taker in Passo Fundo, and in much the same way. A week later I learned that she had escaped en route to Santa Rita.

A few weeks after this incident, Dom Joaquim came to our hut early one morning and announced with great excitement:

"You must prepare to leave, senhors! There has been a great diamond creek discovered a hundred kilometers to the north on the Rio Manso. Tomorrow there will be no one left in Areia, and you will have no one to do business with."

Then, as if suddenly remembering the real reason for his visit:

"Meanwhile, come with me, Senhor Alexandre . . . There is a man just arrived in camp whose life you must save. Otherwise, there will be no one to show us the way to the diamond creek."

Chapter 12

A giant black man had stumbled into Areia shortly before dawn and begged for water. I was not called immediately; but Dom Joaquim had been summoned, and as soon as he talked with the black man, and saw the gunshot wound in his shoulder, he came to my hut.

"This man has come many miles through the jungle," the little mayor said, his eyes bright with excitement. "I think he brings news of a strike."

I hastened with Dom Joaquim to the mayor's hut, where the huge Negro was sitting on a hammock, hunched forward and obviously near exhaustion. A crowd had collected, and the man was looking wildly from face to face. He was muttering something in Portuguese, but his words were not coherent. I quickly examined the wound and found I would have to cut away part of the flesh, which was already rotting. The man's left shoulder was caked with blood from the bullet wound, and his right arm seemed to be smashed.

Someone brought a bottle of *cachaça* and I poured this into his mouth. The liquor seemed to loosen his tongue, and he began to talk more rapidly in a high, sing-song voice. Dom Joaquim had settled beside him on a stool, and was asking questions, his black eyes glittering as he pried the story from the wounded man.

The Negro had made his way over rocky ridges and through marshes and jungles from the headwaters of the Rio Manso. He had found a creek rich with diamonds, which he said he had scooped out by the handful. To prove his story, he jerked a small pouch from his pocket. There were at least a hundred karats of washed diamonds in the pouch, and the miners, crowding around, cursed excitedly. The Negro told a story that was wild and at times incoherent: a rancher and his two sons, known as killers in the region, had found him digging in the creek and fired at him. One bullet went through his shoulder, and he had fallen into the water; but he managed to reach the far side of the creek, where a cascade poured down from the rim of a deep pool, and partly hidden by the boulders, he had plunged into the brush and escaped.

This was the story that started the "Diamantino rush"—the greatest in the history of the Matto Grosso diamond diggings. It was in some respects the most amazing experience I had in more than thirty years in the jungle; and on at least two occasions during that rush, I was closer to death than I have ever been facing a *tigre*.

After I had finished dressing the wounds—and Dom Joaquim had completed his inquisition, squeezing the Negro dry of information—the little mayor motioned for me to follow him. We went to my hut and he said:

"I have been in this kind of thing before, *senhor*. The town will go mad, and by noon tomorrow it will be empty. Now is the time for us to plan wisely."

Ernst and Apparicio had heard the commotion, and had followed us into the hut. My brother's eyes were blazing with excitement; it was the sort of thing that stirred every nerve and fiber in his body.

"Listen to my plan," the little mayor said. "We will join forces—the four of us. The new camp will be in disorder, but they understand the need of control, and will be glad if it is offered. I will lend the black fellow a mule, and he will guide us to the place. This will be a rich treasure, and we must immediately assume the leadership."

Ernst agreed that we should form a partnership; but Apparicio, with a look in my direction, shook his head.

"I have become tired of digging for diamonds," he said. "I will take Valente, Senhor Alexandre, and travel south. Perhaps we will meet later at Senhor Pinto's sugar farm."

I looked at the man from the Rio Grande do Sul, and

understood. The apple was ripening on the bough, and Apparicio no doubt wished to be there when it was ready to fall. Without smiling, I extended my hand.

"It is well understood, Apparicio," I said. "We will meet later in Cuyabá. Take care of Valente—and my regards to Senhor Pinto."

There was a glint in the *gaucho's* eyes as he took my hand. We had been together three years; and although I was several years older, I felt a great bond of understanding with the tall, quiet Brazilian.

Ernst was too much involved in the plans for our departure to pay much attention to what Apparicio and I were saying. It was settled that Apparicio would take one mule and our extra tools, and travel to Cuyabá by way of the São Laurenço. We would meet him there in three months, or send word of our whereabouts.

Meanwhile, the camp began to break up. Those who owned horses or mules began to assemble their packs and take down tents. Others who had no animals patched their shoes. Those who had no shoes wrapped their worldly goods in *mochilas* and began to leave within a few hours. The way would be long and hard for them, and they needed an early start.

Ernst, Apparicio and I worked all night assembling our gear and finishing several repair jobs. The sun's rays were creeping over the ragged trees guarding the town-site when we were packed and ready to mount. Dom Joaquim and Ernst were on their horses, and Apparicio was standing by, waiting for us to leave before he made his final preparations to ride south. I was about to mount, when a wild shout came from across the clearing.

A strange little man rode out of the jungle, bouncing along on a horse much too large for him, and leading a pack-mule. He wore a white pith helmet and his sun-scorched face was framed in a bristling yellow beard, giving him a slightly ferocious appearance.

"What's all the hullaballoo about?" the little man roared.

I recognized the accent. Years before I had worked in a candy factory in Chicago. The little man was a North American.

His equipment was even more strange than his person. Perched on the pack-mule, between two leather trunks, was a gray bulb, that looked like the head of an octopus, lashed down with packing ropes that looked like tentacles. It was the headgear of a deep-sea diving outfit.

"Fred Miller's the name," the little man said, grinning amiably. He addressed himself to Ernst and me—presumably because we were the only non-Brazilians he could see. "From Springfield, Illinois." He sat on his horse, waiting for this information to take effect.

Dom Joaquim, who had been startled by the sudden appearance of the little man, now rode over to him.

"I am Senhor Reis, at your service," he said crisply. "State your business." He waved at the rapidly vanishing camp. "As you see, we are moving out."

Mr. Miller nodded, still grinning cheerfully. He had come to Areia, he said, to dig for diamonds. He was an American businessman, from Springfield; and he had heard that diamonds were to be found in the rivers and streams of inland Brazil. Having the business judgment and enterprise of an American, he had brought along a deep-sea diving rig, figuring that if a few diamonds could be dug from the banks of the rivers, more and bigger diamonds would be found in the middle.

Ernst and Apparicio were staring goggle-eyed at his equipment. It was probably the first diving rig ever brought into the jungles of Brazil.

"Better come along, if you want to dig diamonds," I said. "We are heading north. There's a strike on the Rio Manso."

"A diamond strike!" the little man exclaimed. "What luck! How about joining you fellows, eh? What luck!"

It was agreed that the little man could join us—a decision, I may add, that I had occasion to regret.

It was a four-day trip by horse or mule from Areia to the location of the diamond creek, which was a tributary of the

The Brazilian "battle of the century" . . . handbills announcing the two matches between Sasha Siemel and Leon Beduino, the "terrible Turk." Inset below the picture of Beduino shows the silver medal which Sasha won—fashioned by his arch-enemy, Ricardo Favelle.

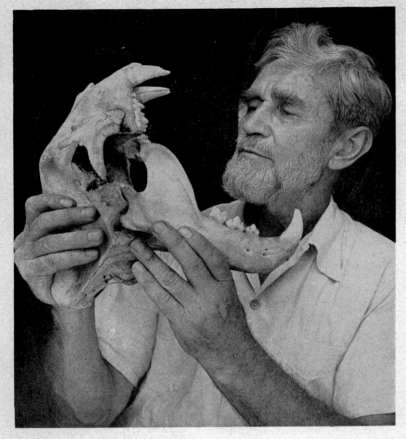

Distended jaws of a *tigre* skull. The jaw-hinge can open wide enough to snap off the head of a man, and the sharp fangs can disembowel an ox.

OPPOSITE—

Top: The oxen killed by the Yanaygua Indians during Sasha Siemel's journey across the "Green Hell." At the left are J. C. Bee-Mason, the English photographer, and Julian Duguid, the English writer. At the right is Mamerto Urriolagoitia, later President of Bolivia.

Bottom: The emperor of the jungle at dinner! A *tigre* is caught in the act of eating a *quexada*, or wild pig, it has just killed. The *quexada* is the only animal in the jungle that does not fear the *tigre*, for it travels in packs; and the *tigre* only waylays the stragglers.

After the spear-fight! The slain *tigre* is the one shown in battle on the opposite page. Left to right: Edith Bray Siemel; Sandra, the first born; Sasha Siemel holding Sashino, the youngest; and Dora.

A scene on the Upper Miranda River, near Barranco Vermelho. In the foreground is an *acuri* palm, while the trees in the background are *anjicos* and *figueras*.

The last act in the jungle drama! At the top, the *tigre* is ready to charge; at the bottom, it has impaled itself on Sasha Siemel's spear. These pictures were taken on the Upper Miranda River, at the Miranda Estancia.

Top: End of a sea raider! This *jacaré*, or marsh crocodile, came ashore at Sasha Siemel's camp at Descalvados to raid the dog pens. *Bottom:* This sting ray was caught on the Upper Miranda River at Barranco Vermelho where Sasha Siemel and his new wife made their home for many years.

A 350-pound *tigre* killed by Sasha Siemel in a spear-fight on the Fazenda Alegre cattle ranch on the Upper São Laurenço River, near the site where he learned spear-fighting from the Indian, Joaquim Guató.

Ernst Siemel, standing over a tapir he shot on the São Laurenço River.

Apparicio Pinheiro, the cowboy from the Rio Grande do Sul—Sasha's hunting companion for many years in the Matto Grosso.

The four members of the "Green Hell" party who, following the route of the ancient Spanish Conquistadores, travelled from the Upper Paraguay River to the foot of the Andes. Left to right: Julian Duguid, Mamerto Urriolagoitia, J. C. Bee-Mason, and Sasha Siemel.

Rio Manso. The country grew rougher as we ascended the higher tablelands of the *Planalto*. Many of those who had taken off at the first news of the strike—some with only a *mochila* slung over their backs—had already stopped beside the trail to rest or patch their shoes; and they stared dumbly at us as we rode past. Others plodded steadily on foot, carrying pots and kettles and the deep-bellied *gameleira* bowls for panning diamonds.

Mr. Miller was cheerful and talkative. After the first day on the trail, we knew about his wife, his friends and neighbors in Springfield, and his automobile business. "Such luck!" he told us again and again. "To be in on a diamond rush like this . . ." He literally licked his chops as he envisioned the stories he would tell the folks back in Illinois.

Ernst was frankly curious about the little man's theory of the diving gear, and asked many questions. Dom Joaquim was not impressed, however. "It is a new kind of thing," he said. "One cannot see diamonds under water. They must be brought to the surface with the other stones from the creek, and this cannot be done in the underwater clothes."

I paid little attention to Dom Joaquim's comments, dismissing them as the product of his inherent disbelief in anything new. To a native Brazilian, nothing is neutral; a thing either is accepted as natural and orthodox, or it is rejected as unnatural, and therefore dangerous.

In the afternoon of the third day on the trail, Dom Joaquim halted the vanguard, which included the big Negro, several *garimpeiros*, Ernst and myself—and Mr. Miller—to wait for the main body to join us. We were approaching the place where the Negro had met the rancher and his two sons, and the danger of being shot from ambush would increase as we neared the diamond creek.

Mr. Miller decided to try out his diving gear during the last few hours of daylight. He and Ernst dragged three logs to the edge of a small river, where the bank fell off steeply, and tied them into a crude barge. Then he strapped himself in his outfit, and with Ernst sitting on the barge manipulating the air pump, he descended into the water.

The macaws swooped down in brilliant red arcs to investigate this strange phenomenon, darting to within a few feet of the helmeted American and squawking furiously. The birds were no more startled than the *garimpeiros* who straggled into camp. They lined the bank, staring at this strange spectacle. Mr. Miller stood in the water up to his chest, shouting last-minute directions to Ernst; and then he clamped the gray bulb over his head, adjusted the screws on the neck-ring and the windows, and waddled down into the river.

Dom Joaquim looked curiously at the demonstration.

"I do not like this," he said to me. "It is certain to cause unfavorable talk. The other miners will think this American plans to crawl under the water and steal their diamonds."

I laughed at this fantastic notion. "If Senhor Miller can find diamonds in that rig, he is welcome to them."

Dom Joaquim shook his head as Mr. Miller emerged dripping from his first trip under water. I felt sorry for the poor fellow. He frankly expected to get to the bottom of the river and collect the biggest diamonds.

"You must talk with him," Dom Joaquim said. "You must persuade him to throw away the diving machine. It is too heavy to carry, anyway."

"It's Senhor Miller's affair," I told the mayor. "I cannot tell him what to do."

We were less than twenty kilometers from the location of the diamond creek; and shortly after noon the following day we rode down to the edge of the creek. The big Negro pointed to a pool where he said he had found the diamonds. He had remained in the rear as we approached, evidently with the memory of the rancher and his sons fresh in his mind; but when there was no evidence of an ambush, he rode his mule boldly into the pool, and waving his hat, claimed it for his own.

No one objected. The miners quickly spread along the banks, each staking out a section of beach. In a few hours there were several hundred claims covering a strip of three miles or so along the creek. And within a short time a shot rang out—the signal that a diamond had been found!

Mr. Miller lost no time setting up his diving gear. Ernst again helped him rig the barge; and this time a second mobile unit was built of two small logs, which could be floated easily with the diver. This prevented the line and air-hose from becoming tangled as it was paid out. By late afternoon Mr. Miller was ready for the first deep-sea diving assault on Brazil's jungle treasures.

The American quickly convinced himself that his theory was sound. He brought up several buckets of gravel from the depth of the river bottom, and early the following morning he turned up a fair-sized stone. He showed this in great excitement to the *garimpeiros* who drifted over to watch the unusual operations.

Dom Joaquim spoke to me about this. He had assumed unofficial leadership of the camp, as he had at Areia; and he knew the habits of the miners.

"Why does the *gringo* boast of his diamonds?" he asked. "It would be better to say nothing. Besides, the stone was not large."

I wondered whether Dom Joaquim was worried, or merely envious.

"It is this business of crawling under the water that makes the others wonder," he said. "How do they know what he does beneath the water?"

"Why don't they watch him?" I suggested. "The water is clear."

The notion that Mr. Miller might be poaching on his neighbors' claims with his diving rig seemed ridiculous; and I told Dom Joaquim the American might be a fool, but I was sure he was no thief. Besides, it was not my business.

I soon found it was my business. The help Ernst had given the American setting up his rig was taken as a plain indication that Mr. Miller was in partnership with us. The first hint that the camp regarded this situation seriously occurred when a burly *valentão*, or bully, came to the hut where Ernst and I were working on repair jobs. He handed me a Smith & Wesson, which was in excellent condition and needed only minor repairs.

"It is my finest pistol," the man, Jose Oliveira, said sharply. "I will expect good workmanship."

His tone surprised me. He seemed to be drunk; and was smiling in a wolfish way, with his lips drawn tightly across his teeth. However, his eyes were not smiling.

"There is little to be done," I said. "It will be ready this afternoon."

"I must have it within an hour," he said, and departed. The man's insolence surprised me; and just to be sure I would be prepared for any further aggressiveness on his part, I laid my own Smith & Wesson .44 on the table beside me.

About an hour later I heard the sound of quarrelling in front of my hut. I stepped to the door, without thinking to take my own gun. As I pushed the flap of the door back, I saw Oliveira. He was drunker than before, and evidently had been arguing with a man. When I appeared, Oliveira pulled a gun from his belt and shot at the man.

The bullet hit the side of the door where I had been standing. I had jumped toward Oliveira when I saw him pull his gun, and now I stepped behind him and quickly pinned his arms to his sides, twisting the pistol from his hand.

"*Gringo!*" he screamed. "*Filho da puta!* Let me go and I will kill you!"

No one could have questioned my actions if I had shot him. But I held his arms, pushing him toward his hut. For years I had trained myself in wrestling, and I knew tricks of subduing men. Oliveira howled with anger, but there was nothing he could do. He was so drunk he could offer little resistance, and I pushed him into his hammock.

Either the man was cunning enough to pretend to pass out, to save face; or he was on the verge of being completely drunk. In any event, he rolled over on his face in the hammock and began to snore.

I tossed the gun into his hut, and went back to my own. A crowd had collected, and I sensed its hostility in the lack of any good-natured comments or laughter. Shortly afterwards, Ernst and Dom Joaquim came into the hut.

"It was not an accident," Dom Joaquim told me, after I

explained what happened. "The man was put up to it by his friends. I have learned that much."

Ernst was even more worried than Dom Joaquim. He suggested that we go to Mr. Miller and persuade him to throw away his diving gear, or leave camp. However, I did not see how this could be done, short of offering to buy the thing— and I did not intend to put out two or three thousand milreis just because some people in the camp did not approve of the American's methods of digging for diamonds.

The next morning I went to Senhor Oliveira's hut. Several garimpeiros followed me; and I knew the camp was expecting excitement. Oliveira, lying on the hammock, was awakened by the noise. He glared at me with bloodshot eyes, and put his hand to his head.

"Devil!" he moaned. "I have one hell of a headache!"

"You were drunk last night, Senhor Oliveira," I said. "In fact, you did not even thank me for preventing you from shooting your friend. You even abused me and insulted me. . . . But perhaps it was the rum talking. Next time, senhor, I will know it is not the rum, but you talking—and I shall act accordingly."

He stared at me sullenly, and shrugged. I turned without waiting for any reply, and walked back to my hut. There were a few murmurs from the crowd, and none of it seemed friendly.

Later in the day Dom Joaquim came into our hut again. He was plainly worried.

"Senhor Oliveira is a bully, and you were right to challenge him," he said. "But the affair is not ended. If you had taken your gun this morning and killed him, no one would have blamed you. But there are those in camp who wish he had shot you . . . And now that you have failed to take this action, they will think Oliveira was in the right."

"My brother and I are the only gunsmiths in camp," I reminded the little mayor. "We administer medicine without charge to those who need it. Everyone knows that."

Dom Joaquim nodded.

"I know . . . but you do not know these people the way

I do. They are Indians—" He spat out the word, with a kind of disdain that only a Brazilian who is part Indian can express. "They dislike this American and his crazy machine which he uses to jump into the water."

I began to think Dom Joaquim was obsessed.

"How can they possibly hold me responsible for what Mr. Miller is doing?" I asked. "It is not my machine. Why don't they take it up with him?"

The old man shook his head, as if my lack of comprehension were beyond his understanding. I began to think one or the other of us was crazy.

"They know he is your friend," Dom Joaquim finally said, simply. "Therefore they look to you to do something."

"And if I do not do something, they will send a man to murder me," I suggested, with all the sarcasm I could command. But Dom Joaquim was quite serious. He left my hut, still shaking his head.

Later Ernst said: "Our friend is worried because he fears this will affect his control over the miners. Nevertheless, he will be loyal to you."

I was rather amused that the little half-caste mayor, who had handled the affair of the lady who killed her "protector" with such shrewd wisdom, should be baffled by a diving rig. However, my amusement was short-lived. Within a few days I began to understand the basis of the mayor's worries. Miners in the camp who had been on good terms with Ernst and myself now avoided us. Wherever I went, there was an atmosphere of hostility.

One afternoon I returned to my hut, after a trip to the storekeeper's place, and found a small, mean-looking man standing near the door. His name was Jose Bahiano, and he was known as a knife-fighter. He was whittling on a plug of tobacco—the old ruse that Pedro Ramos had tried on me in Clevelandia.

Although I noticed the knife, I paid little attention to it, having no intention of talking with the man. However, as I walked past, he started forward, bumping me. It seemed to be accidental, and I stopped to pick up my bundles, which I had dropped. As I bent over, I saw his eyes, shining like small beads, and I knew I was in trouble. There was a fixed smile on Bahiano's face, but his eyes were not smiling.

For an instant I had the cold feeling that I had made a fatal mistake. I was stooping over and completely out of position to defend myself. The knife point was wavering above me, in an aimless manner, but with the point always toward me. My first thought was: "Can I hit his legs quickly enough to drive him over on his back before he can thrust the knife?"

I was sure I could not. On the other hand, if I were to straighten up, he could strike with the knife before I could possibly get into action with my hands or arms to ward off the blow. Since I had only a second or two to make my decision, I decided to move forward and away from him. He was left-handed and I had passed in front of him to the left. Thus, every step I took in the same direction took me a step further from his knife hand.

Without pausing, I scooped up my bundle and stepped forward. My bundle was in my left hand, and as I turned, the bundle was in position to be used as a shield. By this time I was sure I would have to get the knife away from Bahiano or take a bad slashing. However, the uncertainty in his expression, as I straightened up, decided me.

I looked directly at him and laughed.

"For a small man, Senhor Bahiano, you occupy a large space," I said, and walked on into my hut. His surprise probably saved me from attack. Knife-fighters seldom strike unless they have an almost certain advantage; and by the time he had recovered from his surprise, he had lost that advantage.

That night Dom Joaquim again came to my hut; and this time he brought with him a small, compact Brazilian, wearing a tell-tale khaki jacket. The man looked at me with an appraising although not unfriendly eye. He fairly radiated toughness.

"Be pleased, Senhor Siemel, to meet my friend, Dom Marco," the little mayor said. "He is the new *delegado da policia*, and he desires to advise you."

Chapter 13

Dom Marco was a wiry little man, with snapping black eyes, slightly graying hair, and—like Dom Joaquim, the mayor —a composite of various ancestries, including a fair proportion of Indian blood. He had been a sergeant in the Brazilian army before he entered the service of the government at Cuyabá. He had a sound sense of values—particularly when it came to knowing when to kill a man. He lost no time getting to the point.

"You have twice been the victim of attacks by men in this camp," he said, briskly. "In each case, there has been no quarrel between you and the men who have attacked you. Therefore we must assume a conspiracy."

He paused and looked first at Ernst and then at me with his bright eyes.

"Do you mean there is a plot against me?" I asked incredulously.

The little *delegado da policia* nodded.

"The first attack could have been an accident. A second attack is not so accidental. If there is a third attack, you must believe it is a scheme to get rid of you."

This idea stirred my anger. I am normally a peaceful man; but when I understood that a certain group in the village was actively making threats against me, I became unreasonably enraged.

"Then you had better warn them to keep clear of me," I said, sharply. "I have broken no laws—and I know how to take care of myself."

Dom Marco looked at me an instant, as if measuring the

worth of my remarks. Then he spat on the floor, his lips curling.

"Good!" he exclaimed. "In this country there is only one law, *senhor*. Either you must kill those who attack you, or you will be killed. If you fail to kill, you are a fool and should be killed."

I thought of Dom Carlos and his hardy advice—in almost the same words! I felt a growing respect for the little *delegado da policia*. He spoke quietly and without intending offense; and I took none.

"It is my advice that you kill these men who have tried to kill you," he said. "That would settle the matter, because no one will attack you after that. However—" he said this almost regretfully, "if you do not wish to kill your enemies, why do you not go to the stupid *gringo*, and ask him to throw away his underwater machine? That would end the cause of this trouble."

"I will talk to him and see what can be done," I said, as patiently as I could. "But please understand I cannot force him to do anything. It is not my business."

"You had better make it your business, *senhor*," Dom Marco said. "The miners are talking about this thing. I listened to what they had to say at the storekeeper's house, where they meet each night. I think they will soon make it their business. Perhaps they will decide to throw out the *gringo* and then everyone will feel good, eh? Who knows? I shall go down to the meeting presently and break it up, and perhaps I shall break a few heads. But you must do something, *senhor*—I cannot go on breaking heads forever."

Ernst and I talked the matter over. I resented the entire affair as an imposition upon us, but we decided to make a proposal to Mr. Miller in the interest of peace in the camp. Until the present time I had not taken Dom Joaquim's warnings too seriously, but the affair with Bahiano decided me. There was no doubt in my mind now that he had deliberately sought a quarrel with me, and probably intended to kill me. Whether he had been hired by other miners to do this, or was acting in his own sympathetic interest, I did not know;

but the end result would have been the same as far as I was concerned.

We planned to talk the situation over with Mr. Miller the following day. I wanted to explain the growing hostility of the camp toward all of us who were *gringoes;* and ask his cooperation in meeting the trouble. Before we had an opportunity to see Mr. Miller, however, something happened which almost closed the case for me.

A man had arrived in camp a few days before Dom Marco came, who was neither a miner, a trader nor a gambler. His name was Joaquim Carioca, and he had a reputation in the Matto Grosso as a professional killer. He was of medium build, rather slender, and strong. He did not have the manner of the *valentão,* such as Senhor Oliveira. He spoke quietly, even softly; and always stood apart from others, if only by a few feet. He carried a gun in his waistband at all times, which was unusual. Everyone in camp had a gun, but few carried their weapons, since there was seldom much use for a gun except to shoot an animal at night or fire a signal that a diamond had been found.

Dom Joaquim had spoken to me of the man when he arrived in camp.

"I knew him in the South," he said. "There was an argument between two *rancheros* over a disputed calf. They fought with guns and one of the men, Zebú, shot the other. Zebú also was wounded, but managed to reach home before the sons of the dead man arrived, chasing him. The *vaqueros* of Zebú protected him; so the sons retired and engaged this fellow, Joaquim Carioca.

"While Zebú was recovering from his wound, Senhor Carioca rode alone to Zebú's house. Since a single traveller was not suspected, the *vaqueros* let him enter. He was told the *ranchero* lay in bed recovering from a wound. The stranger asked to pay his respects to Zebú and was taken to Zebú's room.

"This, of course, was a mistake. While the wife of Zebú was getting a gourd of *maté,* the stranger—Senhor Carioca— thrust a knife into Zebú's heart. He left the house with no

132

one knowing its master lay dead on his bed. The *vaqueros* in the *galapão* even waved good-by to him as he rode away."

The story of the killing of Zebú, which was well known, added a certain chilling effect to Senhor Carioca's presence. I had not paid much attention to him, and after hearing Dom Joaquim's account of the callous murder of the *ranchero*— not in the heat of argument, but for hire—I was filled with disgust, and avoided the man.

He had not made any attempt, on his part, to become acquainted with me; and consequently I did not consider it more than a matter of routine business when a boy came into my hut early in the morning after our talk with Dom Marco, with a gun which he said belonged to Senhor Carioca.

Ernst had gone out on some errand, and I was alone in the hut when the boy came in and laid the gun on my work bench. It was a pistol of an unusual make, and not easy to repair.

"Senhor Carioca asked me to bring this," the boy said, in a sing-song voice, as if he were reciting. He had a suspicious furtiveness in his eye, and did not look directly at me. "It is to be repaired at your regular rate."

I handed the gun back to the boy.

"Tell Senhor Carioca this is not a pistol of an ordinary type. If he wishes to have it repaired, the cost will be twenty-five *milreis*."

This was more than twice the usual price; but I knew it would take a good deal of work to analyze the construction of the gun and repair it properly.

Within ten minutes Senhor Carioca strode into the hut. I had placed my own Smith & Wesson on the bench. I nodded without looking up from my work.

"That was an unfriendly thing to tell the boy," he said, coldly. "Most people find it safer to be my friend, Senhor Siemel. You have a reputation for repairing guns; I have a reputation for using them. Perhaps we should each of us stay with our talents."

It suddenly struck me that Senhor Carioca was calling upon me in a professional capacity. I remembered Dom

Marco's remarks about the miners' meeting the evening before. I was sure Senhor Carioca would not pick a quarrel with me unless he was paid for it.

I said, as calmly as I could:

"I have stated the price, senhor. If you wish me to repair your gun and will pay the price, give it to me. Otherwise we have nothing to discuss, except—" At this point I picked up my own gun, and rose to my feet, holding the gun in my hand. "If you wish to have trouble, you may have that—without charge! I am not a sick man, Senhor Carioca!"

The reference to the "sick man" surprised him. I had found that men who are killers at heart—like Pedro Ramos and Jose Bahiano—seldom are able to carry out a plan of attack unless their intended victim is in some measure terrified. They become surprised and uncertain when their presence does not produce fear in their victims.

Senhor Carioca was no exception. The cold look went out of his eyes, and his face became flat and expressionless. His lips drew back in a humorless smile, that was like a dog about to snap its teeth. Then he bowed courteously.

"If I should wish trouble with you, Senhor Siemel, I would pick the time and place as it suits me. I shall leave the pistol for you to repair at the price you have set—and perhaps I will see you in the afternoon, senhor!"

He turned and walked out. I watched his back recede, and thought that if Senhor Carioca had been in my place, I would hardly have dared turn my back on him.

When Ernst returned a short time later I told him what happened.

"Let's see Mr. Miller at once," he said. "It is time to put an end to this nonsense."

Mr. Miller was in his hut, tinkering with the headgear of his diving suit. He looked up, as we walked in, with his usual cheerfulness.

"Glad to see you, folks! Sit down." He dropped the headgear and unfolded two camp chairs—part of the equipment which his foresight as an American businessman had told him was necessary for camping in the Matto Grosso.

The canvas backs and seats had almost rotted away, and the hinges were nearly rusted through. He smiled apologetically, as I looked at the chairs with more caution than curiosity before sitting on one. "Things go to pieces up here—most of my junk is about gone."

I decided to come to the point without delay.

"How many diamonds have you got?" I asked Mr. Miller.

He looked surprised; then his red face beamed. He held up both hands, jiggling them to indicate twice that number.

"Twenty," he said. "And I've been at it less than a month. Must be about a hundred karats—and that pays for my whole trip."

"Good!" I exclaimed. "Then you are ready to go home."

"Oh, my goodness, no! I'll be here at least a month or two. This is a great thing for me, Mr. Siemel. I'll have ten thousand dollars worth when I go home. That's a fortune where I live—in Springfield, you know."

Ernst watched, but said nothing. There was a glint in his eyes, and I knew the little American amused him.

"Listen, Mr. Miller," I said. "I've twenty carats of diamonds, and I'd like to buy your diving suit. Will you trade it for the diamonds? That's as much as you've got now."

"But Mr. Siemel—you can use the suit!" he exclaimed. "That's what I told your brother and Mr. Reis. Anyone is welcome to use it! You don't have to pay me diamonds. Why, good heavens—lots of time I'm not using it at all!"

"Mr. Miller," I said, "I want to be frank about this. I don't want to use your diving suit—I want to throw it away. The men in the camp don't like your suit. They don't like your way of digging diamonds."

"But, good heavens, Mr. Siemel—" Mr. Miller was plainly bewildered. "It's perfectly legal. I looked it up with a lawyer in Rio. There's nothing illegal about it."

"The law in Rio and the law out here is different," I said. "You better ask Dom Marco about that. If you feel like taking my offer, Mr. Miller, let me know." I was beginning to feel rather ridiculous in my role; I could not even convince myself that Mr. Miller should get rid of his suit, and

I found it hard to convince him. I turned to go, and he followed me out of the hut.

"Is it really so, Mr. Siemel?" he asked, anxiously. "Do the other people dislike my suit? I wondered why nobody came to see me. Perhaps that's it, Mr. Siemel."

"They come to see me instead," I said, rather savagely, I suppose. I was getting sick of the whole affair; and Ernst, who was grinning, was no help. "If you want to sell it to me, I'll buy it. I'm sorry, Mr. Miller, but you'll have to take my word that the other men in the camp don't like your diving suit."

I left Mr. Miller shaking his head. Ernst and I walked back to our tent, and he left to go down to our claim on the river. A few minutes after he left, Mr. Miller came in carrying an armful of diving helmet, rubber hose, boots and canvas. He dumped these on the floor.

Then he stood for several seconds, wiping his perspiring red face with the sleeve of his shirt. Finally he said, in a rather beaten voice:

"Look here, I've decided to go home, Mr. Siemel. I'm pretty sick of this place . . ." His eyes were wet, like a kicked dog's. "I don't know anybody very well, except you and your brother. You've been pretty swell to me, Mr. Siemel—" He touched the diving helmet with the toe of his boot. "I'd like to leave my stuff with you—just as a present. I don't want any of your diamonds for it."

I felt sorry for the poor fellow. His life in the diamond camp had probably been pretty wretched. He had made no friends, except Ernst and myself. It would have been difficult for Mr. Miller to have many friendships among the hard-bitten men of the diamond fields under normal circumstances; but with the added social stigma created by his unorthodox mode of diamond digging, he was indeed an outcast.

My sympathetic thoughts were interrupted by what seemed to be a commotion outside. I stepped to the door of my hut and pulled back the flap that served as a door. There were perhaps fifty or sixty men coming down the road, and at the front was Senhor Carioca. He was weaving rather erratically back and forth from one side of the road to the other, and I realized he was quite drunk.

I glanced back at Mr. Miller, who was staring rather forlornly at his diving gear. He had not heard the commotion, but when I signalled to him, he came to the door and stared out.

"They are heading this way, Mr. Miller," I said. "Now do you understand why I want you to get rid of that diving equipment?"

"Good heavens!" Mr. Miller exclaimed. His expression was so crestfallen I would have laughed, had there not been more serious things to think about.

"Can you shoot?" I asked him. He nodded, and I shoved a .44 pistol into his hand, and told him to stand in the back of the hut.

"Do not shoot unless someone comes into the hut," I said, looking quickly around to be sure he understood. "I will try to stop them outside—but if anyone except myself comes in, you will have to shoot because they will mean business."

Mr. Miller nodded. He seemed remarkably cool, checking the mechanism of the gun. I had my own pistol in my hand, and by this time I could hear the angry shouts from the mob of men.

I knew our predicament was serious. There was no telling how Senhor Carioca had stirred up the crowd, but I had seen examples of hot-tempered men in this kind of mass-frenzy before, and I knew there would be little chance to stop them once they got out of hand. Except for Dom Joaquim there was no one in camp upon whom Ernst and I could seriously rely.

My first thought had been to wait for Senhor Carioca to come into the hut, where the element of surprise would be on my side. But this was too much like cold-blooded ambush —and I wanted to stop the affair without a killing if possible. However, if I stepped outside, Senhor Carioca would probably begin shooting immediately; and even if I were able to stop him with my first shot, I would be in the line of fire of the others.

Somewhere behind the hut, down near the river, a man shouted; and I concluded it was Ernst. He apparently had seen the marching mob, and was probably running up from the river bank; and I was afraid if he arrived unexpectedly, the anger of the mob might be turned against him. I checked my pistol, and stepped to the door. Senhor Carioca by this time was only a short distance away, and I heard the crunch of many boots on the road. I realized I might be walking directly into the target area of a man who probably had his gun aimed at the door, but I had no other choice. So I stepped through the door.

My gun was in my hand, pointed in Senhor Carioca's direction. He shouted something in Portuguese—apparently cursing me, although I could not understand what he said. Before I could lift my gun, there was a blast, followed by another.

Senhor Carioca had started toward me, raising his gun, but now he suddenly collapsed and sprawled on the ground a few feet from where I stood. Dom Marco clambered to his feet from behind a large stump near the edge of the road. He was holding a double-barrelled shotgun.

"Caught in the act of attempted murder," he muttered, as he kicked Senhor Carioca none too gently, to be sure he was dead. There was no question about that. Half his head was blown away, and the rest of his body was a bloody mess. Then Dom Marco turned to me, almost reproachfully.

"I knew I would have to do the dirty work. I have been lying behind that log—" he pointed with his gun to the huge stump, "for almost two hours in the sun, waiting for Senhor Carioca to approach. Which," he added, looping a rope around the feet of the dead man, "is exactly what you should have done."

The crowd of miners pushed up to the dead man, but the belligerence of the mob vanished in the wake of Dom Marco's two shotgun blasts. He went behind the hut and brought out my mule, and throwing the other end of the rope in a loose hitch around the mule's neck, he hauled the body of the bad man up the road and into a clearing where the burial problem would be solved by the ever-present urubú, already circling in the sky.

I went into the hut and dragged out the diving gear. Mr. Miller had come out of the hut after the shooting stopped, and he watched me with a kind of dazed bewilderment. I took an axe and smashed the helmet, slashed through the hose, and kicked it into a pile beside the hut.

Then I turned to him.

"My offer still stands," I said, speaking loudly enough for all to hear. "Twenty diamonds for your diving rig."

He shook his head and finally held out his hand.

"Thank you for your help, Mr. Siemel," he said. "I'll pack my things now and get out. This has been a terrible day, hasn't it?"

Ernst, who had arrived just after the shooting, suddenly broke into a roar of laughter; and a few miners, not quite understanding the exchange of English between us—but clearly understanding the wrecking of the diving suit—also laughed. One or two came over and gazed upon the mangled equipment, much as they would look at the carcass of a strange sea monster, swept up on the beach.

Later Ernst and I prevailed upon Mr. Miller to accept ten diamonds in payment for his diving suit—a generous price, since the entire equipment could not have been worth more than a few hundred dollars in working condition.

The next morning Mr. Miller rode past our hut on the way out of camp and stopped to say "good-by." He gazed at the pile of wrecked diving equipment, and it suddenly occurred to me that the entire matter could be expunged from the records by a simple procedure.

"Take it with you," I said. "Perhaps you can sell it to someone in Cuyubá or Corumbá on your way downriver."

He seemed too bewildered to protest, but dismounted, methodically unpacked his mule and repacked the remains of his diving suit. The last I saw of him was the white pith helmet as he rode down the trail out of camp, his mule plodding behind him with the dented bulb of the diving helmet bobbing up and down like a huge gray eye. Mr. Miller probably still tells his friends in Springfield how he risked his life digging for diamonds in the Matto Grosso, but I doubt if he ever knew whose life he was risking.

Chapter 14

One morning, a few weeks after the episode of Mr. Miller, Ernst spoke to me about leaving. I knew from his tone it had been on his mind many days, and he was deeply worried. Men who are not related by blood ties can meet or part with a simple understanding; but for those whose bonds are deep, and particularly for brothers whose relationship has been as close as Ernst's and mine, many tangled emotions are involved.

"I have had my fill of this place," he said. "I am willing to go anywhere—even to your damned huts on the São Laurenço! But I cannot endure it any longer in this God-forsaken country. Even the vultures do not come here very often."

Ernst had been growing restless, and I knew he had made up his mind to leave. While I would have stayed another month or two—the diamond strike had not run itself out— I did not want my brother to risk the long trip back to Cuyabá alone. He would have to carry his share of the diamonds we had collected, and although there was little danger of theft in the diamond diggings, there were brigands in the hills— men who were not *garimpeiros* but outlaws from other regions, and who would not hesitate to attack a lone traveller.

"We will leave as soon as our jobs are finished," I agreed. "The old-timers are beginning to leave, and that is a sign the strike is wearing out. Within six weeks we are to meet Apparicio in Cuyabá, and we may as well arrive a few weeks early and wait for him there."

Joaquim Reis and Dom Marco were genuinely sorry to see us go. The tough little *delegado da policia* had become a real friend in the short time we had known him. I found in him the native wisdom and psychological cunning of old Dom Carlos, although Dom Marco was more Indian and less Brazilian, and therefore less subtle than the one-eyed thief-taker of Passo Fundo.

"You are a man for these wild places," Dom Marco confided, when we were alone, "but your brother is not. He requires a woman. As for me, I would rather have a mule. The animal is more sure-footed and can carry a heavier pack, eh?"

He winked broadly at me.

The remark about Ernst "needing a woman" surprised me a bit. It is difficult for those accustomed to the daily contacts of life in cities or well-populated rural areas to understand the basic social attitudes that exist in wild places. Men learn to live with what they have, and to value what they need most; and I am sure that if Dom Marco were given the choice of a woman or a mule, he would choose the latter. This may seem contrary to natural laws and instincts; but actually, there is a great capacity in the human mind and body to fit one's nature with environment. Men who travel long distances between water holes are seldom frequent drinkers; and when they drink, they do it to satisfy the depth of their physical needs, and not lightly or for pleasure.

Ernst could never fit himself to these habits of living, and therefore he was never happy for any length of time. Instead of satisfying himself at the fountain when he was near it, he would drink lightly and be thirsty for long distances between.

As we rode toward Cuyabá, Ernst asked me a question about Apparicio which seemed to bear out Dom Marco's comment.

"He has a woman, has he not—on the São Laurenço?"

I looked at my brother in some surprise; he seldom spoke of women, although I knew he thought about them frequently.

"A girl—not a woman," I said. "But I do not think our friend plans to tarry long. He will be in Cuyabá."

Ernst, slumped in his saddle, showed signs of weariness. The rides were becoming longer, and he was not getting any younger. He was in his late thirties, and headed toward that border line when a man no longer can confuse himself with youthfulness. Long rides and the solitude of lonely camps had taken their toll.

Ernst, I knew, was driving himself to go with me into a country he hated and a life that was miserable for him, partly out of loyalty and partly out of stubbornness. And he was driving himself too far. I could almost watch the seams crack in the skin of his self-restraint.

At the same time, I knew—even though there was some bitterness in the knowledge—that I would not change my plans to follow him back to the coast and the livelier life of the big cities.

"You are too damned stubborn, Alex!" he went on, rather explosively, as if he sensed my thoughts. "You want to go back to that dirty Indian, who hunts with a spear . . . You need not deny it, Alex! I've watched you. I know your feelings."

What Ernst said was true; I had planned to return to the São Laurenço and hunt with Joaquim. It was not entirely a matter of a challenge, as Dom Carlos had said. Perhaps it was to find out . . . to see, first of all, whether Joaquim could stand off a *tigre* armed only with a spear; and if he could—and I was sure he could—I wanted to measure myself against him. I would have crossed a continent to find the answer to that question in my mind.

I found myself thinking frequently of the sinewy, brown Indian, poised on his toes, as steady as a figure of carved bronze under the massive green dome of trees on the banks of the São Laurenço. It was like the memory of a masterpiece, engraved in my mind.

As we rode westward, dipping slightly to the south to reach the curve of the Rio Cuyabá, we could see the flat mists over the great jungles of the São Laurenço far below. It was now the colder season of July, and the floods had receded. The São Laurenço itself was perhaps fifty miles to the south, but the road from Chico Pinto's sugar farm to Cuyabá bent to the west, before it turned south. I thought for a while we might turn southward in the hope of finding Apparicio and Valente still at the farm; but we decided it would take too long to make the detour, and Apparicio would already have left.

It came over me, with rather curious surprise, that I actually looked southward toward the jungle with nostalgia, as if it were home; and I suddenly understood the keenness of Ernst's bitterness. He knew I loved the jungle, with its mighty green temples, its hidden trails and the ever-present noises, the chatter of small monkeys and the sharp calls of birds; and Ernst hated it! The jungle itself had driven us apart.

At Cuyabá we set up shop again and waited for Apparicio; and a fortnight later he rode into town. He was cheerful and quiet as usual; and his eyes were bright. Although I forebore to ask any questions, waiting for him to broach the subject as he wished, I knew at a glance that he had seen the delectable Mariinha.

One evening, the three of us were sitting in our shack. A kerosene lamp dimly lighted our faces, throwing lines into deep relief. I noticed that Apparicio was looking at me with a kind of embarrassment. He said:

"You recall Senhorita Mariinha—the daughter of Senhora Carvalho?"

I nodded; and looking at Ernst, I was surprised to see a sudden sharpness in his glance. He was looking at Apparicio with a fixed, almost bitter expression. The flickering light gave his face a sinister look. I suddenly realized, with astonishment, that Ernst was actually jealous of a girl he had never even seen.

Apparicio, without looking at Ernst, explained to me that the young lady, with her mother, had gone to the *rancho* of their *patrão*—a euphemism, in these hinterland regions, for the father of perhaps fifty or sixty children scattered over an area of several hundred square miles. Mariinha's *patrão* was Senhor Henrique Paes, who owned the big Rancho Triumpho on the lower stretches of the Pantanal do São Laurenço. She had gone with her mother to take charge of cooking and housework in one of the outlying posts of the cattle ranch.

Then, rather awkwardly, he said:

"I spoke to Senhor Paes about you. There are many guns at the *rancho* and tools and other equipment which are long in need of repair. He would be greatly honored if you would visit him."

Ernst, who had been watching Apparicio, jumped to his feet and slapped his hands together.

"Good!" he said. "We have been here long enough, Alex —four weeks, isn't it? We should go south and help Apparicio's friend."

He spoke with great cheerfulness; but I had no difficulty in translating this into a lusty desire to see what sort of apple Apparicio had knocked off the bough. I looked at Ernst, his blue eyes shining like cobalt beads in the lamplight; and while I was inwardly amused at his sudden transformation, I was also perturbed. Here was a fine kettle of fish!

At first I tried to dissuade the pair; but Apparicio, with Ernst as an unexpected ally, argued that we would gain great wealth and have a pleasant visit at the beautiful Rancho Triumpho. It was certainly better than Cuyabá, Ernst chimed in, and finally I agreed. I felt, however, that I had consigned myself to a Pandora's box of trouble. I could not very well explain to Apparicio—or even to Ernst, for that matter—the reasons for my hesitation. I doubt if Ernst actually knew what motivated him. He was like a dog, sniffing a scent he did not understand, but which greatly intrigued him.

Three days later we set off for the Rancho Triumpho. Ernst had developed an unusual air of cheerfulness. His moodiness and disdainful indifference to the country through which we rode had changed to an almost childishly eager curiosity. He even became friendly with Apparicio, plying him with questions about the country surrounding the Rancho Triumpho, and its people.

Ernst hardly realized the reason for his own enthusiasm. He was excited by the prospect of something interesting; his mind had suddenly become filled with a romantic idea, and with characteristic restlessness, he was pursuing the fireflies of his own imagination.

Fortunately, Fate intervened before we arrived at the Rancho Triumpho, in a way that was drastic, but final. About a week's ride south of Cuyabá, near the confluence of the Rio Cuyabá and the São Laurenço, we came upon the Rancho Abobral, owned by a round-faced, cheerful rancher whose name was Francisco Andrade. Senhor Andrade greeted us warmly, and when he found we were travelling repairmen, he let us know of the many items at his *rancho* in need of repair, if we could only find the time to stop and enjoy his hospitality. Price was no problem, if we could restore his collection of rusted guns, broken bridles and other bric-a-brac to usefulness. We looked over his collection, and agreed to stay a few days.

Dom Francisco was a genial host. With patriarchal pride, he displayed the wealth of his possessions—a *rancho* with perhaps twenty thousand head of cattle; the white *casa*; and he proudly introduced his two sons, both in their teens, shy and gawky. He even introduced us to his wife, Dona Rita, a fat, waddling woman with a completely resigned and unintelligent expression in her dark eyes. It is not usual for Brazilian women in these remote places to have any part in the social affairs of the house, and guests seldom see them; so that this departure from custom, slight as it was, might have been regarded as significant.

Its significance became apparent when Dom Francisco mentioned another possession, a daughter, Maria, who as it turned out was of marriageable age. In the Matto Grosso, any unmarried female of fifteen or over is of marriageable age.

Apparicio who had been given quarters in the *galapão*, or bunkhouse, heard of this when he joined us in the evening. It brought a slow smile, and he winked at me.

"The old man senses a catch," he said. "He is about to rope a young bull for his herd."

We had been at the Rancho Abobral several days when Apparicio and I returned one afternoon after a short hunt. Ernst was puttering with a pistol, trying to dislodge a rusty hammer. Suddenly he hurled the weapon across the room.

"Damn the country!" he said. "Damn the people! Damn the rotten smell!"

This was the dry season, when fish lay on the ground, stranded by the receding floods, and rotting in the sun. The stench was in the air, like something unclean; and only the natives seem to be able to ignore it. I have been caught by a puff of this foul odor out in the open, miles away from the place where these rotting carcasses lay, and almost retched.

Neither Apparicio nor I spoke; in such cases it is better to let a man get it off his chest. After a few seconds of fuming and growling curses against the mosquitoes, the weather, the dirt and the bad food, Ernst walked over and picked up the gun. He examined it, rather shamefaced at his outburst, and went to work again.

That evening, sitting in front of our hut after the usual dinner of dried fish, *charqui*, rice and beans, Ernst spoke more quietly about what was on his mind.

"I have had enough of this wandering life, Alex. I cannot stand any more. You like it, and so does Apparicio—but I do not!"

I nodded. There was no use fighting the issue. Ernst was right; and inwardly I was glad he had finally reached the conclusion.

"We will divide what we have," I suggested, after he had made it clear that he had definitely reached this decision. "Will you go back to Cuyabá, or to the coast?"

Ernst shrugged.

"I will find a woman to live with," he said slowly. "I am sick of living alone. Some stupid, uneducated woman who is good enough to sleep with and not too good to cook for me! You can live with the sunsets and the jungle noises and the mosquitoes, and Apparicio can live with his beautiful Mariinha—but damn it, Alex, I want a woman who is flesh and blood! I am sick of this lonely riding, I tell you!"

147

His voice had risen, so that it was quite audible in the *casa*.

I heard a slight giggling, and glanced up. A few feet from our door there was a wooden grating between the kitchen walls and the eaves of the main house. I knew some of the feminine ears of the household had been listening.

In a backwoods Brazilian household, the women spend most of their time in the kitchen. It is their part of the home; and what they lack in direct communion with the men of the house, they make up in the sensitivity of their hearing. There is hardly a whispered word that does not somehow find its way into the grist of chatter that is constantly being ground out in the cooking room.

That evening, as we were retiring, Dom Francisco came to the door and in a mysterious whisper, called to my brother: "Senhor Ernesto! May I speak with you, please?"

Ernst left, and Apparicio, who had not gone down to the *galapão*, rolled his eyes expressively. I felt a deep pang—partly regret, and partly resentment. Perhaps I could not quite forgive Ernst for not loving the jungle trails as I did. Nevertheless, I knew the issue was now final.

Ernst came back an hour later. He said nothing and I did not ask questions. The next morning Dom Francisco, bustling in like a real estate salesman who has closed a deal, invited us all into the kitchen where we met, more or less formally, the women of the household.

Dona Rita, her huge frame rolling at every step, came forward to greet us. Her usually expressionless eyes glinted with a kind of feline satisfaction. Behind her, in a long, blue dress, was the girl, Maria—tall and solidly built. Her glance was a combination of maidenly restraint and defiance; and her glance caught Ernst's and hung there.

My brother had the grace to blush. He bowed slightly and accepted Dona Rita's hand. Her fat paw clasped his as if she had a slippery fish in her hand and was not going to let it go.

A week later the wedding was held. Father Marco, a shambling man, lanky and unshaven, arrived on a mule to perform the marriage with Catholic rites. He expressed regret that Ernst was not of the Faith, and prepared briskly for the ceremony. My brother was married that afternoon in Dom Francisco's bedroom.

I watched in silence as the tall girl, dressed in white cotton that hung glowingly upon her shapely figure, made the responses for Ernst as well as herself. Under the rites of the Church, he could not even answer for himself. He stood in dismal solitude, his head slightly bowed, accepting the fate he had chosen.

Two days later Apparicio and I headed south for the Rancho Triumpho.

Chapter 15

We rode southward for many days across drying swamps and bare ridges scarred by the receding floods; and to my surprise, I felt an actual relief, almost a sensation of freedom. With Ernst, our journey had to end at some town or village. But Apparicio and I loved the open trail, and each deep-throated call of an organ-bird was like a note of joy, welcoming us home. There was no particular end to our journey.

I found that certain ideas, which had remained half-formed beneath the surface of my thoughts, now took shape in my mind. I had become tired of travelling from camp to camp, repairing men's guns; at times I went to sleep dreaming of rusty hammers and broken springs. There was a notion that had been dormant in my thoughts for many months, born of my brief experience hunting with Joaquim Guató. I mentioned it to Apparicio as we rode along.

"Why do we not become hunters, Apparicio?" I asked. "Perhaps we can make a better living than working on other men's mistakes as we do—fixing broken guns that have been treated with less respect than most men have for their wives."

The tall *gaucho* laughed; but his eyes looked at me seriously.

"I have promised Senhor Paes we would stay to repair his broken tools and his guns," he said. "We cannot abandon him."

I assured Apparicio that we would keep the promise he had made, although I wondered—knowing the roving nature of his kind—what had been so sacred in the promises he had made. But I had a plan of my own which I would present at a later moment.

The continuously new aspects of the jungle always amazed me. On one occasion, we rode through a tangle of *acuri* palms and I saw a strange battle to the death between two kinds of trees—the *figeira*, or wild fig, which drops roots from its branches into the ground, and a cluster of *acuri* palms. The palms had grown so heavily around the huge fig tree that they were sapping the water and nourishment from the ground around it; and the fig tree, with ruthless barbarism, had coiled its hanging roots, which fell like tentacles from its spreading arms, around the nearest *acuri* palms and had actually strangled the life from the palm trees, so that they were shriveled and dead, while the fig tree raised itself toward the sky overhead.

I called this to the attention of Apparicio.

"This is an example of a place where there is no morality," I said. "There is only the natural law of survival."

Apparicio laughed deeply. He was not inclined to philosophize with words, but I knew there was a deep well of thought within him; he interpreted the signs and habits of wild life with the cunning of an Indian.

"A man also knows this law of survival, Senhor Alexandre—but a woman knows of two laws."

"What are they?" I asked curiously.

"The law that says she must have children, and another law which says she must have a man in order to have children." Apparicio paused, as if uncertain how I would take his comments. Then he said, quite cheerfully: "Your brother will understand this law better after his new mother-in-law has fastened her fingers in his neck. That old sausage wanted a stud for her daughter, and perhaps for herself."

I was a bit startled by his crudeness, as well as the cynicism, of his remark. But Apparicio, with the curiously natural directness of his kind, went on seriously:

"In this country, Senhor Alexandre, a woman has a special position, perhaps more than anywhere else. A man may forget God in the jungle, but he will never forget the

Mother of God . . . She lives always, like the earth. He may fear other men, or the jungle, or death. But he will never fear woman—and yet he should fear her. Her love is like the caress of a *tigre*, whose next blow will snap off his head."

I had seldom heard Apparicio talk so freely. Usually we rode with that strange interplay of men's thoughts as they ride along jungle trails, each thinking and understanding according to his own lights . . . and with an underlying feeling for communication that needs few words.

"You have made a special study of women, I suppose," I put in, with the idea of prodding him to further comment, rather than jibing him. Apparicio laughed shortly.

"No, Senhor Alexandre . . . I have a little knowledge of them. I know that men can be brothers, and ride together and perhaps fight together. But a woman is always alone. She is like the *tigre* in many ways. And she alone can stand between two men who are brothers."

I was thinking of Ernst; and it was later . . . many months later, that I realized, recalling Apparicio's words, that he might have been thinking of ourselves.

"Have you ever thought of taking a wife, Apparicio?" I asked. "What of Senhorita Mariinha?"

His thin lips tightened, but he was good sport enough to realize that what was sauce for the goose was sauce for the gander. He had commented freely about my brother; therefore he could not object to my remarks about his affairs. He had thought of it, he confessed; but not too much.

We rode up to the square mud-walled *casa* of the Rancho Triumpho, and were greeted warmly by Senhor Paes, a genial, graying man with a sense of humor as robust as his capacity for populating the countryside. When he asked why Ernst was not with us, I explained the fate that had befallen my brother. The old man laughed with lusty enjoyment.

"The old sow set a trap and got her buck, eh?" It seemed that Senhora Andrade's predatory maternalism was known to everyone along the Rio Cuyabá.

On his last visit to Rancho Abobral, Dom Henrique told us, the lady of the house had appeared rather desperate, referring to the advancing age of her daughter, who was then eighteen, as if she had been approaching senility.

"She would have worried some of the fat off her," Dom Henrique said, "if your brother had not come along. A girl who reaches eighteen in this country with no mate in prospect is an ill-omen in a household. Tell me, Senhor Siemel," he said, fixing me with a rather searching look, "have you given no thought to attaching to yourself a wife?"

I must have looked startled. The thought occurred to me that there might be a *senhorita* of marriageable age among the scores of Dom Henrique's own personal population on the Rancho Triumpho, whom he wished to dispose of. The *ranchero* caught the expression on my face and his laugh boomed out.

"Do not fear, my friend. I can see· that you are a lone hunter!" He winked, almost lecherously.

We quickly agreed upon arrangements for repairing a collection of bridles and stirrups, and several badly rusted guns that needed attention. The guns I would handle myself; but by this time Apparicio was sufficiently skilled in welding broken bridles and such items to be able to do this work. I knew that Apparicio would want to remain on the Rancho Triumpho for a time, and I had another plan in mind for myself.

It was perhaps ten days after our arrival that something happened that made it possible for me to broach this plan to Apparicio. We had ridden eastward up the edge of the river, looking for small wild pigs that are found in the *pantanal*; and Apparicio obviously had intended that our route take us past a certain outpost hut.

"We shall stop only a few minutes," he said. "The old man who watches Senhor Paes' cattle in this area will have a jug of *canha*."

It was not the jug of *canha*, however, but a black-eyed *senhorita* that had lured Apparicio to the outpost. She was standing in the doorway, a rather short, well-formed girl, with black, shiny hair drawn close to her head and hanging in a twisted braid down her back. Her dusky complexion and wide features indicated a strain of Indian and perhaps some Negro blood, the olive color of her skin contrasting delicately with the blackness of her hair and eyes.

Her eyelashes dropped as we rode up; but she raised them and looked at me, and I remembered her. This was Senhorita Mariinha of Chico Pinto's sugar farm. I threw a sidelong glance at Apparicio, but he was studiously inspecting the corral in the rear of the hut, presumably to locate the mother or the old man for whom she kept house and cooked. The hut was a line-camp, and vaqueros for the Rancho Triumpho often stopped at the place for food and rest on their ride over the thousands of acres that belonged to Dom Henrique.

Senhorita Mariinha remembered me well from Senhor Pinto's farm, and she curtseyed, her dark eyes alive with a burning intensity as she looked first at Apparicio and then myself. Her figure was compact, neither too slender nor too plump; and her dress, clinging loosely to her body, brought vividly to my mind Apparicio's remark about the ripest apples on the tree. Senhorita Mariinha had ripened noticeably since we were at the Pinto sugar farm.

The old man rode in a few minutes later. Senhora Carvalho bustled out of the hut to cast an appraising eye over Apparicio.

The girl said little, moving quickly into the hut after we arrived; and now and then I caught a flash of her red print dress in the rear room, where the cooking was done and where the women lived. It is never the custom of inland Brazilians to allow their women to mingle with guests, although in this outpost it was evident that the custom was not scrupulously observed on all occasions.

Apparicio walked around to the rear of the hut, and I caught the flash of Mariinha's dress near the corner. I said nothing, and I knew from the studied indifference of the mother and the old man—Jose Vaca, or "Joe Cow," to translate literally into English—that Apparicio's visits were not unfamiliar to them, nor were the reasons particularly obscure.

On the ride back to the *casa* I outlined my plan to Apparicio.

"There is some work remaining at Senhor Pinto's mill," I said. "I will return there and complete the job, and meanwhile you can remain here and finish what we have agreed upon with Senhor Paes." Apparicio nodded, and I could not refrain from adding, "I do not doubt that you will be well occupied while I'm away."

Again he nodded gravely; but I knew from the slight quirk of his mouth that he understood my meaning quite well.

A few days later I loaded two large *bruacas* full of tools on one of the mules, and taking Beduino as my own mount, rode eastward along the river. Apparicio rode with me as far as the Carvalho hut.

"Old Joaquim is hunting again," he told me as we followed the winding trail along the high marsh grass at the river edge. "He inquired of you when I was there . . . You have made a friend of that old Indian."

Mariinha was at the door when we rode up, and this time her glance was less reserved. Her eyes, glowing with dark fire, were turned directly at me, and I felt a strange apprehension . . . possibly mingled with a slight twinge of regret, or perhaps resentment—I could not be sure which. But I thought, as I watched her body turn gracefully, and her eyes shift from me to Apparicio: "Ernst has got his Maria, and Apparicio is at least on the way to having his little Mariinha, while I am on my way to a rendezvous with a withered old Indian, probably drunk with *canha* and snoring in his hammock in a filthy hut on the São Laurenço."

I must have grimaced outwardly at the notion, because Mariinha's dark eyes suddenly widened, as if she were startled by what she saw in my face. Later, as I sat at a table and ate from a plate of rice and *charqui* and fish stew, which Senhora Carvalho had set out for me, Mariinha came near the table, and stood a little behind me; and I was suddenly physically conscious of her presence.

When I said "good-by" to Apparicio, I was even more

conscious of the presence of the girl. She stood in the doorway while I mounted Beduino and waved at the *gaucho* and old Jose Vaca. I glanced at Mariinha, and became acutely aware of the living movements of her firm, full body under the red cloth dress as she lifted one hand tentatively in an uncertain gesture of farewell.

For several miles, as I rode eastward along the river, I was pursued by strange fancies, until I shook them off and pushed Beduino into a faster gait. Valente, running along at one side of the trail, glanced up, his brown eyes full of remarkable understanding, as if to say: "Well, master—I'm glad you have left that nonsense behind you, and are ready to hunt with me again!"

The cold season was on the wane, and the drying pools in the deep marshes along the *pantanal* were clear mirrors in the centers of caked mud flats. A few fish bones lay on the banks, dry and fragile as spiny blossoms of white cactus; and now and then a half-rotted body of a *jacaré*, the marsh crocodile, gave off a sickening stench. For the most part the trail was clear and fairly easy to follow. The jungle has strange moods that vary with seasons and with the wind; and now it was quiescent, with a kind of lurking calm, as if it awaited the onrushing floods that would sweep over thousands of square miles of trackless waste in the wake of the torrential rains that come with the hot season.

The *urubú* and *carancho*, or hawk-vulture, now and then circled over a lonely patch of forest, dipping to investigate some stray bit of carrion; and the migrating barn swallows, Eskimo curlews and buff-breasted sandpipers that had flown north with the approach of the southern winter, were now filtering through the forests of the Matto Grosso on their way south to the *pampas*. Great yellow-billed toucans, with purple-rimmed eyes and enormous beaks, swooped down along the river edge, looking for stray fish that might linger too long near the surface; and deep within the forests the honking roar of the organ bird mingled with the raucous croak of the cock-of-the-rock and the harsh screams of macaws.

For three days I rode eastward, covering seventy-five kilometers, and on the afternoon of the third day I rode through the forest where Joaquim Guató and I had shot the puma. I followed the river trail that led past Joaquim's hut, and found it in the same disreputable state it had been when I last saw it. Now it was apparently uninhabited. I looked into the reeking interior, and noticed that the seven-foot zagaya was gone. I concluded Joaquim was away on one of his journeys into the jungle.

Chico Pinto was visibly glad to see me. The mill machinery had broken down and had been temporarily patched up, but he welcomed my arrival and the opportunity of having the machines repaired permanently.

After I had settled myself in the same hut I had lived in before, I asked about Joaquim, and Senhor Pinto shrugged.

"He goes and comes . . . I do not know where he is now, but he will be here in a day or two."

True to Senhor Pinto's prophecy, the old Indian shambled into the sugar farm two days after my arrival, wearing his oversize boots and herding a pair of mongrels ahead of him. His tough brown torso was covered with a ragged remnant of what had once been a military shirt, and he grinned when he saw me, exposing sharp yellow teeth.

His first words were of Valente.

"The dog has been good, senhor?"

Valente crowded against my legs for an instant, and then darted toward the Indian. Joaquim's hand licked down and slapped the dog good-naturedly on the neck, and Valente, with a tact that would have been enviable in a diplomat, returned to rub against my legs, his tongue hanging out as he panted eagerly, his brown eyes searching mine for a mute understanding. It was exactly as if he had said: "This is my old master, and I must greet him; but it is you to whom I belong. Please do not be offended at any attention I show him."

I patted the dog's head and he whisked off, investigating each bush as he trotted around us, thoroughly satisfied that his attachments had been properly and securely understood.

Joaquim turned toward the rim of the forest which encircled the sugar farm and then announced:

"The *tigres* have moved into the upper *pantanal, senhor.* They leave the lowland when the rains come. In two days we will find them within ten kilometers of this place. On the day after tomorrow I shall call for you."

He said this quite simply, as if we had already discussed the matter of hunting and were merely setting a date. Nothing further was said; but on the second morning after my arrival at Chico Pinto's farm, I was ready an hour before dawn when Joaquim came to my hut.

Four dogs were held on leash, heavy-chested, square-faced brutes, slightly larger than Valente; but Joaquim signalled that Valente was to be the lead-dog.

"He is the best dog since Dragão," the Indian said. "He knows you now, and he will know exactly what to do on the hunt. The others may become excited and lead you into some mistake."

We set out along the river trail, Joaquim stopping—as he had done before—to toss his boots into the hut. For the second time since I arrived in the jungle I felt that tingling of suppressed excitement; the other time had been on the hunt with Senhor Cajango's two boys at Bananal. Whatever caused the sensation, it was by far the most intense and concentrated feeling of physical anticipation I had ever known. I have seen several hundred *tigres* and have participated in hunts too numerous to mention; and perhaps the sensation has become a bit commonplace to me. In any event, I have never quite experienced the same feeling since that day.

For one thing, I was certain we would track down the *tigre*. Joaquim had said they would be found within a few miles of the sugar farm, and by this time I had learned to rely upon the old Indian's crafty judgments with the utter confidence that a farmer reposes in the almanac.

And I could not help but realize that this was in all probability to be the actual fulfillment of an anticipation, almost a dream, that had been lodged in my mind since the night Dom Carlos first told me of Joaquim Guató.

As we threaded through the thickets that fenced in the forest, with its sheltered corridors of sunless shadows, I felt as if I were in the last act of a great drama, playing only a bit part, to be sure; but part of the play, just the same. It was an exhilaration which, mingled with the profound beauty of the forest, amounted almost to a religious ecstasy . . . an ecstasy, I may add, which became more than religious at the climax of the drama.

Chapter 16

Among the Indians of central Brazil, the women do the work and the men fight and provide food by hunting and fishing. Although Joaquim had left the villages of his tribe many years before, and had lived alone just as he hunted alone, he had never overcome his inherent aversion to work; and this may explain the fluctuations in his personal conduct —at one moment a worthless derelict, lazy and sodden with *canha* and slobbering his words with the unintelligible vacuousness of an idiot; and the next a hunter with senses as sharp as a knife blade, tough as rope-weed and as deadly as a serpent in the coiled concentration of every nerve and fiber of his body.

I marvelled at this transformation as I followed his wraith-like path through the green labyrinth of the forest. At one moment he would be trotting effortlessly over the bare ground, hardened by the months without rain; and at the next he would suddenly dart through what seemed like an impenetrable wall of tangled ferns, laced with the twining tendrils of vines and hanging roots, and emerge into an opening beyond without seeming to dislodge a branch . . . I marvelled, too, at his sure instinct for the right trail, and the almost perfect economy of movement as he fled silently through the dim jungle. There seemed to be an inexhaustible store of strength in his sinewy legs, and in the rippling muscles beneath the smooth, bronze skin.

The sheer pleasure of watching this poetry of human movement, while I followed as well as I could, striding through open areas of tall brush grass, and jogging across stretches of shaded forest, actually helped me keep up the pace. It lent a kind of rhythm of motion as we moved along. I was tougher than I had been two years before; my endurance and wind were better. Still, I was breathing with considerable agony when we finally slowed down as we approached the edge of the *pantanal* beyond the forest.

We had been travelling at a fairly good pace for perhaps three hours, covering a distance of about a dozen kilometers, when we broke out of the dense forest into a more open area, covered with high marsh grass. Beyond this, perhaps two miles to the west, was the edge of a patch of *capão*, an isolated island of jungle. There would be a water hole in this area, and Joaquim stopped and held up his hand for silence.

We proceeded now more slowly and with the greatest caution, until we reached the edge of the *capão*. The dogs were sniffing furiously, and now and then a whine would give evidence of their excitement. We followed the course of a shallow stream, almost dry except for a muddy channel along the middle, until we came to the edge of a small lake, or tarn. There were many animal tracks along the muddy rim, most of them quite old; but Joaquim suddenly pointed to two tracks near the mouth of a small inlet.

He crouched, and pointed at the tracks, his finger indicating the moisture along the soft edge of the footprint. Then he held up two fingers.

"Two hours," I whispered, and he nodded. The dogs were unleashed and they bounded into the marsh grass, Valente leading the way as the rest of the pack set up a chorus of sharp yapping, Valente's deep bay making a bass accompaniment. I listened carefully to the dogs as we followed, since I wanted to be able to distinguish each animal by the sound of its voice. In the high grass it is well to know which dog you are following.

We followed the dogs for perhaps a quarter of an hour, when a sudden crescendo of shrill barking in the grass ahead told us the dogs had flushed their prey. Joaquim was a few steps ahead of me, and as we pushed through a belt of shoulder-high thicket, I saw the dogs about a hundred yards ahead. They were gathered near a bank of brushwood, surrounding a stand of *acuri* palms.

The *tigre* was out of sight, in the thicket; but by the direction of the dogs' barking I knew the approximate location. All at once, I saw a flash of black and yellow and the big cat, weighing perhaps three hundred pounds, prowled out of the thicket into the open. His great paw lashed out at the dogs, who were snapping and bouncing furiously in a semi-circle.

Joaquim advanced to within perhaps twenty yards of the *tigre*, which was now thoroughly angry. It was a completely different animal from the one in the tree at Bananal, or from the puma I had shot in the forest. The big cat was on the ground, moving in sinuous half-circles, now this way and now that. There was no disdainful aloofness in this cat's demeanor, as there was in that first *tigre* I shot at Senhor Cajango's ranch. Its huge head was lowered and the eyes gleamed wickedly as it turned furiously from one pestiferous dog to another, now and then giving utterance to a low, throaty rumble that ended almost in a cough.

Joaquim had moved up to the far side of the *tigre*, and I stood perhaps fifty feet back with my Winchester ready. Without any signal from Joaquim, I knew this was to be his kill; and I sensed, moreover, that it was to be in the nature of a demonstration. The old Indian was about ten feet from the cat, which had turned to regard this new enemy balefully. Joaquim's spear was almost parallel with the ground, held with both hands. He was crouched forward, so that the point of the spear was not more than two feet above the ground. The grass was short and there was no obstruction between Joaquim and the *tigre*.

Joaquim's foot suddenly darted forward. By this time I had recovered from the first moment of frozen suspense, and was concentrating on every movement of the cat and of Joaquim. There was a puff of dust. The cat flicked his head and its paw lashed out. A great, gnashing roar came from the red throat; and I realized that I had seen almost a duplicate of what Dom Carlos had described. Joaquim had kicked a clump of dry sod into the *tigre's* face.

The core of the conflict had now shifted. It was as if the *tigre* understood that it had a new enemy, of a different caliber than the dogs. From that moment, the *tigre* paid no attention to the dogs. The great head was now turned full at Joaquim, and the cat seemed to be lashing itself into a rage, wagging its head back and forth, and breathing in dry, husky gasps. For what seemed an eternity—but probably was only a second or two—Joaquim seemed to hang in poised suspension, his body tilted slightly forward. Then the point of the spear darted out, like a boxer feinting with a left jab. The *tigre* tore at the iron blade with a sweep of its paw, and for an instant seemed to settle on its haunches.

Joaquim's spear was pulled back toward him again. Then like a one-two punch of a boxer, he drove it out again just as the cat lunged. The spear met the shock of the charge, driving into the *tigre's* neck. It seemed to me Joaquim, frail and wavering and astonishingly small in front of the huge, tawny body, must dissolve in that charge. It was like a fantastic and unbelievable wrestling match. The cat was a snarling, clawing ball of fury, its haunches curving forward as it strove by every slash of its four paws to drive away the thing that was stinging its throat and throttling its breath. Joaquim was only visible in glimpses of brown flesh. Now and then I saw his legs shoot out in a sort of devilish dance, and his bare feet seemed almost to cling to the ground, as he fought to keep his balance and keep driving the spear deeper into the *tigre's* throat.

The cat gave ground first, trying to withdraw from the goring blade of the spear; and the instant it retreated a step, Joaquim pulled out the spear point and drove it again, almost faster than the eye could follow—this time straight into the chest of the writhing animal. Joaquim's feet danced sideways, and I realized that the cat was now on its back, squirming away the last bit of ebbing life as the Indian pushed the blade deeper into the animal's chest.

The whole affair could not have lasted longer than a minute. I felt as if I had held my breath throughout the duration of the battle. As Joaquim straightened, I exhaled my breath; and then I realized that I was sweating. My hand, on the stock of my gun, was wet with perspiration. The dogs by now had moved in and were worrying the hide of the dying jungle king. Joaquim looked at me as I walked up, and his wrinkled face was wreathed in a quick grin.

"You have seen the fight," he said simply, and began pulling the spear from the bloody chest of the dead cat. I stood over the body, my gun pointed at its head ready to shoot if it showed the slightest sign of reviving vitality; but the big beast was dead.

I looked at Joaquim, and knew I ought to say something. He had put on this show primarily for me . . . Yet I could find no words to express myself. What I had seen, it seemed to me, was reserved for the gods, and not for human eyes. I finally reached out and rather awkwardly took the old Indian's hand and shook it. He seemed unfamiliar with this gesture at first; then he pumped industriously, grinning at me and displaying sharp, uneven yellow teeth.

"You are a *tigrero*, my friend," I finally said. "Now I have seen what my friends in the Rio Grande do Sul promised I would see!"

Joaquim continued to grin and to shake my hand until it was becoming embarrassing; finally, he kicked the dead carcass with his toe, and said:

"You shall have this skin, my friend, to remember this day. Later you will have one from your own kill."

I nodded and we went about skinning the cat—which must be done leaving plenty of fat and meat on the hide. Later it is pared off with a razor-sharp knife, washed with soap and water and stretched on a frame.

During the trip back to the sugar mill, my mind burned with one consuming idea: I must learn to do what Joaquim had done. It was as if all the underlying fire of imagination, which had been smouldering in my thoughts since the night I talked with old Dom Carlos, had suddenly been stirred into flame. It had become a passion as primordial as the fire of love or hate: I had to match myself against a *tigre!* Actually, it was a feeling not unlike love or hate; because if underlying passion can be stirred by the sight of a beautiful woman, why not at the enormously more rare spectacle of a man fighting a beast?

Joaquim, I believe, understood my feelings; because now and then he glanced at me and grinned, as if we now shared a secret. I did not speak to him of my intention to learn spear-fighting while we were walking homeward; but after that, several times a week, I met him before dawn and we went out into the forest together.

Fortunately, my desire was not as ardent as that of a lover requiring immediate satisfaction. I knew that only time and patience would teach me what I needed to know. And old Joaquim was a patient teacher! Sometimes we went into the forest with dogs, and sometimes alone. He helped me make a zagaya, and showed me how to hold it, pressing the staff firmly against the side to give added weight of the body to the force of the thrust. He also showed me how to meet the charge, with the knees slightly bent, to give resilience at the impact.

The old man was thorough as well as patient; and it was well that he was, or I would not have survived the first test of combat. He knew with the natural wisdom of an Indian how dangerous the eagerness of a young man might be; and he guarded against my overconfidence, that might lead me to trust too soon in my own skill.

With my first actual fight—not alone, for Joaquim never would let me go into the jungle alone—I was able to prove, almost fatally to myself, the wisdom of his caution. He had instructed me in the habits of animals, telling me how a tigre might be expected to charge. But he could not tell me—since only experience can teach certain things—how to sense the mood of the tigre. The hunter must know from the way the cat bunches its claws and raises its haunches slightly, whether it will charge or slink away. And he must be able to judge in a split second whether it will charge low or come in a bounding leap, since each requires different tactics with the spear.

One morning, perhaps a fortnight after the spear-fight,

our dogs struck *tigre* spoor about an hour after dawn. It was a deep print, but Joaquim decided it was not a large animal. The softness of the ground can measure the time since the track was made, as well as the weight; and he judged the track was about an hour old.

I had my newly made *zagaya*, about equal to Joaquim's in size, but with a better blade and finer temper. I also had my pistol in my holster. We unleashed the dogs and started after them; and it was only a few minutes before Valente's sharp cry told us the *tigre* was at bay. We broke through a stand of thicket and saw him, pacing in a nervous half-circle, facing the dogs. It was a young male, obviously angry as well as surprised by the yapping of the dogs, but it did not seem ready to attack until Joaquim and I started across the clearing.

Suddenly, with that unpredictable nature that is so characteristic of the beast, it turned and started toward me. I had my spear in my hand, and Joaquim suddenly flashed his arm forward in a signal for me to take the charge. I held my spear staff in both hands, one two feet from the cross-bar, as Joaquim had instructed me, and the other back toward the butt-end. The point was held low, ready to bring it up quickly as the animal jumped for my head.

There is no use saying I was not afraid. Although only a few seconds elapsed from the moment we stepped into the clearing until the cat was loping toward me, it seemed like a lifetime of suspense. Fortunately, there is no time for rumination when a *tigre* is charging. The cat was still perhaps thirty feet away, and I was gripping the spear-handle and getting set for the charge, when it swerved suddenly and ran a few steps broadside to us, in that curious way jungle cats have of feinting for an opening. I remained in frozen suspense, moving the spear-head slightly and turning my body to keep the spear pointed at the animal.

Vaguely I saw Joaquim to my left, but I was concentrating entirely on the movements of the cat. At that instant it charged. I held the point low, as Joaquim had taught me, intending to bring it up as the *tigre* leaped. But it did not leap. It came running right at me, its snarling face almost level with the ground. In desperation, I lunged forward, hoping to drive the spear into its throat, but I missed the head completely, striking the shoulder.

The force of the blow threw the *tigre* slightly to my left, which got me momentarily out of range of the flailing paw. But it also carried me sprawling forward, so that I almost pitched headlong to the ground. The spear had bitten deep, because I felt its spring-like tension as I lunged forward and past the animal.

At the instant I pitched forward, the *tigre's* snarl became a scream. I flung myself sideways, trying to keep my left hand gripping the spear, and scrambled away, almost on my knees. Joaquim had risen like a brown wraith on the other side of the cat. As I rolled out of reach, I saw the *tigre* twist over, its claws distended as it struck in furious but helpless sweeps at the ghost-like figure of Joaquim, dancing almost above the prone beast.

It was over in a few seconds. I had rolled out of reach and was reaching for my spear, which apparently had been pulled out of the shoulder and was on the ground, when the *tigre* suddenly became limp. I did not realize immediately how close to death I had been; but after Joaquim had pulled his *zagaya* from the side of the animal's throat, I felt a coldness in my stomach.

The old Indian looked across the dead body of the *tigre*, and all he said was:

"You charge too quick, *senhor*."

Later, when I reviewed my performance on this first spear-fight in which I took part, I realized why Joaquim did not want me to hunt *tigres* alone. The lightning strokes I had now seen him deliver twice against a cat charging past him—first at the puma when Dragão was killed, and now at the *tigre* charging me—were not the things one learns in a few days of hunting. The timing and the sureness of the spear-thrust were the result of many spear-fights, and perhaps were learned at the cost of other men's lives.

During the weeks that followed I began to absorb the old Indian's cunning. His art was not merely that of spear-fighting.

Although I was no giant, Joaquim was physically almost frail beside me. But he had learned self-control and economy of movement; an effortless style; and above all, he knew how to *think* with the animal. It was not skill and courage alone that made Joaquim Guató a great hunter. It was a power of concentration upon the fight itself that was intense while it lasted; and it enabled this old Indian, who must have been well over sixty, to pit his puny strength against an animal twice his size, and possessed of a fury and a desire to kill that for the moment outweighed all other instincts.

Joaquim could actually outthink a *tigre*, using cunning where physical strength could not have prevailed. And from his great store of jungle knowledge, he sought to teach me. Why he did this I do not know. Perhaps he had an inner desire to pass on to someone not of his tribe or origin the knowledge and skill he possessed and which, so far as I know, was not achieved by any other Indian of his day.

Sitting beside the fire of a night camp in the jungle, with Valente crouched nearby, watching us from between his paws with his soft brown eyes full of affection and mild bewilderment, I listened to the old Indian pour out his hunting lore in anecdotes of great battles. He explained how to tell, from the roar of a *tigre*, whether it is on the ground or in a tree. The big cats seldom roar while they are perched in a tree, since it is their instinct to crouch quietly in comparative concealment, and not disclose their presence until they pounce on their prey.

Studying tracks, to determine when a cat has passed by, is the first rule of hunting. Each footprint bears the marks of a story. A soft track in wet ground is new if the ridges between the toes are still moist; since they dry quickly, the tracker can gauge almost the exact hour that the track was made. The best clue to the age of a track, however, is the dog. If it is an old footprint, the dog will sniff and worry around the spot; but if the track is fresh, the dog will immediately bound off in the direction taken by the animal.

These and many other things I learned, prowling through the jungle with Joaquim. He showed me, by demonstration and later in spear-fights, how to judge which way the *tigre* will attack—whether at a full run along the ground, charging or leaping; or by an evasive, worrying attack, like the slippery, shifting attack of a dog.

The old man seemed to delight in having a willing audience for his stories; and now and then, his tongue loosened by *canha*—which he never drank on the hunt, although he seemed to find no reason for avoiding it at other times—he would boastfully recite his accomplishments.

"Only a man without fear can face the *tigre* and come out alive," he said; and pointing a long, gnarled finger at me, he said: "If you are such a man, Senhor Siemel, you will profit by my knowledge and you will become a *tigrero*. If you are not without fear, you must never hunt the *tigre* alone."

I have since come to believe that what Joaquim said about fear actually concerns an entirely different emotional complex. I have felt fear, even when facing a *tigre*, because of something that went wrong at the moment and left my plan of fighting confused for a second or two. But two things a man must never lose: his confidence and his power of concentration. The latter is perhaps the most valuable asset of all; and Joaquim had it to an inordinate degree. Together, they give the spearman the use of all his fighting facilities—mental as well as physical; and when a man is facing an eight-feet-long *tigre*, nothing short of all his fighting assets will help him.

Joaquim taught me the patience of a hunter; the care that must be given to every detail of tracking. I have watched him study a track and the area around it for an hour; and then return to re-examine it when some further detail of the tracking fails to develop as he expected. Each thing that happened, as we roved through the forests and on the *pantanal*, would be explained, carefully and patiently; and his black eyes would bore into mine, until he was certain I understood.

In later years I realized how deeply the old man understood hunting; and—as they say of airplane pilots—there are many old hunters and many bold hunters; but there are few old bold hunters. Confidence and concentration are needed;

but recklessness and carelessness are never assets of the true hunter.

During these weeks I fought side by side with Joaquim against several *tigres*; and on our second trip after my first blundering and almost fatal effort, I drove home the spear that killed the cat. It was a moment of exultation, but the edge was taken off by the knowledge that I had not done it alone. Joaquim was with me, diverting the *tigre* until I was set for the charge; and had I failed to meet the charge, that iron blade of his would have been driven home.

My confidence grew with each spear-fight, yet I could not persuade Joaquim to let me tackle a *tigre* alone.

"You have many years for hunting, *senhor*—but only one moment to die," he said, rather sententiously, it seemed, even if quite true.

The hot season moved in, with the steaming breath of the jungle in the air; and the torrential rains swept over the *pantanal*. We were on the fringe of the marshes, above the low area where flood waters made a treacherous morass of the ancient swamps. The animals of the jungle began their annual exodus from the lowlands as the rains started, and the *tigres*, driven to the higher grounds, began to prowl at night through the grasslands of the Fazenda Alegre.

"I must go far to the northwest," Joaquim said to me one day. "There are reports of a *tigre* who kills not only cattle, but men in the *pantanal*."

My work on the machines was not finished, so I remained at Senhor Pinto's place to complete the job. It was while Joaquim was out in the *pantanal* that word was brought of a *tigre* spotted in the *capão* about a day's ride from Senhor Pinto's farm.

I had not wished to hunt alone while Joaquim Guató was at the sugar farm, for fear of hurting the old Indian's feelings; but this seemed to me to be the opportunity I had wanted. Senhor Pinto wished to send one or two of his *vaqueros*, but I declined, explaining that I would take my gun as well as the spear, and my dog Valente, with two other hunting dogs from the farm that I had used on several trips.

"You will do well to remember the old saying, my friend —a dead hunter brings home no rabbit for the pot," Senhor Pinto said. "Perhaps you had best leave your spear at home. The *tigre* may not know that you are a pupil of the great Joaquim, eh?"

The old man grinned at me; I think he understood the desire that had been burning in me for so many months— since I had first witnessed the spear-fight that day on the *pantanal*. At any rate, he made no further effort to dissuade me.

Long before dawn I was up, preparing to leave. Senhor Pinto came to my hut, bringing a tray with a steaming pot of *maté*. I had sharpened and tested the blade of my spear the night before; and now I had it carefully placed in a leather sheath. I took the Winchester, but I had mentally resolved that *el tigre* would not die with my bullet in its heart if it decided to fight on the ground.

"*Vay' com Deus!*" the old man said, after I finished the *maté* and was ready to depart. "Bring back a head that I can mount over my gate as a warning that a *tigrero* lives here." He laughed jovially, but I felt he was really worried about my safety.

Perhaps I was, also; but I did not admit it, even to myself. Just as the gray streaks of dawn were dividing the sky from the forest in the east, I mounted Beduino, and with Valente and the other dogs on leash, started down the trail toward the river on what was to be the greatest adventure of my life.

Chapter 17

For a half day I rode through high marsh grass, descending gradually with the river. My direction was to the south and west; and now and then from a rise in the rolling terrain I saw the gleam of the São Laurenço where the sun, far to the north, caught an open expanse of water. Forests filled the lowlands along the river, and for the most part obscured the river itself from my view; but I could determine my general position from the curving body of the jungle, winding along the valley like a massive green snake.

I kept to the higher ground south of the river because I did not want to become lost; and after travelling some twenty kilometers over wild brush country, I began to look for some of the landmarks Senhor Pinto's *vaquero* had described. The *tigre* had been seen from a distance by a rider who was returning from a trip to a small cattle ranch on the *pantanal*. The man had followed the cat into the high marsh grass, but having no dogs, quickly gave up the chase and returned to the *casa* to report the marauder. It was late in the afternoon when I rode out upon the edge of a line of red clay cliffs (*Barranca Vermelho*) and looked down from this eminence upon the rolling country beneath, sloping westward toward the São Laurenço. Far to the south was the wide green path of a southern tributary of the São Laurenço; and in the narrowing neck formed by the converging rivers was the area where the *tigre* had been seen.

Valente stood beside my mule, surveying the country in a serious and dignified way, as befitted the leader of the pack; while the other dogs ran along the rim of the cliff, sniffing vigorously. The loneliness of the country was deeply etched in the vast panorama of marshlands, mottled with great patches of forest. I felt almost a shiver of apprehension . . . perhaps at the silence of this wild place. Except for the rustle of the dogs in the thickets (I had unleashed them for a brief rest, and they were wandering through the brush) there was nothing to mar the profound stillness. We were above the forest, on a flat ridge that curved in a great semi-circle—possibly the bank of an ancient inland sea. Beyond the sharp break of cliffs, about fifty feet down, the land sloped away gradually toward the sweep of rolling country that spread for miles to the west. The clear outlines of a green mass of *capão* in the foreground, perhaps five miles away, was gradually lost in the shimmering haze that hung over the rivers beyond.

I have never felt fear of the jungle; but at this moment I felt its solitude. In an area of perhaps a hundred square miles, I was probably the only living human—and certainly the only white man. All of the ancient mystery of this age-old land, that had been steaming in alternating cycles of floods and parched heat for millions of years, seemed to rise in the flat mists that hung over the deep jungle below. If my bones were left to bleach under this tropical sun, they would bleach unmarked and untended until the slow corrosion of nature would reduce them in actual fact into the dust from which they came.

Finally I gathered the dogs, climbed on Beduino and we rode slowly along the rim of the cliff until we came to a depression where flood waters had eroded the bank. We found a way down to the floor of the valley, and I followed this dry stream-bed across the marsh grass, knowing it would lead to a water hole.

The water hole was not large; but it was probably the only one in the immediate vicinity. The *cápao* was perhaps a mile and a half wide, and the trees were not tall, like the *cedros* and *anjicos* of the deep jungle. The ground was heavily blanketed with thickets, which were almost impenetrable in places. Even the dogs would back away and Beduino and I would have to turn aside for as much as a hundred yards to find a breach in the thorny fortification. Finally Valente yelped and dived toward a small tunnel, apparently an animal trail, made by *peccari* or *caytetú*, boring through the brush.

I had dismounted, and using my *machete*, I cut through several yards of thickets until I could lead Beduino into the more open space beyond. A few yards ahead the gray bank of a water hole was visible through the tangled brush. It struck me that this would be an extremely unfavorable spot for a meeting with the *tigre*. In all the spear-fights I had seen or taken part in, there had been an open area, apparently selected by the cunning Joaquim in some instinctive way; but here, except for the area immediately around the water hole, there was nothing but brush thickets.

Valente gave a sudden tug at the leash, and was almost dragging me forward. I followed to the edge of the depression, which was partly covered at the center with a pool of dark, turgid water. There were many animal tracks in the caked mud surface near the bank, most of them quite old. At the far side, near a wet but waterless inlet, where the bank was only a few feet from the edge of the water, I saw the large tracks of a *tigre*. Holding the tugging Valente on leash, I crouched down and examined the marks of the big cat. The ridges between the claws seemed moist, and I concluded the *tigre* had been there during the morning.

Valente was whining and the other dogs, sniffing vigorously as I circled the watering place, were yapping in sharp, eager voices. I was confronted with a problem: if the *tigre* were close by, it would be better to tether Beduino and follow the dogs on foot through the brush; but if it had gone some distance, I would have to return for the mule and thus lose the trail.

There was also the possibility that if the *tigre* had not gone far, it might circle behind me and attack the mule, which would be powerless to defend itself or to run. Valente meanwhile was looking back at me feverishly, as if to say: "All right, master—we have found the track of the brute! Why do we not start after it?"

It struck me there were many problems that had been

previously solved by Joaquim to which I did not know the answers; and in addition to having responsibility for my own success now, I also had the responsibility for the animals.

Finally I decided—while Valente was nearly yanking my arm off in his haste to be on the track of our prey—that I would follow the trail on Beduino; and if we had the *tigre* within range, I would unleash the dogs and go after it afoot. This seemed the wiser course; and it turned out to be the best one. We followed the tracks of the *tigre* through perhaps a mile of thick brush and low, spreading trees of the *cãpao*, and then came out upon marsh grass.

The *tigre* apparently had headed out across the marsh grass toward the deeper jungle beyond; and I was now confronted with the problem of following it through the high grass and perhaps in the end being stalked by the *tigre* itself. It was not unusual, I knew, for a big cat, finding itself trailed by dogs, to circle and pounce on its pursuers from ambush; and since a *tigre* makes far less noise in the grass than a dog or a human, this is not too difficult a trick.

I was beginning to feel more than the solitude of the jungle; I was learning the deeper problem—not of loneliness, but of survival. My fate and that of my dogs would rest on my making the proper decision. It was also getting close to nightfall, and I wanted a place to make night camp where Beduino and the dogs would be safe from attack in the darkness.

We pushed across perhaps three kilometers of thick, head-high grass, Valente following the tracks of the *tigre*, until we were almost to the fringe of a deeper jungle beyond the marsh grass. Then, from the changing tone of Valente's whining yaps, and the way he circled back and forth, I realized he had lost the trail. I unleashed the dogs and after several minutes of scurrying about, they came back to gaze at me, as if waiting for my infallible divination as to what to do next.

It was nearly night, and I had only a small amount of water; but there was evidence of water from the *buriti* palms which were visible among the trees. I decided to push a little way into the forest. Water can usually be obtained by driving a hole near a *buriti* palm, and letting it fill up—a trick Apparicio had taught me. However, we came to the edge of a small stream with pools of clear water, and after carefully selecting an open space with no heavy tree branches above it for a lurking cat to crouch upon, I hobbled the mule and set up night camp.

Valente crouched with the other dogs on a blanket I had laid near a small fire which I had built—not as protection against prowling beasts, because a *tigre* will attack around a fire as soon as any place, but to provide a circle of light in which I could see the dogs and the mule. After feeding the animals and myself (I warmed a piece of *charqui* and with *mandioca* flour and a drink from my water bottle, made my supper), I sat with my back against a tree and my rifle beside me, prepared to sleep as well as I could.

Whenever I awoke, I replenished the glowing fire with a few sticks, and the crackle would arouse the dozing dogs for a moment. Each time they would lift their heads and gaze furtively into the blackness that swallowed everything that surrounded us. Then I would close my eyes and attempt to take another nap, but I did not feel much like sleeping. On the whole it was not a very restful night.

On many nights, travelling with Apparicio, I had remained awake for long hours, listening to the myriad sounds of the jungle, and seeking to identify them and to interpret their meaning. This is instinctive with those who travel in wild places and sleep by a camp fire at night; but that was nothing like the feeling I experienced this night.

I found myself staring into the blackness beyond the dull rim of light from the glowing fire, and feeling the strange mystery of the jungle at night. There were things not identifiable, or even capable of being sensed outwardly. Yet I felt them within my own senses. They were like ingredients of my solitary vigil . . . For example, I closed my eyes at one moment, and tried to understand what the *tigre* would do, if it were prowling around the camp site. I concluded it would watch us, and then skulk off, having no possible reason—unless it were hungry—for attacking that red glowing spot in the blackness. I looked into the black ring of trees and tried to understand the deep quiet of the jungle at night; and I think I actually understood how an animal would feel, crouching in suspension between sleep and wakefulness, having no desire to attack any living thing, but ready to defend itself at the slightest unfamiliar sound. There are many animals that prowl in the jungle at night, and a few of these I heard . . . the soft gnashing of teeth of the *cayetú*; and once I saw a gleam of eyes beyond the fire. I reached for my rifle, but whatever the animal was, it scurried off and I resumed my vigil.

By the time the first streaks of light began to outline the trees and the marsh grass to the east, I was fully awake and actually refreshed; and above all, I felt as if I had passed through a kind of inner change. The vigorousness of the morning air, which was cool at this time of the year, filled me with a sensation of strength and sureness which I had not felt the day before. It was as if the night I had passed alone in the deep silence of the jungle had poured into me a confidence and an awareness of the jungle's power, and also of my own power. I still felt that sense of solitary responsibility for what I was doing—for my own life, and the lives of the animals; but I no longer had any doubt as to my own capacity.

Valente picked up the trail less than an hour after we left the night camp; and before the sun was above the rim of the *capão* to the east, Beduino was running along after the dogs. I knew from the tone of Valente's bark—a deep baying, that came full out of the dog's throat, rather than a whining yelp—and from the straight run the dogs made, without scurrying to one side and the other, that the *tigre* was not far ahead.

I rode along the rim of the forest, keeping within range of the dogs' barks; and as Beduino plunged through patches of thorny thickets I began to wish I had Joaquim's uncanny knack for picking his own fighting ground.

However, I had no chance to make such a selection. After a mile of rapid pursuit, the dogs' barks changed from eager baying to a sharp, snarling crescendo, and I knew the *tigre* was at bay. I rode close to the place from which the noise was coming, dismounted and fastened Beduino's reins to a thorn bush. I pulled my spear from the sheath and also took my rifle, since the cat might be in a tree where it could not be reached with a spear. Then I pushed forward through the high grass.

The brush country was not good for spear-fighting . . . I knew that, from all Joaquim had told me. Also, it was unfamiliar ground. But I had no choice in the matter—since I could not return to Beduino and leave the dogs. So I shoved my way through the grass and brush.

I saw the dogs sooner than I had expected. They were near a patch of brush and grass that surrounded a thicket of *acuri* palms. From the direction of their snapping and barking, I knew the *tigre* must be in the thicket. I laid my rifle against a branch, and holding the spear in readiness, shuffled cautiously toward the bank of brush.

As I approached, I could hear the low, throaty snarl of the *tigre*, even in the din of the dogs' barking and growling. It seemed to say: "Leave me alone, and I'll leave you alone."

I got close enough to probe with my spear into the grass; but still I had not located the position of the *tigre*. The hoarse grumbling was now a snarl, as if the patience of the big beast was rapidly thinning. The sounds from the cat were quite audible; but I had no idea of the direction from which they came.

My hands had become slightly damp, from the heat and from sweating in the palms. I knew the next few seconds would decide my fate—and probably that of the dogs and of Beduino. But I had no way I could think of that would provoke the cat into revealing its position. Once I heard a slight rustle in the brush, and turned to face that point; but the next instant I heard a low, throaty snarl ending in a cough, several feet away.

By this time I dared not retreat or change my tactics. If I turned away for an instant, I would expose myself to an attack I might not be able to meet; and if I shoved the spear into the brush, I would be out of position to meet an attack.

While I was concentrating on this problem, the *tigre* suddenly increased the tempo of its growls. The first rumble of protest changed to a snarling roar. The dogs were at one side, and I was afraid the animal might charge them, forcing me to defend them from the flank. It would be almost impossible to drive the spear into a vital spot of a *tigre* charging the dogs; and I was just about to go for my gun, and take a chance on a shot at the *tigre* as it came out of the brush, when I caught a flash of black and yellow in the grass, almost instantly followed by a terrifying roar.

The *tigre* was charging at me, and almost instinctively, I lowered the spear to meet it. The charge was low; and the sight of that snarling face, contorted with animal rage and the screaming sound that came from the pink cavern of its throat, was so sudden I was startled, rather than frightened. I believe surprise saved me, because my own reaction was as instinctive as anything I have ever done. I had no time to decide between one thing or another; and I think I reacted automatically. As the *tigre* hurled itself at me, I jabbed sharply upward with the spear and caught it full in the chest.

Then the *tigre* did something else I had not expected. It wrested itself from the spear and backed off. The blood was spurting from the wound in its chest, and I knew the *tigre* was badly wounded—but I did not know how soon it would die. All at once, my mind concentrated on one thought; I must provoke the *tigre* into a quick charge, so that it would have enough force to impale itself on my spear.

I have said earlier that I believe it was the sense of sureness and of confidence in myself that saved me. The *tigre* could have turned aside and struck at me with a slashing, side attack; and I do not think I could have fended it off with the spear, since I would have had to use the weapon as a stick or club. Then my own survival would have been only a question of how long the animal could live, with the slash in its chest.

But I remembered Joaquim's trick of distracting the *tigre*. Carefully keeping my balance, so I would be ready for a charge, I quickly kicked out and knocked a cloud of sand toward the cat. The effect was instantaneous. With a roar that came like a horrid gargle from its bleeding throat, the cat lunged at me again, and this time I drove the spear into its chest, aimed straight at the dying heart.

The *tigre* had almost no fight, once I drove in the spear. There was very little of the furious wrestling between man and beast that I had seen in the first fight between Joaquim and the *tigre*. The great spotted body was writhing and the claws were slashing through the air in a fury, but within a few seconds the hulk of the cat suddenly softened and grew limp. I lurched against it with a final heave, and managed to pin it on its back, where the animal threshed out the last bit of draining life.

I stood for a moment, leaning on the shaft of my spear, the blade sunk deep in the *tigre's* chest. For the first few seconds, I doubt if I was conscious of anything except a terrible weariness. Oddly enough, my first thought was that if the battle had lasted another minute, the *tigre* would have killed me. It seemed to me that I was in such a state of weakness, I could not have held the spear. Later I realized that this was merely a reaction from the concentrated energy I had used up during the short time that the fight lasted.

I looked down at the face of the *tigre*. The eyes had closed, and the regal face was still; but the lips were drawn back over the white teeth in the last agony of death. At that moment I felt a bond between myself and that *tigre* which nothing can ever efface.

There are psychologists who believe there is a sensual relation between a murderer and his victim—a sensation of intimacy that is almost akin to the ecstasy of love. The dying victim is so closely bound up with the living killer that each, for an instant, is wholly dependent upon the other for his existence—for what he is. I do not know how true or how fanciful this theory may be, since I have neither deliberately or knowingly killed a man, nor am I a psychologist. But I know that there was such an intimacy between myself and that dying *tigre* in the jungle.

I have seen death and I have been near death many times; but this, for the moment, was not the spectre of death.

It was almost a feeling of purification, if I may be pardoned a leap into the limbo of spiritual fancy. I had fought this beast in a lonely arena, deep in the jungle, with only my dogs as witnesses; yet no Olympic champion or Roman gladiator ever felt more profoundly, I believe, the ultimate exultation of triumph. I actually had a desire to leap on the carcass and yell, but I restrained this impulse.

While the dogs worried at the limp legs of the animal, I removed the hide—not as a trophy of victory, but because I wanted some visible reminder of this moment. And I thought of Joaquim, and wondered how he would take my lone hunt. I had, in a sense, violated the injunctions of my teacher not to hunt alone—although I owed no particular obligation to him in that respect. Yet I wanted his approval.

I rolled up the bloody hide of the animal that a few hours before had been a lord of the jungle, and strapped it on the back of Beduino's saddle; then I started back to the sugar farm. Valente, who seemed to understand every mood and thought that passed through my mind, trotted solemnly ahead, tossing his head back now and then, as if to render to me his own peculiar dog tribute for my triumph.

As I rode back across the marshlands and over the ridge with the red clay cliffs, I had a strange feeling that I had left something unrecoverable in the jungle behind me. Perhaps my depression was a reaction from the climax of the hunt. I had been physically and mentally keyed up to this task; and now that it was over, it was as if the strength were suddenly drawn from my legs.

Later I learned from Joaquim that this is a common reaction for any spear-fighter—even those who hunt in packs. I have also heard that in Africa, the Massai spearmen, who attack lions in hunting packs with spears, are often sick for days after a spear-fight. I do not know whether this is true; and in my case I doubt if it was entirely due to the reaction from the spear-fight with the *tigre*.

This was a turning point in my life. I had lived for six years with the thought of this conquest of a jungle *tigre* burning like a living image in my mind. I remembered old Dom

Carlos' words . . . "This was not a hunt. It was a battle of the gods!" I had fought alone in the jungle with a man-killing animal that is, in its way, the lord of that part of creation. I was alone among men, and the sense of loneliness persisted.

My mind went back to my boyhood days in Libau, and my little half-sister Olga, who was a year younger than I. My brother Ernst did not like her, and very often whipped her; while I strove to defend her. She remained with my family for ten years, and many years after I left I learned that she killed herself by drinking acid. Why I should have thought of Olga at this moment I cannot say . . . except that she was like a crippled animal, and I hated to see an animal crippled.

I rode back into the yard at Senhor Pinto's *casa*, dumping the hide at the corral where I asked one of the animal handlers to salt and tan it. Senhor Pinto came out and examined the skin carefully, noting the rents in the throat and chest, and nodded. He looked at me.

"Joaquim said you would kill a *tigre* one day with the *zagaya*. Praise be to God, you have come back alive! Did you have serious difficulties?"

I shook my head. A few days later, Joaquim returned from his hunting trip to the north. He looked at the skin, which was stretched out to dry. He had heard of my hunt from the *vaqueros* who tended Senhor Pinto's small herd of cattle, and his black eyes glittered.

"You did well to kill that animal," he said. "It is a big cat, and I see from the skin you had to strike twice."

I told him what had happened; and again he nodded.

"A wounded *tigre* may run away," he said. "A dying one never! You might have retreated, but your dogs would not have left. And a dog is made reckless by the smell of blood."

He looked at me with his dark, beady eyes; and then he awkwardly put out his hand. I took it, and he pumped mine up and down like the handle of a well-pump. It suddenly occurred to me that in all probability the only time the old Indian had shaken hands with anyone before this, was when I shook hands with him the day he killed the *tigre*.

"You are a *tigrero!*" he exclaimed. His crooked yellow

teeth were exposed in a grin, and his wrinkled old face lighted with pleasure. It was the old hunter's accolade.

Joaquim and I hunted once more together; and then, my work completed on the Pinto sugar mill, I made my plans to head west and rejoin Apparicio at the Rancho Triumpho. I thanked Senhor Pinto warmly for his hospitality. He bowed, his eyes crinkling with a friendly humor, and extended his hand.

"My home shall always be proud to remember that the *tigrero*, Senhor Siemel, was my guest."

I clasped his hand. He was a warm, kind man; and I knew I was leaving a friend. He asked gravely after "Dom Ernesto," and I told him I would extend his greetings to my brother. As I rode out of the compound, made up of the *casa* and the big, shed-like mill and the small huts surrounding it, I felt that I was leaving a place that had been more of a home to me than anywhere I had lived since I left Libau.

With Valente trotting along the trail beside me, I headed for Joaquim's shack. The old Indian was there—sober this time—leaning in the doorway of the dirty little hut. He lifted his hand, grinning.

"*Saude, senhor!*" he called; and I dismounted and walked over to him.

"Good-by, my friend," I said to him. "Drink of the *canha* for me. Perhaps we will meet again one day."

He dashed suddenly into the hut and brought out the inevitable jug, and two dirty cups. He poured the liquor into the cups. We raised them and drank—and only my knowledge of the cauterizing efficacy of the *canha* permitted me to drink from the grimy vessel without some physical revulsion. I knew that no germs could withstand Joaquim's *canha*.

My last sight of the old Indian was the ragged brown figure, slouched in the doorway of his hut, his eyes wet and glistening as he waved farewell. It was the last time I saw him alive.

Chapter 18

Apparicio was at the Rancho Triumpho when I arrived at the casa of Dom Henrique Paes again, and I knew from the expression of gravity on his face, and the barely perceptible nod he gave me, that he had news of importance. As soon as as I could gracefully complete the amenities of greeting, I walked down to my hut and found Apparicio waiting for me.

"I have two things to tell you, one of a serious nature," he said gravely, "and another matter which I believe will be joyful news for you."

"Tell me the bad news first," I said, immediately thinking of Ernst. "Has something happened to my brother?"

Apparicio shook his head, but his dark eyes glinted; I had come to understand the expression of his eyes as well as if he had spoken.

"It is about Ernst," I said.

The gaucho nodded. "A drunken Matto Grossense was at the rancho a few days past. He stopped at the galapão. He called himself Pedro Vaca. A dirty caboclo, senhor! I told him of our travels and in the course of our talking, your name was mentioned." The tall man from the Rio Grande do Sul dropped his eyes toward the ground an instant, as if in silent apology for having been so careless.

"This animal flew into a stupid rage. I thought he was speaking of you, and I would have throttled him as he stood there, but it was not you he spoke of, senhor—it was your brother."

I remembered the scar I had seen on Ernst's shoulder, the night we sat together in the little hotel in Passo Fundo.

He had spoken savagely of a "present from a damned *caboclo*."
I told Apparicio of this incident, and he nodded.

"Perhaps," he said. "At any rate, it was an affair over a
woman. I said nothing further, since it did not concern you.
But the man is in Cuyabá now, and your brother should be
warned."

I reflected, rather wearily, that the issue of life and death
in Brazil seemed to hang upon the word "insult." If Brazilians
only had less tender feelings . . . But I had no knowledge of
the extent of Ernst's offense against the man, and I also felt
a slight twinge of disappointment that he had become involved in such an affair.

"I will ride to Abobral in a day or so," I said. "Ernst
must be told of this."

Apparicio agreed; it was highly probable, he said, that
the man would learn of Ernst's presence at Abobral and set
out to ambush him. In this wild country a man might lie
dead on the *pantanal* for weeks within a few kilometers of
the *casa*, and not be found except by vultures.

Apparicio also had a bit of news that concerned Favelle.

"Your enemy from the Rio Grande do Sul has been in
Amolar," he said. "He spoke with a *vaquero* from this *rancho*
and inquired of you. The man told him nothing . . . or so
he says. Nevertheless, you and your brother now have enemies
in this area."

Amoral was a small settlement of about thirty houses on
the Rio Paraguaya, perhaps fifty kilometers below the Rancho
Triumpho. I turned to Apparicio:

"First of all, you must explain to your friend, the
vaquero, that he is quite at liberty to tell anyone who asks
where I am. I am not hiding . . . nor am I running from anyone. As soon as I have returned from Abobral, Apparicio, I
will ride to Amolar."

Apparicio shook his head, and his thin mouth broke into
a smile.

"You cannot ride down the river. The floods have risen,
and there is no trail beyond the landing. However, I have
found a new way for us to travel!"

This, it seemed, was his "joyful" news. Apparicio had located an old river scow, gray from disuse, partly hidden among the reeds in a small creek branching off the Rio Cuyabá. It was the property of a man who operated a prison farm, Dom Francisco Pinto de Oliveira.

"I have spoken to the old man," Apparicio said. "He does not wish to sell it for what we can pay. But the machinery on his sugar farm is badly in need of repair. We can make a bargain with him."

I had heard something of Senhor Oliveira's farm. It was known as Aricá, and was an official place for minor criminals whom the government at Cuyabá wished to repent of their crimes, without necessarily costing the provincial treasury anything for their period of penance. The problem was solved by Senhor Oliveira; he needed workers for his sugar farm and mill, and one of the by-products of his industry was *canha*. As long as the prisoners had *canha*, they would remain at the farm.

The following day Apparicio and I rode down the Rio Cuyabá past the river boat landing, and found the small creek. The flood waters had risen so that it was impossible to cross the creek; but there, against the mud bank on the opposite side of the creek, lay a gray hull. On the weathered side was painted: *Aventureira*. In Portuguese, this is "Adventuress."

It struck me that if the old scow proved sound, and we could acquire her, here was a way for Apparicio and myself to travel down the Paraguay and set up hunting camps wherever it was most convenient. We would keep our equipment aboard, and be able to establish a base camp wherever we anchored.

I became as excited as Apparicio. Stripping off my clothes, I swam across the creek to the side of the barge and clambered aboard. I had to pull aside the weeds to find the hatch, but there was only a small amount of water in the hold, and the hull seemed to be sound. Apparicio, sitting on the other side of the creek, waved directions at me, and was almost crowing with delight at my own excitement.

"We need two poles and a big paddle for a rudder—that

is all!" he said, as we rode back to the ranch. "We shall travel as masterhunters of the Rio Paraguaya, and when the rains are coming down, we shall not even get our feet wet!"

It was the first time I had seen the usually reserved Apparicio display such enthusiasm—and it was not long before I discovered the reason.

Senhor Oliveira's sugar farm was along the Rio Cuyabá, but could be reached by a more direct overland route. Since the floods were beginning to pour across the jungle, we had to use a dugout, poling it through narrow channels among the sponge-like hummocks that rose treacherously in the murky forest.

We found Senhor Oliveira at Aricá. He was a man of perhaps sixty, with a bristling, iron-gray beard and an expression of patriarchal dignity and benevolence that contrasted rather strangely with the kind of institution he operated. However, the prisoners apparently were happy as long as they got regular rations of *canha*. This was dispensed at the rate of one cup a day and a liter each weekend, resulting in an unrestrained debauch on Saturday night which ran well into Sunday. Senhor Oliveira retired to his *casa*, locked the doors to his wine cellar and let the celebration run its course. By Monday the inmates had finished their *canha* and were too drunk to fight, so there was nothing else to do but sober up working at the cane-presses and in the fields.

"It is not an unpleasant form of servitude," the old man told us, "and is peculiar to this region. I doubt if it would be successful anywhere else, but here—" he shrugged. "There is no other source of *canha*. Where else can they be assured of food, a place to live, and regular rations of *canha*? They have their orgy once a week, and are quite fit for work again."

The institution was, in a sense, coeducational; and we found the men and women living and working together in apparent harmony, at least during the *canha*-less week days. We were to find out later how the plan worked on Saturdays.

We had no trouble reaching a bargain with Senhor Oliveira.

"Keep the mill running until the crop is finished and

worked through the cane-press, and the *Aventureira* will be yours," he said. "I shall be well repaid!"

We arranged to return to Dom Henrique for our tools. It was almost a fortnight, however, before we reached Aricá again. I left Apparicio at the Rancho Triumpho to patch up the scow, stripping off the roof of the aft cabin so that we could carry our horse and mules on board; and meanwhile I rode north to Abobral.

Ernst was in a sour mood when I arrived. Life on the Rancho Abobral had proved even less charming than he had expected, between the overbearing maternalism of Dona Rita, who had assumed a kind of spiritual partnership in Ernst's marital adventure, and the physical assets of Dona Maria, which apparently were not inconsiderable. In addition to these trials, Ernst's wife was with child—which he regarded as a calamity. Those infrequent moments of spontaneous gaiety, which were Ernst's greatest charm, were being ground out of his personality, leaving him with only a sulky hostility toward life. I learned that he and Dona Maria planned to leave soon to live in Cuyabá.

When I was able to talk with him alone—after the first effusive greetings of old Dom Francisco, and a few moments of suspicious inquiry on the part of Dona Rita as to why I had returned—I told Ernst of the black native who had passed through the Rancho Triumpho.

"I do not wish to inquire into your affairs, Ernst," I said. "You probably have old enemies . . . just as I have. But in this case, the man seems to be stalking you. And it is only a matter of time when he will find you, particularly if you go to Cuyabá."

Ernst shrugged, indifferently.

"I suspect it is that damned Pedro Vaca," he said, "although there are several others who would like to slip a knife between my ribs." He laughed abruptly. "He became annoyed because I amused myself with a little *chiquita* whom he regarded as his own property. I hardly considered the man as a rival, Alex . . . Besides, he was a pimp and I was a lover. How would any girl choose? He shot at me from behind a shed in Campo Grande. But as you have seen, he did not shoot well enough. So I thrashed him, and that is all. I have not seen him since."

I thought of Dom Carlos' prophetic advice . . . it is better to kill a Brazilian than to beat him with your fists. Ernst was watching me with amusement. To him Pedro Vaca was just a name, a "dirty little *caboclo*," as he had called him. But he was more than a name: he was a human being, dangerous with wounded pride; and in his own mind, he was the one who had suffered—not Ernst.

Suddenly I said to my brother:

"Look here, Ernst—I will go to Cuyabá in advance of you and Dona Maria, and find this fellow, and end this thing once and for all. Then, by God, I will find Favelle, and settle with him. I am sick of these fellows stalking us, as if we were hunted men!"

Ernst laughed, but shook his head.

"I am going to Cuyabá, Alex . . . Maria and I will go there to live. It has already been settled. I will take my tools and establish a shop there. Cuyabá is not Rio, but it is better than Abobral."

There was little use arguing; and I had become sufficiently fatalistic to know that the laws of the jungle and its people are not subject to change or improvisation from the outside. Ernst had made his bed, and he must lie in it.

I left him and his *senhora*, whose future motherhood was already becoming evident from the tightness of her dress, disclosing the outlines of a well-rounded and growing belly; and I thought as I followed Valente down the river trail that each parting with my brother was becoming more dismal.

We rode at a steady pace through the marsh and down into the patches of deep jungle which clustered along the river. I had acquired an easy friendship with Valente. He was a dog of singular intelligence, and at times it seemed to me that all he lacked to make him human was the power of speech. And even that might have been superfluous, because he could turn his brown eyes upon me with such expression that I experienced at times the strange feeling that we had spoken to each other.

As we travelled into the jungle, which formed a heavy bridge between the *pantanal* of Fazenda Abobral and that of Fazenda Triumpho, I felt once more the challenge of the deep forest. It is something I have never felt anywhere else; and like the animals of the jungle, who have no real enmity against humans, the challenge bears no malice. To live in the jungle, one must know it . . . every tendril of vine or rope-weed, every root swinging from a massive fig tree and searching hungrily for a spot to clamp itself to the ground, every animal sound and every bird call. At one point I stopped to listen to the most massive orchestration the jungle can produce—a concert of howler monkeys, a cacophony of monstrous noises that swelled like the roaring of a great organ against the green domes overhead. It was a magnificent natural orchestra, and I was the only human in the audience.

Riding back to the Rancho Triumpho, I realized that this time there was an emptiness left by my parting with Ernst. It seemed to me that a crime had been committed against Ernst . . . but it was a crime of nature, not of people. He was lost in this wilderness, and no one could save him— not even himself. At times I blamed myself for not having turned him back before it was too late; but there is one thing a man learns in the wilderness, and that is that each must account for himself. Nature has no other way of assessing responsibility.

Apparicio was cheerfully completing the carpentering work on the *Aventureira* when I returned. A few planks had been replaced in the hull, the deck was repaired. Our "Noah's Ark" was almost ready for launching.

There is a certain pride that comes to a man with his feet on the deck of a ship. It is a floating world all to itself, and the man who commands the craft—whether a ship or a barge—is master of that world. Standing in the stern of the scow, which was perhaps forty feet long, I surveyed the bulky bosom of the old river barge, resting on a mass of water lilies like on old woman who has fallen asleep on her face, and in my romantic eyes it began to assume the maidenly proportions of a young girl. I envisioned her slender prow biting into the waves of a stormy inland lake, or cutting a silken furrow through the placid surface of a jungle lagoon. Actually, we seldom let her drift far enough from the bank so that our poles, known as *zingas*, could not hold to the bottom of the shallow river. And she was almost as wide six feet aft of the prow as she was amidships.

Nevertheless, Apparicio and I were quite pleased, and as proud as a pair of *Conquistadores* as we prodded the old barge loose from the clutching marsh grass, swung her prow across a mass of water lilies and gently pushed her with our *zingas* down to the mouth of the inlet and out into the Rio Cuyabá.

We were four days on the winding jungle route outlined by Senhor Oliveira, until we reached Aricá—and our arrival, unluckily, fell on a Saturday night, which was "pay day" for the prisoners. The sun had gone down, and only the light of a lantern on the small jetty guided us to the landing. As we rounded a bend that brought the little sugar mill settlement into view, a glare against the trees behind the jetty greeted us, and at first I thought the mill was on fire. As we poled the *Aventureira* up to the jetty, which was completely deserted, I saw that the glare was man-made. A huge bonfire had been built in an open space behind the wharf shed, and around the fire, silhouetted in the fantastic light of the flames, half-naked men and women were dancing.

This macabre celebration apparently was the finale of the prisoners' pay-day ration of *canha*. The dancers were close enough for us to see them quite clearly, and also hear them. It was a brand of Portuguese with which I was not entirely familiar, but the sense of what they were saying was not hard to understand, and the cackling laughter of men, slapping the women on their buttocks, made the whole business quite intelligible. This was the "orgy" of which Senhor Oliveira had spoken, the "pleasant kind of servitude" which made life endurable for the prisoners.

At first I was afraid the merrymakers might rush to the

Aventureira when we poled her alongside the jetty, but the dancers paid no particular attention to us. We got the dogs ashore, in the face of the flickering glare of the bonfire, and led them along the edge of the settlement, skirting the bonfire area, to the main house. After that we aroused Senhor Oliveira, and he greeted us warmly, assuring us of the safety of the *Aventureira*.

"They are far too drunk by now to become inquisitive about a boat," he said. "If any should be foolish enough to remain sober and go aboard the barge, we can easily find them in the morning and thrash them to within an inch of their lives."

The varieties of Brazil's jungle had always amazed me, but the varieties of its people were even more astounding, and Dom Francisco Pinto de Oliveira was among the more astounding. It seemed to me the jungle, by sheer force of nature, carved each person according to his own special mould, but in a form that was like a caricature. Old Dom Juão Cajango, and his singular lust for getting the best of a bargain; Dom Joaquim Reis, the little "mayor" of Areia, with his shrewd perception of social requirements in a village populated chiefly by riffraff; Dom Marco, the rugged little legal philosopher of the diamond fields; my brother's new father-in-law, Dom Francisco Andrade, who asked only a man's soul as a dowery; Dom Henrique Paes, whose robust paternalism had virtually populated a country half as big as Belgium; and Dom Francisco de Oliveira, who organized this unique system of criminal reform without cost to the government, and apparently with satisfaction to the inmates and considerable economic reward for himself.

Shortly after Apparicio and I arrived at Senhor Oliveira's sugar mill at Aricá, I acquired a monkey, and just before I left I acquired a dog—or rather a puppy. I mention these two additions to our jungle family because the monkey, Chico, became my constant companion, and the dog, Tupi, saved my life. The latter incident occurred some months after I left Aricá, but it concerned an almost legendary *tigre* known as

Assassino about whom I first heard reports at Senhor Oliveira's farm.

In fact, one of the nearby cattle ranchers had asked Apparicio and myself to hunt the marauding cat, which had destroyed as many as a dozen cattle in a single night of raiding. But Assassino had a reputation for eluding human trackers and killing dogs, and I saw little reason to risk my small pack in a futile hunt.

I had heard of a dog of such fabulous cunning as a *tigre* hunter, that I set out one day with one of the prisoners—lent me by the affable Dom Francisco—to find an old Guató Indian who owned the dog. The Indian was known as a *tigrero*, although I never found out whether he had killed *tigres* singlehanded with a *zagaya*, as Joaquim Guató did. He lived on a remote *aterrado*, a refuge built by the Indians long before the *Conquistadores*, and used as a haven against enemies. These *aterrados* are artificial hills, raked up from the swamps, rising well above the flood-marks. They usually are about a hundred and fifty yards long, and perhaps fifty yards wide; and they lie hidden in almost inaccessible swamps, protected by a maze of streams and lagoons, and only the Guatós knew the routes. Here the ancient men of the tribe dwelt alone, gradually dying out after four centuries of stubborn refusal to accept the conquest of the white man. They were not molested, chiefly because no one except a Guató could find them—and also because they did no harm to anyone.

The old man lived in a triangle of jungle and swamp between the sugar farm and the Rio Paraguaya; and to reach the place required two days of poling a dugout through marsh channels. The prisoner, lent to me by Dom Francisco, guided the boat unerringly through this jungle labyrinth, apparently recognizing each hummock and fig tree. His accuracy as a navigator fascinated me, and I found that he had been born in this swampy area on one of the long, mound-like *aterrados*, where the families of refugees from the *Conquistadores* once lived—but which now were the solitary refuges of the Guató hermits who lived and died there.

The *atterado* itself was a blinding mass of color—the

lavendar plumage of a *lapacho* grove, surrounded with thickets of brushweed blooming with pink and carmine flowers. It was in the middle of an immense, flat country, spotted with lagoons and murky marsh pools. The water was almost tepid in the wake of the rains and under the blistering heat of the tropical summer sun. An old Indian crouched on the bank, beside a dugout canoe, and he apparently had just landed a fish, which he clutched to his hairless chest.

He was aged and withered, yet his black eyes gleamed with sudden hatred when I made known, through the prisoner who acted as my interpreter, the reason for my visit—that I had come to buy his dog. The subject of my bargain, a lean, square-jawed hound, stood stiff-legged beside his master, neither accepting nor rejecting the visitors to his island.

"You wish to buy my dog—to shoot *tigres?*" the old man said, baring his unclean teeth in a snarl. Through the interpreter, I assured him that my only reason for wanting the dog was to hunt with a spear.

The old Indian seemed to sneer at me. For an instant I felt sorry I had come; the utter disdain of the old Indian was obvious. But my interpreter jogged me in the ribs with his elbow.

"Offer him two bottles of *canha*," he said. "His pride will drop like a withered leaf!"

I went to my *mochila*, which was in the dugout, and took out a bottle. The old Indian's face had undergone a remarkable transformation. Pride and temptation seemed to be contesting for supremacy in his expression; and his eyes squinted as if he were also calculating how many bottles he could gain in the bargaining. I was suddenly sick of the effort. Here was an old Indian, living on an island in the swamp, alone except for his dog—and I was trying to bargain his only companion away from him with the most debasing lure a white man can offer.

"Keep the dog," I said, "and you can also have the bottle."

The black man with me uttered a little grunt of dismay. The old Indian seemed puzzled at first; but I explained that

I also hunted with a zagaya, and knew the value of the dog. Amazed at the sudden turn of fortune, he led us to his hut, a few steps from the river, and offered the hospitality of the house—which was a drink from the bottle I had just given him.

The dog, a half-starved creature, whimpered at his side, and the old fellow alternately petted it and slapped it. He began to recount his exploits as a hunter, in a sing-song voice. I learned that he, too, was a spearman—a zagaya hunter. I mentioned Joaquim Guató.

The old man regarded me with a sly squint; and I realized that he was probing my own qualifications, with infinite cunning. Possibly Joaquim, in his solitary journeys, had stopped at the aterrado of this old man.

"Only a short time ago, at the beginning of the summer sun, I left Joaquim many miles to the east." I pointed in the direction of the São Laurenço. "He is a great hunter. I have hunted the tigre under his guidance."

The old man smiled and nodded, apparently satisfied. He told me of one of his inventions—a hollow shell, made of bark, with which he could simulate the mating call of the tigre. He explained to me how he had crouched in a dugout canoe, blowing the bark-horn until the tigre, prowling to the river edge to investigate the amorous call, had swum out and been speared in the neck.

We remained that night on the aterrado, and the following day set out for Aricá again. I tried to persuade the old man to come back with us, but he grinned and shrugged. I last saw him standing with his dog at the edge of the aterrado, a thin, solitary remnant of a very small segment of humanity —but a segment that for four centuries had declined the infinite benevolence of the conquering white man.

Later I heard from a Guató, who had visited the neighboring aterrado of one of the old man's sons, that he had died alone on the island. As the old man had prophesied, the urubú had closed his eyelids.

Chapter 19

The rains ended in April, and the sugar crop was harvested in the dry, cold season. During the months at Aricá I fulfilled my bargain with Dom Francisco. His chugging old steam engine was kept in operation. Her joints were creaking, and rust spurted out of leaks in the steam-pipes; but I learned to know every whim of the old wood-eater, and by September the cane crop was squeezed dry of its juice and Dom Francisco was a happy man.

"Next year you will make money with me," he said, squinting in a calculating manner; but I shook my head.

"My bargain was for the *Aventureira*," I said. "I have done my job, and now she is ours."

The old man smiled with the flawless courtesy of his people; and as an additional reward, presented Tupi to me. By this time Apparicio and I had decided on our future career; we would drift downriver on the *Aventureira* and hire out to the great ranches along the Rio Paraguaya, killing the *tigres* that destroyed their cattle. It would be both pleasant and profitable.

As it was in the Garden of Eden, there is always a serpent and an apple.

Apparicio came to me, a day before we were due to leave; and I knew from the way he looked at me—or rather from the way he did not look at me—that he had something on his mind.

"I would like to ride upriver to the Rancho Triumpho," he said. "I gave my word that I would return before the rains

196

began again. Senhorita Carvalho is now two years older than when I first knew her."

I snorted.

"The apple is ripe, eh?"

Apparicio grinned; but he was quite candid.

"She would be a fine companion on these lonely nights on the barge," he said.

"You are suggesting we bring her with us?" I exclaimed. "Apparicio—do you plan to marry Senhorita Carvalho?"

He shook his head.

"I cannot afford to go for a priest," he said. "It would cost too much. But before we left on the boat, she said she wished to come with me."

A sudden recollection crossed my mind. It was the remembrance of a red dress, and the rather pleasing movements that went with it. I shook my head, to rid myself of the thought. For a few seconds I tried to consider the matter objectively. The Matto Grosso was a wild place; but there were limitations upon that wildness, and this was particularly true where women were concerned.

"Does Senhor Paes know of your intentions?" I asked Apparicio. He shook his head.

"Of course not, *senhor!* He would probably shoot me."

There was more than one aspect to Apparicio's problem. Dom Henrique was my friend, and I did not want to offend him. Yet I knew Apparicio, and if he and Mariinha had made up their minds to elope, they would do so. The barge was Apparicio's home as well as my own . . . and so in the end, I agreed.

"I will not be a party to any theft of a girl," I said. "But if you and Mariinha arrive at the junction of the Rio Cuyabá and the São Laurenço in two days, I will be there with the boat."

Apparicio helped me load the tools and our other belongings aboard the *Aventureira*. Then he set out overland, since the ground was now dry and it was less than a day's ride to the Rancho Triumpho. I poled the barge downriver, meditating a good deal on the recklessness of what I had agreed to. The notion of a girl aboard the barge was so startling that I could hardly believe I had made the arrangement. Yet I had; and the evidence was the sight of Apparicio, sitting on the bank, waving at me from beneath the shadow of a *lapacho* tree with a smaller figure beside him when I poled the barge through the shadows of trees that lined the creek and out into the sunlit glare of the São Laurenço.

Mariinha looked at me at first with a questioning glance; then with a sudden blaze of dark fire that I had come to recognize in the eyes of women of the Matto Grosso. I had seen that flame in the eyes of Dona Maria Andrade; it was as if a smouldering secret lay behind the dark lens of the soul, a dull fire that might break out any minute into a flame that could—for a moment—melt the stoniest heart.

We arranged our quarters aboard the *Aventureira* according to natural convenience: I took the forward section of the deck house, where I had set up my work bench and tools; Apparicio occupied the middle room, and Mariinha was mistress of the kitchen.

This arrangement was adequate for the moment; but it was not long before I realized that two men and a woman from time immemorial have been an impossible number of people on any boat. A man is aware of a woman in the way an animal senses another living creature—whether a friend or an enemy. The moment Mariinha stepped aboard the *Aventureira*, it ceased to be a drifting home for Apparicio and myself, and became a crucible for our emotions—subtle at first, but more definite as the days lengthened one upon the other.

As I sat in the forward end of the drifting scow, dragging my pole through the water and now and then thrusting at a partly submerged ledge or rock, I was conscious that Mariinha was there. She said very little to me, and I saw little of her at first, except at meal times. But the dark flash of her eyes would catch mine as she put a dish of steaming rice and *charqui* on the table in the kitchen where we ate. I could not be unaware of her presence when she looked at me.

Apparicio seemed outwardly unchanged by this addition

to our group; but I knew it could not help but change his attitude—if not toward me, at least toward the life we were leading. I observed his attitude toward Mariinha, and I realized he was in love with the girl—perhaps more than he had ever been before, since he was hardly twenty when I first met him and had not developed any serious affairs of the heart until he met Mariinha.

She proved to be a cheerful soul, working quietly and efficiently in the kitchen, cooking our meals and washing our clothes. At times I would hear her humming strange melodies, probably of both Indian and Brazilian origin. Now and then I stopped to talk with her about trivial things. Once I asked her, rather blunderingly, if she and Apparicio planned to get married when we reached Corumbá. She turned and looked at me, her dark eyes very large.

"No, senhor!" she said. "We have no such plan. It was not for that reason that I came on the Aventureira!"

I did not ask her the reason. Apparicio came out of his cabin at that moment, and came toward us; and I made an excuse to return to my own place at the forward end.

After the first few days, the routine aboard the scow became more settled. Brazilian women are outwardly patient and docile by nature; and Mariinha was no exception. She worked quietly in her kitchen, preparing our food; and I seldom saw her except at dusk when she would come out to the rail and stand, watching the darkening bank of green slide endlessly behind us.

After several days of drifting in this leisurely fashion, we nosed out through a wide gap in a flat expanse of marsh grass on either side of the river; and the prow of the old barge swung gently southward. We were on the Paraguay, the ancient dividing line between Spanish and Portuguese claims in the New World. On the western bank a sheer bluff of reddish earth rose from the water, an iron-ore mountain that contrasted sharply with the unending flatness of the jungle.

A short distance below this was the village of Amolar, consisting of perhaps fifty huts along the river bank, with a single jetty. I indicated to Apparicio that we would pole the *Aventureira* alongside the bank.

"If that jackal is still here, I will find him," I told Apparicio. "I am not going south with him running all over the Matto Grosso making threats."

Apparicio was disturbed; I suppose he was as much concerned over the possibility of some of the men in the village interesting themselves in our charming passenger as he was with my feud with Favelle. He asked one favor:

"Let me go into the village and see if he is there. If not, we can go on."

An hour later Apparicio returned. His thin face was quite grave.

"Your enemy has not been in the village for many months. He was not well liked . . . and he left to go south to Corumbá. He was there until three months ago, working in a small machine repair shop on the river. One of the men who hated him saw him. Since then, nothing is known."

I knew that Apparicio was worried about the matter. He knew the nature of a man like Favelle, his entire character festered by what he regarded as an irreparable damage to his pride; and I think Apparicio feared he would ambush me if I showed up in Corumbá.

However, his fears were groundless. We arrived in the big port town, which is the commercial center of the Matto Grosso, about two weeks later, and in spite of my inquiries, I could not find any trace of the man. However, something else occurred at Corumbá which temporarily interrupted our plans for heading south to the great cattle ranch at Barranco Branco, where we had planned to begin our careers as hunters.

We had tied up at the wharf, and I left Apparicio in charge of the barge while I went up to the main part of town, which lies on a shelf of land above the river facing east across the Paraguay. I was prowling through a hide store when a man in a white *sombrero* came up and spoke to me.

"Is your name Siemel, *senhor?*"

I was startled at first, and thought perhaps this was an emissary from Favelle, for whom I had been inquiring along the waterfront. The man was rather heavy, wearing loose white clothes; and his fat, florid face showed signs of worry. He mopped his forehead with a dirty handkerchief. I told him my name was Siemel.

"My name is Gomez," the man said quickly. "It is about your brother—Dom Ernesto . . . May we talk privately?"

We went to the rear of the store, and the fat Senhor Gomez told me quickly that he had come down only a few days before from Cuyabá, where he had spoken with Ernst.

"Your brother has killed a man," he said, still wiping his red face with the dirty cotton handkerchief. "He has been taken to Santa Rita do Araguaya to be tried. The killing of the man was not serious, but your brother made unfortunate comments which were resented by the populace. They were quite enraged against him, and it is only because of my personal regard for your brother that I dare tell you this."

The man seemed so frightened I wondered for a moment if Ernst had been engaged in some political activity; but a few questions quickly explained what had happened. The man Ernst killed was Pedro Vaca; and Ernst was not drunk at the time . . . even his enemies admitted that, Senhor Gomez said.

"Your brother lost his head," the man explained. "At the hearing on the case, he made some remarks about the man—about his blood."

I knew what had happened. A black man to Ernst was a Negro; and in Brazil's vast interior there is a strain of the blood of black men in more than half the population. After gleaning all of the information I could from Senhor Gomez, I returned to the Aventureira, and told Apparicio what had happened. I had decided to leave the next morning for Cuyabá.

"Keep the Aventureira here, or take it south—whichever you wish," I told the gaucho. "I will find you when I return."

A small river launch was leaving the next morning for Cuyabá, and I took passage on this; but it got stuck so often on sand bars that I left it at Aricá and rode overland to Cuyabá. Here I learned more of the incident that had caused

Ernst's arrest; and although it was the end of the dry season, I decided to strike immediately eastward for Santa Rita, which is on the border of Goyaz Province. The rains were drenching the *planalto* but the trail was not as treacherous as it would have been further south in the jungles and swamps.

Ten days later I rode down into the town of Santa Rita, built of reddish mud. From a distance Santa Rita looked like a pink scar on the hillside; and it actually lay across the border from Goyaz to Matto Grosso, with one-half of the town in each province. The jail was on the Matto Grosso side, and I found my brother in a small windowless cell. He looked wan and sick; his eyes were feverish, and it seemed to me he had lost hope.

I quickly learned the details of the affair; and I found also that Dona Maria, his wife, had followed him from Cuyabá and was living in a house near the jail.

"The jailer is quite reasonable," Ernst said, with a twisted smile. "He lets me go home at night, knowing that I will not embarrass him by escaping."

As a matter of fact, the situation was less serious than I had feared. The government had no intention of convicting Ernst, but desired to let the matter rest until the public indignation over Ernst's slur upon the natives of Matto Grosso had subsided. The jailer, a wiry fellow, came in while I was talking with my brother, and assured me with elaborate gestures that Ernst's crime would diminish with time, and if he stayed in jail long enough the case would collapse.

I went home with Ernst to a single-room hut, made of four corner poles, the walls laced together with sticks and plastered with the red-clay mud that scarred the land along the river. It was a dingy little place, but sufficed for Ernst, his wife and their child, a chubby, blue-eyed boy, who had been brought overland from Cuyabá.

Dona Maria was already spreading into the shapelessness which so quickly changes the well-formed girls of inland Brazil into ponderous drudges. Her eyes had lost their challenging luster, as if she were already growing weary of life.

She welcomed me to their house, however, with a cordiality that was quite genuine; and I realized as she sat holding the baby against her breast as she talked, that she loved my brother and held no malice against me.

I remained for two weeks, until Ernst's case came up in the provincial court; and it turned out exactly as the little jailer had predicted. The government prosecutor droned his charges in a monotonous voice and the judge commented upon the fact that Ernst was a foreigner, and therefore not familiar with the customs of the land. A small fine was assessed, the judge and prosecutor shook hands with Ernst and wished him God-speed.

Ernst and his little family decided to remain in Santa Rita until he could take in what money there was in the town for repairing firearms; and I wanted to get back to the Aventureira, so I decided to push ahead. Parting with Ernst this time was one of the deepest moments of sorrow I had known since I left Buenos Aires. As we stood beside my horse, clasping hands, the past seemed to pour over me, and I felt as if I were talking to a dying man.

That feeling may have been prophetic; because I never saw my brother again. A year later, while I was at Fazenda Barranco Branco, I received word that he had been ambushed and killed by friends of the *caboclo* he shot near Santa Rita.

Chapter 20

When I returned to Cuyabá it was mired with rain and the floods had swept southward along the Rio Cuyabá and the São Lourenço; so I sold my horse for the price of passage and took the little mail launch again, chugging down the tortuous course Apparicio and I had followed in the *Aventureira* many weeks earlier.

The barge was still at Corumbá when I arrived, lying against the stone jetty where we had tied her up. I talked over future plans with Apparicio, and since we were low on funds, we decided to remain in Corumbá long enough to earn a few *milreis* and buy supplies for the journey downriver. There were few men with real mechanical skills in the Matto Grosso in those days, and we had little trouble finding special jobs at the repair shops, which paid us well.

The atmosphere of uneasiness on the barge, gradually built up by the presence of a woman aboard, had settled somewhat; Mariinha remained in her cooking room or on the after deck, and I saw little of her except at meal times. She seemed afraid of the bustling river port, and seldom went ashore, and then only for a brief trip with Apparicio to buy a piece of cotton or some household needs at one of the shops just back of the waterfront.

We pulled out of Corumbá, late in April of 1925, in order to reach Barranco Branco in time for the early hunting. By this time I had settled in my own mind the problem of the girl on the *Aventureira* by the simple expedient of remaining very much to myself.

We drifted southeastward along the broad river, which

holds with its teeth even after it is out of the water. As Favelle staggered the last few steps across the beach, some of the fish still clung to his flesh with their teeth, wriggling and twisting. Part of his chest and stomach were torn away, and he was bleeding and almost dead by the time he reached a shack. Several people were running toward him. He lunged through the door and then I heard a shot.

I turned and saw that Apparicio was at my side. An old man in shirt sleeves, his eyes round with fright, turned to me and said: "Was he your enemy, senhor? My God, what a way to die!"

Apparicio took my arm and pushed me back from the edge of the jetty. I was sick from what I had seen. I did not go to the shack to look at Favelle. I found out later that he had been living there for several months. I doubt if he knew I had come on the *Aventureira*. Whether he met me accidentally on the jetty, or had found I had landed in the village and was looking for me, I never found out.

Those who went to the shack to look at the bloody, half-eaten body, later told me the *piranha* had ripped off half his stomach, tearing through cloth to get at the flesh. He would probably have died in another minute if he had not dragged his gun from a holster on the wall and shot himself.

Apparicio walked with me across the jetty with deep concern in his eyes, as we headed toward the *Aventureira*, and finally he said:

"You must not blame yourself for this, Senhor Alexandre! The man's own hate killed him—you were not the cause of it!"

I knew I was not; yet I wished I had killed Favelle. As Dom Carlos had told me years before, it would have been the kindest thing I could have done.

We pushed out into the river a few days later. I was sick of the memory of that horror in the river. The death of Favelle meant no more to me than he had meant as a living person; but the way he died left a deep depression in my mind. I looked forward only to getting back into the wilderness again.

Chapter 21

For perhaps two or three weeks we progressed slowly down the broad surface of the Paraguay, drifting on the current and hugging the west bank as closely as possible. We could steer to some extent by the rudder, although we depended more upon the *zingas*, or poles. At times we would float into deep water, and then Apparicio and I would take stations at opposite ends of the barge and try to find shoals or rocks which we could thrust against and work ourselves in to the shore.

It was a familiar pattern of jungle: vast green stretches, as flat as a billiard table except where it was broken by craggy towers of *anjico* and *cedro* trees; and now and then a patch of *buriti* palms, silhouetted gracefully against the sky from a slight rise, the slender stalks looking like the filaments of a gigantic green comb; and then the endless flatness of the drab marshlands as we drifted southward and westward toward the *pantanal* along the Paraguay border.

I had a small assortment of books which I carried in my mule packs— Goethe's *Wilhelm Meister*, some essays of Schopenhauer and Heine, and in English the works of Poe and Coleridge. I read Schopenhauer and Heine particularly because they fitted my own mood.

One afternoon, after we had drifted past Pôrto Esperança and tied up at a small inlet, which led inland to a lagoon, Apparicio came to me.

"You are too gloomy, Senhor Alexandre!" he said. "I have spoken to a *vaquero* from a *rancho* not far away. There is a *fiesta* tonight, and perhaps we should attend."

I laughed, and shook my head.

"Go and enjoy yourself," I said. "Take Senhorita Mariinha with you and have a good time. I will watch the *Aventureira*."

Apparicio hesitated, then said:

"Mariinha is indisposed—she wishes to remain here." Then with an odd twist of his mouth, he added: "Perhaps you can cheer each other, Senhor Alexandre."

There was something curiously restrained in Apparicio's manner, almost as if he had intended saying something, and then decided against it. I wondered about it for a while, and then thought nothing more about it. I had become so gloomy in my own thoughts that I had not paid much attention to what was happening on the boat.

After Apparicio left, the girl came forward to my end of the barge for a few minutes, and spoke to me in a low voice, saying only the commonplace things familiar to her in the limited life she had lived. Then she returned to her quarters in the kitchen. In the early morning hours I heard the thud of Apparicio's boots as he stumbled aboard, apparently drunk, his voice raised sharply as he talked to Mariinha.

Several days later, when Apparicio was ashore cutting poles for animal cages we planned to build on the barge, the girl came over and stood beside me at the rail.

"Senhor Pinheiro is quite angry with me," she said in a low voice, her dark eyes cast down so that all I glimpsed were the long black lashes and now and then a sparkle as she raised her glance for an instant. "He believes I have become no longer his woman."

I looked at the girl, wondering what kind of role I was about to be cast in. My experiences as a father-confessor were extremely limited; and besides, my sensations with regard to this girl had not been entirely fatherly. She looked up at me unexpectedly, and I caught the almost fateful glow within her eyes, like a smouldering heat about to burst into flame.

"He is right, *senhor!*" she went on, in a rush of words, before I could say anything. "I have not been his woman . . . I came to this boat because of you!"

I was startled to a point that I was unable to make any reply. In fact, there was very little I could say, although all manner of thoughts raced through my mind. The girl, her eyes now looking almost pleadingly into mine, went on to explain in words that were half-choked and uttered with great agitation, that she wished only to stay aboard the barge, and would continue to wash our clothes and cook . . . Only I must not let Apparicio drive her away because he was angry!

Apparicio returned a short time later from his trip ashore, and I went into my own cabin. I did not even go aft for dinner, pleading that I was not hungry. When I did walk back to the after deck during the evening, there was no indication of an estrangement. I found Apparicio talking quite cheerfully with Mariinha, and there was not a trace in her manner of anything that pertained even remotely to what she had said in the afternoon.

That night I thought long and seriously about the matter. My own actions thus far were unimpeachable, but my thoughts had not always been entirely so . . . The jungle is a dangerous mistress, and she breeds strange fancies in men's heads. I remembered the curious feeling that had been awakened in me the day I first saw Mariinha at the Rancho Triumpho. She had been hardly more than a girl at Senhor Pinto's sugar farm, and I had not particularly remembered her . . . But I remembered her very distinctly after I saw her with Apparicio that day.

For an instant, I wondered whether there was some purpose in this. Perhaps Mariinha was planning some casual infidelity, and was cleverly setting a stage for it by enlisting my sympathy in advance. But I discarded this idea. If what Mariinha said was true . . . what would my future conduct be?

Needless to say, the voyage downriver now took on quite a different aspect. I found myself for the first time wondering what was happening in the after cabin—a speculation from which I had sedulously guarded myself up to this point. Now and then I watched Mariinha as she stood beside the kitchen shed, gazing into the deep jungle with those dark, unfathomable eyes. I seldom looked directly at her; but once, as she stretched to fasten some washed garments to the clothesline which we had rigged across the stern, the contours of her body were silhouetted against the bright glare of the afternoon sun on the river with such startling and unmistakable beauty that I found myself staring at her, and I realized that things could not continue this way indefinitely.

I found myself wondering what Apparicio had said to Mariinha . . . that might concern me. When the three of us were together on the *Aventureira*, the days passed in long silences. It was far different from my days with Apparicio in the jungle.

Often Apparicio and I would leave on short trips to nearby *fazendas* to arrange for our hunting services. On our return from these trips, Mariinha would always greet Apparicio; but her eyes invariably sought mine, and I became uncomfortable with the realization that this situation must inevitably be threshed out between Apparicio and myself. I had even thought of speaking to him quietly and directly when we were alone in the forest; but what could I say? A man cannot go to his friend and say: "Look here, your mistress seems to be attracted to me. What shall we do about it?"

One evening, when Apparicio had left on a journey up-river in our dugout to bring some cartridges and splicing wire, which we badly needed to fix our animal cages, Mariinha came forward to where I was sitting, near the door of my cabin, and spoke to me. Her voice was almost inaudible at first, and I was not sure whether she had spoken or the wind had rustled the arms of a great tree branching overhead.

"Yes, Mariinha," I said, trying to conceal the sudden agitation I felt at her nearness. The river seemed to be motionless in the hush of the sunset. Somewhere ashore an ant bear gave a raucous grunt, and a few feet inland there was a slap of a *jacaré* slithering down from the bank of a small inlet. I found myself wondering, without much relevance, whether Mariinha had felt and understood these noises.

"What is it?" I asked.

"I have poured hot water into the *maté*," the girl said. "Shall I bring the gourd to you, *senhor?*"

Maté, the native drink of Brazil—and of most of South America—is prepared first by pouring cold water over the crushed, dried leaves of the *maté* tree; the cold water is then sucked from the leaves through a tube, and expectorated; after which hot water is poured into the leaves, and the resulting brew is sipped steaming hot by the drinker.

I thanked Mariinha, and she brought the gourd. I had drunk *maté* hundreds of times in the kitchen; but for some reason, the way she handed it to me seemed like a ritual. I looked at the girl's face, now turned toward the jungle. Her face was broad and heavy; yet in repose there was an indefinable delicacy and even beauty in her features. Something in her expression, the faint glint of her eyes under the long dark lashes, and the slightly petulant sadness of her mouth, made me think of the sadness I had seen in Dona Maria's eyes, as she held her baby, rocking it gently against her breast, and talked with me at Santa Rita.

I rose, after drinking the *maté*, and handed the gourd to the girl. She looked directly at me as she took it, and once again I saw the dark fire in her eyes. I wished fervently at the moment that Apparicio were not my friend.

"Mariinha," I said—it was so dark by this time I could hardly see the outlines of her face—"it is becoming dark and you will get lost in the night. Go back to your room and Apparicio will be home very soon."

The girl seemed to shrink away in the darkness, and all I heard was the soft shuffle of her sandals on the deck.

The following day I had to go inland on a journey of two days to talk with a *fazendero*, or cattle rancher, who wanted Apparicio and myself to hunt *tigres* that had been destroying his cattle. We agreed to anchor at the Rio Tereré, several miles below our present camp, and work out of this camp until the end of the rainy season. We would be given beef and other supplies, and would be paid in *milreis* for each *tigre* head we brought in.

It seemed like a good proposition; and I returned and told Apparicio of our arrangements. He said little; his thin face seemed to be drawn tightly, as if he were suffering in some way, but did not wish to disclose it. Within a short time we had collected our cages and loaded them aboard the *Aventureira*, and prodded the barge off the bank and headed southward.

At Rio Tereré we found a camp already prepared. Two *vaqueros* sent by the rancher, and a woman of middle age, part Indian and dark as the bark of a tree, had established our headquarters. The *fazendero*, in his eagerness to please us, had even provided a horse for our use.

"Look, Apparicio!" I exclaimed, as we poled the *Aventureira* toward the bank. "They have set up camp for us!" The three ashore waved to us, the old Indian woman, fat and waddling, grinning from ear to ear as we shoved the barge against the bank. Mariinha stood by the rail, her eyes dancing with eagerness; and even Apparicio smiled—something he had not done for weeks.

We took our gear ashore, and set up camp. It was a broad, flat bank, about level with the deck of the *Aventureira*, and I could envision the makings of a comfortable base camp which would last us until April or May, when the rains would end and the cold winds would blow up from the *pampas*.

This would have been a hunter's paradise for Apparicio and myself—had we been alone. It was a camp on high ground, secure from the floods; for, while the torrential rains made vast inland lakes of ground that was parched and dry in the cold season along the Xarayes marsh, the great trough of the Paraguay easily drained the water from these banks.

One of the *vaqueros*, Rosenzo, was stationed at a nearby outpost of the ranch a few miles up the Rio Tereré; the other man, Pedro, had ridden down from the main *rancho* to help us set up camp. These two soon departed, leaving the horse; and Apparicio and I were left with the two women, a strange quartet in the jungle.

We arranged our living quarters so that we could have our meals ashore, and sleep on the *Aventureira*, Dona Rosita taking up quarters on the barge with Mariinha. During the evenings, as we sat beside the glowing cookstove, I watched the girl listen to bird calls. The sounds in the jungle at night are far more distinct than in the daytime, or at least the ears pick them out more clearly. A bird, trilling with such infinite tenderness that it seemed to be the passionate melody of a human throat, would break the silence, and I would notice the girl, tilting her head slightly. Now and then a smile would interrupt the smooth expression of her face, but her eyes remained sad; and I noticed that Apparicio would look at her wistfully, and then turn and stare out at the blackness of the slowly moving river.

One night when Apparicio had gone with Rosenzo on a trip to the west to check on a report that *tigres* had been heard in that region, I sat alone with the girl. Dona Rosita had gone aboard the *Aventureira*, and darkness had settled over the river, swallowing the outline of the barge. Suddenly, with a mental caprice that I suppose had some reason but certainly had no sense, I said:

"Do you ever want to return to the Rancho Triumpho, Mariinha?"

"No, *senhor*," she said, shaking her head and looking up at me from where she sat by the fire. "The Rancho Triumpho was not my home—it was where I lived. I would like to live here—with you—forever, *senhor*."

Her head was only a foot from my knee, and I found myself stroking her dark hair. She leaned her head against my knee, her feet curled under her, and she seemed like some small, harmless creature of the woods . . . an animal that needed to be petted and protected.

For a long while we remained this way, talking in low voices. Finally I suggested it was time that we get some sleep. She rose, straightened her red skirt, and said simply:

"I shall go with you tonight, *senhor*, if you wish."

I took her hand and we walked across the plank to the barge. There was a faint light from a late-rising moon, just beginning to show above the trees. I felt less fatherly toward Mariinha than I had ever felt before; but I also knew that our camp on the Rio Tereré was fast becoming an impossible place for both Apparicio and myself. Even the jungle moon, leering from the roof of trees along the river, appeared to be mocking me. Loneliness had never been hateful to me, as it had to Ernst. I was always a solitary man. But here, it seemed, the very elements were combining to thwart my desire to be alone.

I led Mariinha down to the after end of the barge, and she stood for a moment, her head thrown back so that her dark hair fell away from the pale oval of her face in the misty moonlight. Her eyes were black pools in the night, and I could sense the quick rising and falling of her breasts. I found myself still holding her hand; and finally I said—possibly more sternly than I intended, since my heart was not in my words:

"You must go to your cabin, Mariinha. We will talk about this later."

The girl bowed her head, with a docility that is a part of the nature of women with Indian blood; and without another word she turned and faded into the blackness of the kitchen.

I cannot say that my friendship for Apparicio was uppermost in my mind as I walked back to my cabin. Mentally I cursed myself for a fool. I doubted that Mariinha, being a woman, would have the slightest respect for me after this night. But somehow I knew that I had made it possible for Apparicio and me to remain together on the *Aventureira* . . . for a while, at least.

Apparicio returned the next day, and although he gave no sign, by word or otherwise, that Mariinha had spoken to him, I knew she had. Something in his manner, perhaps the fact that he seldom spoke unless on a matter of common camp affairs, told me that the old comradeship between the tall *gaucho* and myself had ended.

We had been at the camp on the Rio Tereré for about a month when Rosenzo rode into camp one morning and announced that a *tigre* had raided an outpost of the *fazenda* and killed a *vaquero*. This was the most serious news that anyone could bring in this country, because a *tigre* that has killed a man becomes a roving assassin. Most *tigres* are cautious when humans are around; they seem to sense an unequal force, and will skulk off into the underbrush if they meet a man riding through the jungle. Even when they are hungry, they will seldom attack.

But a *tigre* that has killed a man apparently learns how defenseless the human animal is against his claws, and often becomes a wanton killer. Therefore he must be hunted down and destroyed.

I quickly assembled my dogs—Valente, the leader; Vinte, Pardo and Tupi. Apparicio wanted to join me, but I knew that someone I could trust must be left to guard the camp and the women. He came over to my horse, just before I left, and extended his hand. This was unusual, since he never shook hands.

"God go with you, Senhor Alexandre," he said.

I rode off, wondering at his strange manner. However, my worries about Apparicio were soon forgotten. We reached the line camp where the *vaquero* had been killed and found the grisly remainder of what had happened. The body of the *vaquero* had been removed, but there was evidence of the terrible struggle that had taken place in the cabin. From what Rosenzo told me, it was evident the *vaquero* had gone out to look for the *tigre* and had lost his dogs in the brush. He had hurried back to his hut and in turn had been stalked by the *tigre* which caught him in the hut. This would indicate that it was a killer, already experienced in tracking down and destroying human enemies.

We found the track of the *vaquero's* horse, and saw the *tigre's* footprints superimposed above the hoof marks. Valente picked up the scent and we started off through heavy brush, the four dogs in single file ahead of us. In less than an hour the sharpening cries of the dogs told me they were close on the scent; and a few minutes later, to my surprise, I found them ringed around a tree. The *tigre* was crouched on a branch, perhaps twenty feet from the ground.

I had my Winchester carbine, and also my bow and arrow, which I had learned to use during my hunts with Joaquim. Motioning Rosenzo to take the horses back into the brush, I dismounted and pulled the bow and an arrow from the leather case strapped to my saddle. Rosenzo led the horses away, and then came back and took my rifle, ready to shoot if the arrow failed to take effect; but the first shaft I let fly drove deep between the *tigre's* forelegs, and the big cat toppled to the ground.

I turned to Rosenzo.

"We have not caught the man-eater," I said. "He would never have taken to the tree."

Rosenzo nodded; man-eating *tigres* seldom leave the high marsh grass, apparently sensing the inability of their human enemies to see them in the tall grass, where they can also stalk their pursuers. Rosenzo and I rode back to the *vaqueiro's* hut, and I saw a fresh *tigre* track above those made by our horses that morning. I quickly ordered Rosenzo to ride back to our camp and warn Apparicio that the man-eater was at large.

"Tell him to remain on guard tonight," I said. "I will return tomorrow."

It was two days, however, before I finally tracked down the *tigre* and shot him—this time with my Winchester, to avoid injury to my dogs. Weary from the hours of tracking, I rode back toward our camp. Dona Rosita was at the oven, tending the evening meal, when I rode in and handed the reins of my horse to Rosenzo. She motioned me to come with her to the barge. I followed her across the plank and when I stepped on board the *Aventureira*, I realized there was no one else on board.

Dona Rosita waved her hand at the empty deck.

"They have both left for Pôrto Esperança," she said.

Dona Rosita told me that the day I had left with Rosenzo, a terrible quarrel had taken place between Apparicio and the girl. Apparently things had reached a climax between them. She had told him, in Dona Rosita's hearing, that she would have stayed with me on the *Aventureira* if he had not remained with us. The *gaucho* had raged through the camp, swearing he would shoot me.

After Rosenzo came back and reported the man-eater was at large, Apparicio went to Dona Rosita and told her that he intended to leave—now that there was a man to protect them —and that the girl had agreed to leave with him.

"Little Mariinha had a big heart for you," the old woman said. "And so had Senhor Apparicio."

It was an unhappy ending to the only real comradeship I had known in the Matto Grosso. Later I heard that he had married Mariinha and they had gone to live on a cattle ranch east of the Rio Miranda.

Chapter 22

The jungle along the Paraguay thins out into flat pantanal marshland as the river curves westward below the Rio
Miranda, toward the southern tip of Bolivia and the Gran
Chaco; and then southward again along the eastern border of
Paraguay. In this high marsh grass, spotted with patches of
capão and laced with swamp channels, the tigre prowls more
freely than anywhere else in the Matto Grosso, preying upon
the stock of large cattle ranches along the Paraguay, the Nabi-
leque and the Branco.

For two years after Apparicio and Mariinha left the
Aventureira, I remained in this area. Most of the time I was
alone; although now and then I had the help of some vaquero,
on loan from a cattle ranch or hired for a few weeks to help
me pole the barge from one base camp to another.

The fazenderos knew of my hunting, and often sent word
of tigres destroying their cattle; and I would set out across the
marshes on horse or mule, with my four dogs—Valente, Vinte,
Pardo and Tupi—which were as well known as I was. The
fazenderos would pay me in supplies, or with a horse or mule;
and I had the privilege of slaughtering a young heifer or bull
for food for my dogs and myself. It was a lonely but satisfying life; and it was here, as I learned many years later when
Mamerto Urriolagoitia, who later became President of Bolivia,
and his English friends, Julian Duguid and J. C. Bee-Mason,
came by on the expedition which Duguid made famous in
his book Green Hell, that I became known as the "wild Russian engineer."

I had many occasions in which I could reflect upon the

course of my life; and at times when I watched the black *urubú* circling in the hot sky over a lonely stretch of *capão*, I wondered if Alexander Siemel would some day lie in a small pile of bleached bones on the marshes, gnawed clean by the foxes and vultures, and turned to a glittering white under the baking heat of the tropical sun.

Once it almost became more than a matter of wondering. I had gone inland to the *rancho* of Dom Antonio Cardozo, known as Firme, on the Rio Branco, in response to a rumor I had picked up that *tigres* were raiding his cattle and destroying as many as a dozen a night.

"I prayed to my patron Saint Anthony that you would arrive," the old man told me fervently when I rode in.

A group of Chamacoco and Guaraní Indians, squat and stolid, with broad faces and their hair hanging over their brown flat foreheads, stood by apparently ready to go on the hunt in a pack; but I asked only for a tall Guaraní Indian, Jose Abá, who had hunted with me before. The big Indian smiled with pride at my selection, and we arranged to meet the next day at a place on the Rio Branco where he would bring horses.

The land around Firme was mottled with deep pools and hummocks of marshland surrounded by treacherous swamps; and although we could use horses for the first part of the journey, we were forced finally to leave our horses at the river edge and slog through the morass of sunken trails on foot. It was here that I came as close to being dessert for the *urubú* as I ever had come during my time in the jungles—and not from the claws or teeth of a *tigre*. I had been following the dogs, carrying my rifle, with my bow and arrows strapped to my back. The dogs had caught the scent of the *tigre* we were following and were racing along ridges of swamp grass; and we were stumbling after them. I suddenly found myself over my boot tops in treacherous slime. I tried to stop but slipped forward, until I was waist deep in murky water.

Grasping at the branch of a heavy bush, I saw the thin filament of a tiny skeleton, hanging from the branch. I knew instantly that it was a *piranha*, and the knowledge struck me with a kind of cold terror. At the same moment I felt a blow against my leg, and although my legs were shod with leather, I knew it would not resist the murderous attacks of the flesh-eating fish if they were in this water. These shoals were stranded during the dry season, but they were lakes during the rains, and *piranha* often came in schools from the river during the wet months and remained in these isolated pools or channels, starving and ravenous, during the short cold season.

I flailed my arms backwards, clutching my rifle instinctively, and managed to get back on a solid bank. I lay there exhausted—mentally as well as physically—listening to the fading bark of the dogs. I had been jogging through the marsh for several hours, following the dogs, and was utterly spent. Finally I rose, cleaned my rifle as well as I could with grass, and then found to my dismay that I had come out on what appeared to be a peninsula threaded by channels from which I could see no retreat. I would have to swim across the channel, perhaps infested with *piranha*.

I must have fallen asleep as I crouched on the bank, because the next thing I knew, I was awakened by something cold and wet on my face. I looked up and saw Valente, licking me. The dogs had chased the *tigre* in a circle, and the cat had gone by, almost exhausted from the day-long chase, a few yards from where I lay. I rose, rather unsteadily, picked up my gun and spear and started after the dogs, who were bounding along in short, lumpy jumps about a quarter of a mile away.

Jose Abá caught up with us a short while later and we slogged across the marsh after the dogs, who instinctively found a solid bank that led from the peninsula. The sun had gone down in a blaze that made a sea of gold out of the entire western sky. We reached the edge of a patch of forest and plunged through to higher ground, following through the dark lanes between the trees. We were following the dogs by sound alone; and finally a staccato of hysterical barking indicated they had cornered the weary *tigre*. I unstrapped a flashlight, which miraculously still worked although it had been fastened to my belt when I went into the water; and boring a hole of light through the darkness, we soon located the cat.

I handed the flashlight to the Indian, deciding to use my

rifle. The first time I pulled the trigger, the hammer fell with an empty click. From the sullen growl of the *tigre* I knew it was going to charge, and I quickly threw another shell into the magazine and fired again. This time the gun blasted with a roar that echoed against the forest walls, and the *tigre* toppled from the tree.

We stripped the hide from the beast, using the flashlight, and headed back along the Rio Branco to where we had left our horses; and when I traded the hide to Dom Antonio next day for the horse he promised me, I felt I had earned my fee.

In my second year at Barranco Branco, I received word from the captain of the little mail launch, that chugged each fortnight downriver from Corumbá to Asunción, that Ernst had been killed at Cuyabá. I was sick with remorse; it seemed to me I had abandoned my brother—and now, with Apparicio gone, I was entirely alone.

I returned to Cuyabá, leaving my dogs and the *Aventureira* in care of a camp helper. It was during the dry season, and I knew I could make quicker time overland. I set out, travelling with a native guide, and once I almost starved, due to lack of game. In desperation I ate some old honey in a dried comb, which the Indian warned me against, and became blind for several days. After eight weeks I reached Sta. Rita, and found Dona Maria living in a hovel, destitute and utterly discouraged, with her small son.

"They brought his body home to me at night," she said, in a low voice. Her eyes were dull, and all hope seemed to have been washed out of them. "He had been shot many times by several men who waited for him." She told me the whole story, now and then glancing at the small, golden-haired boy, with Ernst's blue eyes and an incredibly dirty face, who toddled around the squalid little room.

I gave Dona Maria what money I had, and asked her if she could not go home to her family home at Abobral. She shrugged, and then nodded.

"Perhaps now. Before you came I had no money on which to travel."

I remained at Cuyabá a few days, trying to locate the

murderers; but I found they had disappeared after the murder of my brother. Years later I found the ringleader, and it was my intention to kill him. But his face was gray and his body wasted with sickness, and I left him to die of his disease. In all my years in the jungle there were only two men I hated: this man, and Favelle. Of the two, Favelle was less evil; he had something in his nature which he could not conquer.

I stopped at Aricá on my way south, and found a message from the rancher who had wanted me to hunt the devil-tigre, Assassino. There had been many raids in the area, and Assassino, who had been believed either killed or gone away, was now reported to be the author of these wanton killings. I left word that I might return later in the year, but I must now get back to my camp and the dogs on the Rio Branco.

As I rode down the São Laurenço trail, threading through a stretch of capão, I found something else that left my depressed state of mind at an even lower ebb. About a quarter of a mile off the river trail, I noticed something that looked like a broken half of a canoe. I rode over to see what story was left.

It was a Guató canoe; and a few steps above it I saw a rusted iron blade, and part of the broken shaft of a zagaya. I was sure—even before I looked further—what I would find. Tangled in the bushes was a collection of rib bones, most of them snapped; and a short distance away lay a human skull. I examined the spear shaft, chewed by some animal in its frenzy, and recognized it. I had come upon the scene of Joaquim Guató's last jungle fight.

It was not difficult to reconstruct what had happened. He had apparently driven his canoe ashore, following a tigre, and perhaps was not aware that the cat was lurking in the brush. As he reached back to haul the dugout on dry land, the tigre must have struck—and the rest was the end of a saga that might happen to anyone who hunts alone in the jungle.

I dug a shallow grave and buried the bones of the old man. Had he had a choice of ways to die, I was sure he would have chosen this way.

It was well toward the end of the dry season, with the

threat of rains in the weeks ahead, when I returned to Barranco Branco. Valente pounced on me with an eagerness that brought the only stirring of happiness I had felt in months. I had been in the Rio Branco country less than three years, but it seemed to me I had lived half a lifetime here. During that time I had learned the power of the jungle to create living things and to destroy them; I had felt its power as I have felt no other force in my life. The blaze of morning throwing shafts of light into the dim caverns of the trees . . . the harshness of the sun, burning pitilessly upon animal and plant alike, on the great stretches of bleak earth along the *campo cerrado* and on the lush depth of the *capão* around the water holes— and finally the sound of the organ bird like a dirge of death in the hours of twilight . . . all were part of a vast natural drama, which I was only beginning to understand.

A report had come in my absence of a new raid of *tigres* on the *pantanal* below our base camp, at a place called Palmas Chicas; and I decided to move the *Aventureira* downriver. The region around Barranco Branco apparently had been cleared of the big cats, and I needed more hunting to replenish my supplies and funds.

At Palmas Chicas I was received with a real welcome. The *rancho* had been losing from its herds through almost nightly raids of prowling *tigres*, and two days after my arrival I set out at dawn with Valente, Pardo and Vinte. I was afoot, because the *vaqueros* had reported a big *tigre* less than a dozen kilometers inland.

The hunt was wrong at the start. A hunter learns to sense things that may be trivial at the time, but which point to miscalculations and often disaster. The dogs split less than an hour from the camp, Vinte heading back toward the river on a scent, while Valente and Pardo worked rapidly up a steep slope. It was still almost dark, the false light before dawn shedding a gray, misty light upon the silhouettes of trees. The brush was thin, and I had no difficulty following; and since Vinte's bark seemed to show the stronger scent, I turned with him back to the river.

For perhaps half an hour I could hear the ringing barks

of the two dogs who were above us; then they ceased, and I concluded they had lost the track. Meanwhile, Vinte's yelps also ceased, and a few minutes later he bounded out of the brush, and I knew he had lost the track of the cat he had been following.

The dog bounded up the hill after the other pair, and I followed. There were thickets of wild pineapple and thorny brush along the crest, and my clothes were ripped as I pushed through. I was becoming uneasy at Valente's silence; and my fears became real when Pardo suddenly appeared, loping out from a heavy stand of trees. He was whining instead of barking; and without pausing, I plunged into the thicket from which he had emerged. Several times I stopped to utter the long-drawn call that the dogs recognized; but there was no answering sound.

For two hours I smashed through the forest thickets, with a tightening fear. The ground now sloped downward from the crest of the hill; and just as the sun rose high enough to throw the full force of its blazing light into the forest, I pushed through a clearing and saw a brown body lying in a patch of sunlight.

It was Valente. His side was slashed open and he had been partly eaten. I knelt down to look at the face of the dog, who had been with me for more than five years, and had taken part in a hundred *tigre* battles. He was probably the only creature in the world who would have given his life for me without question or hesitation.

I have seldom wept in my life. Not even Ernst's death, nor my parting from Elsa, had brought tears. But the sudden realization that I had lost this old friend was overpowering. I have a vague recollection of Pardo and Vinte, standing a few feet away watching me curiously, while I knelt beside the body of the dog. Then I arose and dug a hole with my spear, burying Valente in the forest where he died.

I returned with the two dogs to the *Aventureira*, feeling more alone than I had ever felt before in my life. Except for Tupi, the fox terrier Dom Francisco had given me at Aricá, there was not a man or animal with me who had been on the

São Laurenço. Ernst and Joaquim were dead . . . Apparicio had left in bitterness . . . and now Valente was gone!

Perhaps my thoughts had already been forming when I left Cuyabá, but the death of Valente brought my decision. The next day I began to crate my animals and equipment; and a few days later I arranged to have the *Aventureira* taken upriver to Pôrto Esperança. I rode ahead and arranged for shipment of the animals to São Paulo.

I had decided to leave the jungle.

Chapter 23

At *São Paulo I realized, perhaps for the first time, how* remote the inland jungles of Brazil were to the people of the coastal cities. There was a barrier of land over which few people travelled that left the vast wilderness of the interior a land of mystery. Even the animals were not known; and the sight of *tigre* cubs in cages astounded the cultured citizens of São Paulo.

I decided to make some profit out of this curiosity, and built a small zoo where I exhibited my animals. The venture paid off, as far as box-office returns were concerned; but it soon became apparent to me that if the people of São Paulo understood little of the people and habits of the interior, the ignorance was mutual. Most of the proceeds of my zoo were exhausted in paying for help and maintenance. In a few months I decide to salvage what I could from the sale of the animals, and head for Germany, where I wanted to visit my sister Selma, and tell her of Ernst's death.

It may have been a realization of the lack of knowledge of the inland wilderness on the part of most Brazilians—and possibly a desire to remedy that ignorance; or it may have been nostalgia. In any event, on my trip to Germany I was already planning to buy new photographic equipment and return to the Matto Grosso to record my wanderings in film.

For almost half my life—and I was nearing forty—I had wandered on lonely trails. It is not an easy habit to dispose of. Possibly the memory of those strange fears that obsessed me when I saw the *urubú* wheeling across the hot sky over the *pantanal* affected my decision. The human mind can stand a great deal in the form of emotional reverses; it can endure the loss of loved ones, and even anticipate death. But I do not believe it is possible for mortal man to endure the idea of annihilation.

However the idea was first formed in my thoughts, it grew until it was a fixed decision. I knew that I must return again to the jungles of the Matto Grosso, and that I had to record what I had done in some permanent way that would not be destroyed if my bones were left some day to bleach under the hot sun of the *pantanal*.

Call it what you will—perhaps vanity, or the hope of immortality, or even the simple desire of a man to make a record of what he has done; but in four short months after I had departed from the Matto Grosso "forever," I had returned once again to the lonely trails, to the roaring orchestration under the domes of the green cathedrals, to the life of a solitary man living with his dogs in a thatched hut on the banks of a jungle river.

Some quirk of imagination—perhaps a fragment of hope that I might recapture certain lost memories and take them back to the jungle with me—caused me to turn south on my journey inland, so that I passed through Passo Fundo. I found old Dom Carlos, now well past seventy, his solitary eye aglow with joy when I walked into his *patio*. He recognized me immediately, although I had changed in the years since he saw me crouching over what I thought was the dead body of Ricardo Favelle.

He waved me to a chair. Lobo was gone, but there was another dog in his place, and Dom Carlos was scratching its neck.

"Ha!" he exclaimed. "The dog has come back to his first bone! Tell me, my friend—did you find the old man?"

I told him of my days hunting with Joaquim Guató; and of the journey to the diamond fields with Ernst, and all that had happened since. His brown eye, now moist with age, squinted steadily at me; and when I told him of the death of Favelle, the old bandit-chaser shook his head.

"He had to die, that one! As long as you lived, it was impossible for him to live. Yet I am sorry he could not have died more pleasantly. You should have killed him as I advised you."

"And you and Lobo would have brought back my ears, eh?"

Dom Carlos chuckled. He had mellowed somewhat; and was now living in semi-retirement. He made me repeat with the greatest detail my spear-fighting experience with Joaquim Guató, and he frequently slapped his leg and laughed with relish. Then he asked me what I planned to do.

I told him of my exhibition in São Paulo, and my trip to Germany to get photographic equipment. The empty socket of his lost eye narrowed in a familiar squint, and I prepared myself for a philosophical utterance. He said, rather abruptly:

"Go back to the jungle and die with your friends, the animals, my son. You have nothing else to live for."

I explained my plans for capturing the jungle life in celluloid.

"Pictures, eh? You have conquered the beasts with your spear, and now you wish to conquer them with pictures!" Dom Carlos cackled gleefully, as if he had discovered some satanic bit of humor. I began to think, as he raked his gnarled fingers through the thinning aura of white hair, that the old man was becoming senile. But he quickly stopped laughing, and looked at me seriously.

"Go with God, my son—and perhaps He will find some new kind of brute for you to challenge. Perhaps a woman, eh? You have said nothing of your women!"

I made no reply. There was still a soreness in my thoughts when I remembered Apparicio and "Little Mariinha with a big heart." My experiences with women were not among the more notable achievements of my life, and I did not particularly want to hear Dom Carlos' callous cackling on this subject.

He continued to regard me wisely with his single eye, which was like a probe for use on the human soul. I sometimes felt the old fellow could read my innermost thoughts.

He finally gave utterance to a short chuckle and slapped his leg, as if he had suddenly discovered the answer.

"Perhaps you will find a woman who will be as good a hunter as you are," he said. "Only she will use different weapons." He ruminated a bit on this bit of devious wisdom; and it was a piece of the old man's thoughts that I had occasion to recall many years later when I was on the Upper Miranda River.

Finally Dom Carlos said, conclusively:

"Otherwise, my son, you have nothing else to do but go back to your jungle and die."

I left Passo Fundo with the old man's admonition ringing in my ears; and I must confess the prophecy left me feeling depressed. At Pôrto Esperança I found my shipment of camera equipment had not arrived; and also certain arrangements I had made with a cameraman at São Paulo had not come through. However, my dogs were there—still in the care of a *fazendero* with whom I had left them; and I decided to push north to the Ilho do Cara Cara, near Amolar, where I intended to establish a base camp. This area was on the southern range of the big Fazenda Descalvados, where I planned to hunt and at the same time to immortalize the Matto Grosso in film.

Of the four dogs—Raivoso, Pardo, Vinte and Tupi—only the little fox terrier was untrained in *tigre* hunting. I took him along, however, as a camp pet; and it was well that I did.

Shortly after I had set up camp near Ilho do Cara Cara, an outpost rider from the big *fazenda* rode in and brought grave news. His name was Jose Ramos, and he lived with his wife at a small *fazenda* about ten miles upriver from my camp. He ran his own small herd, and also watched the herds of the big *rancho*.

"You must come with your dogs!" the man said. "Assassino has begun raiding again, and has already killed twelve of my cattle!"

There was an air of desperation about the man. His khaki shirt was stained with sweat from the ride, and it was evident he had ridden in great haste for help.

Ordinarily I would have agreed to go. But I had lost my lead-dog; and except for Raivoso, a dog that had been well trained but not tried out as a master-dog, there was no one to lead the pack.

"I am sorry, Jose," I said. "I cannot risk the dogs I have left with that devil. He will kill the dogs as fast as I send them after him. I would as soon send little Tupi—" I pointed to the little fox terrier, who had grown rapidly during the time we had come downriver, but was still too small for a *tigre* hunt. Tupi cocked his head to one side as I pointed, regarding me with sudden suspicion.

I laughed.

"Do not worry, Tupi," I said. "I will not send you."

The story of Assassino was well known along the Pantanal do Xarayes. Several years before this enormous *tigre* had been wounded by an inexperienced hunter, who shot too hastily while the cat was crouched on the limb of a tree. The infuriated *tigre* had bounded from the branch, and the hunter fled, leaving his dogs to the mercy of the big jungle cat.

The dogs were destroyed by the animal; and apparently through some kind of jungle cunning, the *tigre* understood that a hunter with a rifle could not kill him in the tall grass. It was never again seen in a tree; but it would rove through the marsh grass, killing cattle wantonly. Apparently the early experience had also left a deadly enmity for dogs, because the big cat had learned to draw the dogs into pursuit through the tall marsh grass, and then circle and crouch beside its own trail, springing at the dogs as they ran by. One sweep of the razor claws would destroy a dog, and then the cat would lope on, repeating the maneuver on each dog that followed. It was this trick of ambushing pursuers that gave the *tigre* its name —Assassino.

Since I was the only hunter in this region who killed with a spear, the big *fazendas* had often sought my help; but I also knew that it would be impossible to track the *tigre* without dogs, and Assassino was so crafty that sending a dog after him was virtually a death sentence.

Jose, of course, knew this. But his situation was desperate.

"If you do not go after him, Senhor Siemel, he will destroy all my cattle, as he has done in the South. I shall lose everything I have, and the big ranch will not pay me any more."

Twice before I had been asked directly by the big *fazenderos* to hunt this devil. Once I had refused because of the risk to Valente; and on the other occasion I was on my way south from Cuyabá and could not take the time to hunt. Nevertheless, the feeling persisted that I must finally decide to hunt this *tigre*.

Jose watched me with dark, smouldering eyes. He knew the risk to the dogs; and he had no dogs of his own capable of tracking the *tigre* and bringing it to bay. I finally said:

"I will promise this much, Jose. If I see the *tigre*, or know that he is near, I will go after him."

Jose looked out across the flat marshland, shimmering in the sultry heat. Then he turned back to me.

"In that case, *senhor*, I shall go after Assassino, myself—without dogs," he said quietly. "Either I must kill the devil, or he will ruin me."

He whirled his horse and rode off along the river trail toward his *rancho*. I had visited the place shortly after I moved to my camp, and I felt sorry for him. His wife, Maria, was young and sturdy, and they worked hard to make enough to live on in this lonely marsh country.

I knew, moreover, that Jose would go after the *tigre*. He was one of those plain men who live in small outposts of civilization, in whom is bred a stubborn courage. I wondered if I should have refused; and at the same time, the notion grew in my mind that I must finally face this *tigre* and destroy it.

A few days after Jose's visit, I saw the *urubú* circling in the still, hot air west of the river. I leashed Raivoso, Pardo and Vinte, and started across the *pantanal*. Within a short time the dogs found the kill—a small marsh-deer.

The deer had been badly clawed, the flesh ripped from the neck and side; but no part of it had been eaten. I knew it was Assassino, because the devil-*tigre* killed wantonly, for pleasure and not for food.

The dogs were off baying through the grass, and I followed. Within a mile we found a second kill, also a marshdeer, destroyed in the same way, but not eaten. A third and fourth kill were found in the same way, all marsh-deer, and all showing no signs of being eaten. The fiendish jungle cat was marauding through the marshlands, killing simply for the enjoyment of it!

Suddenly Raivoso, the lead-dog, let loose a sharper bark, and I rode up to find a small ocelot, or *jaquaterita*, feeding on the fifth kill of Assassino. While I was examining the carcass, after driving off the ocelot, I heard Raivoso's deep bay in the grass beyond, and I knew from the sound that he was on the track of Assassino himself.

I collared the other dogs, and this probably saved them from destruction. It was useless to follow Raivoso through the marsh grass. The sudden staccato of shrill yaps, ending in a shrill, screaming bark told the story. He had caught up with Assassino and had been trapped by the *tigre's* ambush.

Back in my base camp that night, I carefully thought over the situation. In my years of hunting in the Matto Grosso, this murderous killer was by far the most unusual I had encountered. I knew the natives had a superstition about "deviltigres." They did not believe they could be killed by a human weapon—bullet or spear. I knew, of course, that Assassino's survival was purely the result of an instinctive knowledge of the fundamental weakness of hunting in the marsh grass. A gun was useless, because the target could not be seen; and without a gun, it was necessary to bring the *tigre* to bay with dogs—and Assassino killed dogs as fast as they were sent after him!

It posed an impossible problem; and finally I decided the only way would be for me to go out on the *pantanal* alone—which would be like trying to find the proverbial needle in a haystack.

The loss of Raivoso was serious. Pardo was the next best dog; and I needed several hunts to train him sufficiently to take the lead. My plan was to use the dogs to pick up the *tigre* trail, and perhaps bring me within a reasonable distance of the cat.

My plans were unexpectedly changed. The following morning, while I was cleaning my rifle in front of my hut, little Tupi set up a great yapping. I looked down the river trail and saw Maria Ramos, Jose's wife, galloping toward the camp. Her hair was flying and her red blouse was out at the waist. As she pulled up the horse, I saw that her eyes were wide with terror.

"Senhor Siemel!" she gasped, as I started toward her. "Jose—"

I helped her off, and tried to calm her. She looked wildly from me to the edge of the jungle from which she had ridden.

"What's happened to Jose?" I asked.

"He went after Assassino—and this morning only the horse came back!"

I glanced at the horse, and for the first time noticed that the flank was gored with two gashes, which had bled freely. Blood was smeared on the wooden saddle. Meanwhile Maria, a pretty, dark-eyed girl of about twenty-five, was pouring out her story. Jose had returned from his visit to my camp, determined to track down the beast that was killing his cattle.

He had neither a good gun, nor experience as a hunter. But he had an old muzzle-loader, which he filled with chopped nails; and he also had a pair of mongrels I had seen at his house. With these he set out across the marsh toward a place where his last dead cow had been found.

"After he rode away," Maria said, "I lighted a candle before the image of São Antonio and prayed for him to come back."

The girl said she prayed all night, but Jose did not return. The next morning she found the horse in the yard, with the saddle covered with blood. She had mounted the horse and ridden to my camp.

I quickly saddled my horse and coupled four hunting dogs to the leash—Pardo, Vinte, Amigo and Leon. As I started away, little Tupi set up a great yapping, and since I knew the dog would try to follow me, I tied it to the corner of my hut.

Then I rode off along the river trail with Maria Ramos. When we reached the point where she said Jose had apparently turned off into the marsh grass, toward the place where the dead cow had been found, I asked the girl to ride on to her *rancho*.

She shook her head. "I must see for myself," she said.

I knew the poor girl was nearly crazy with the dread of what she would see, yet she had the rugged courage of a frontier woman. We rode for perhaps two kilometers through the high grass, until we came to the edge of a *capão*, where the grass was shorter and a grove of trees, crested with *buriti* palms, indicated the presence of water.

I had spotted *urubú* circling above the patch of jungle, and I was afraid to let the girl see what I knew must be lying a little way ahead of us. We broke through a patch of underbrush, and I saw the figure of a man, lying face down on the ground. His shirt was ripped and the body had been badly mangled. Even before I turned the poor fellow over, I knew it was Jose.

I heard a small cry behind me, and turned to see Maria slipping from her horse. I jumped over and caught her. She recovered quickly, and after a minute or two agreed without further protest to ride back to her *rancho*.

During the ride across the *pantanal* I had determined on a plan which offered some chance of success. I was sure the *tigre* would be close by, probably around the water hole in the *capão*. Assassino had not wandered from this area for several days, and I doubted if it would move very far from its last kill. From the marks around Jose's body, I knew the *tigre* had leaped for the back of the horse, probably knocking Jose from the saddle. I found Jose's gun a short distance away, loaded but not fired, and I knew it had fallen from the saddle as the terrified horse galloped away.

If the *tigre* had once attacked a man on a horse, it would do it again; and if it came from ambush I could not use a spear from the back of my horse. So I tied the horse to a tree in a fairly open clearing, unstrapped the shaft and spear-head, and also took my bow and a couple of arrows. I had a pistol in my holster, but no rifle—since it would be useless in the high grass.

My plan was to unleash the dogs and follow as fast as I could on foot. If I could stay close enough, I could force the *tigre* to attack me. I took the bow and arrows hoping for a distance shot, since a *tigre* will always fight the arrow rather than the one who shot it. Holding the bow and arrows in one hand, and the spear in the other, I started after the dogs, running low through the grass.

I had been running for perhaps ten minutes, when I heard the sudden baying of Pardo in the lead. Then there was a shorter yapping and a shrill scream; and when I reached the spot, Pardo was on the ground, his side ripped open. I did not stop, hoping to overtake the other dogs; but a second scream told me the *tigre* had made another kill. The murderous Assassino was following his usual technique, circling back quickly on each dog and ambushing it with a sweep of its paw, and then loping on before the next dog could reach it. This circling back took only a few seconds—a short turn through the grass with the dog close behind, and then the deadly slash of its paw.

It was over in a matter of minutes. I had run perhaps a quarter of a mile since the first dog was killed, when I found Leon lying near the edge of a clearing in the *capão*. I stood over the dog, sick with rage, and not knowing what to do next. At that moment there was a yapping in the grass behind me, and out bounded Tupi, my fox terrier. He scampered across the clearing, barking joyously at the sight of me. I saw from the trailing length of rope that he had chewed his tether and followed us.

As the dog scampered past, I jammed my heel down on the trailing rope, and brought him up short. At that moment I heard a rustling in the heavy grass across the clearing, and with a sudden inspiration, I stepped forward with my free foot, landing on Tupi's paw.

The dog let out a startled yelp, tugging at the rope which I still held under my heel, and barking in high protest that sounded across the *pantanal*. I had dropped my spear as I stepped forward, and I quickly fitted an arrow to the string, and as soon as I saw a movement in the grass, I let fly.

The arrow apparently struck something, but how vital the shot was I did not know. I was relying on the frenzy of the *tigre* and Tupi's sharp barking to send the beast in my direction. There was a sudden commotion in the grass, and although it was so dense I could not see five feet through it, I was sure of my target now. I picked up the remaining arrow, fitted it to the bowstring and took careful aim. When I had isolated the movement of the animal in the grass, I shot again, trying to hit close to the center of the commotion.

Suddenly I saw a long, yellowish shape break from the grass and streak across the clearing toward a low scrub tree. Assassino, in pain from the arrow which had been driven through its shoulder, reverted to its first instinct, and ran for the tree.

The *tigre* apparently saw me as it neared the tree, and swerved toward me. I had to release my foot from Tupi's tether, and the dog scampered off to one side, barking with ridiculous futility. I had recovered my spear, and now I was ready to lure the big cat into a charge.

The open area in which Assassino and I faced each other was roughly thirty yards across; and I knew I must keep the cat within that area or my problem would be tremendously complicated. Unfortunately, I had no dogs to carry out that phase of the battle. Tupi was useless; and the *tigre* was so maddened with pain that I knew its actions would be completely unpredictable.

The big cat was weaving back and forth, stepping first in one direction, then reversing. Every so often it would fling its head and let out a snarl that ended in a scream. I edged toward the animal, anxious to get close enough so it would have to charge me. If it should suddenly turn and slink into the tall marsh grass, I would not only lose my advantage with the spear, but I would have no way of following its movements.

As I moved closer, my ears caught the whirr of an *urubi*, apparently lighting on a nearby tree. That vague premonition, which had shadowed my thoughts so ominously, crossed my mind. Perhaps this was the moment of my grim foreboding. Whether it was the sound of the *urubi*, or the morbid fancy that flickered for an instant in my thoughts, my attention was deflected, and the *tigre* chose that instant to charge.

A single second of diverted attention can be fatal in a spear-fight; and this missed being fatal by a single step. I had been caught off guard, and perhaps the cat sensed that momentary lapse. As it lunged toward me, I managed to pivot and drive the spear at the charging animal's neck. The spear did not bite deeply, but it was enough to throw the cat off balance. One paw, cutting through the air, actually grazed my right shoulder, and the force of my side-step threw me off balance. Had the cat swerved toward me, continuing its charge, I doubt if I could have met the attack. But it drew back, possibly from the new pain in its shoulder, and I had a chance to roll over and get on my knees. I still had the spear firmly in both hands, and I rose quickly to meet the next charge.

As I braced myself, I realized that I was rapidly becoming exhausted. There is something in the concentrated effort and the unrelieved tension of a spear-fight that quickly drains the strength. It is the kind of fight that must be finished quickly, because a man cannot physically stand up for any length of time against the greatly superior strength of a big cat.

Assassino also seemed to be drained of strength. As the *tigre* drew back, I saw the great slash I had made in its neck, with blood gushing out; and I knew that if I could stand up to another charge, the cat would not last for more than one more thrust of the spear. I could vaguely hear Tupi's shrill yapping, but this time I dared not let anything deflect my concentration. It seemed to me that Assassino and I had—each of us—one more charge, and whoever stood up to it would be the victor.

The big cat was sideways to me, its head turned and the white teeth flashing, but it did not charge. I could not attack, since he might escape into that tall grass. I was breathing rapidly, and sweat was pouring down my face, almost blinding me, but I could do nothing about that. I tried kicking dirt at the *tigre*, but this had no effect. Suddenly, while I was desperately casting about for some way of provoking a charge, the cat gave a terrible, snarling roar and leaped straight at me.

I barely had time to lift the point of my spear, and then it was a bit too high on the throat. I could feel the hot, foul breath against my face and arms as the spear-head drove into the animal's throat, high over the chest; and for an instant I had the horrifying thought that I had misjudged the distance and was too close to the raking claws.

With every ounce of strength I had left, I rammed the blade deeper into the dying animal's chest. Any other *tigre* I had fought would have had the life drained away by this combination of wounds; but Assassino clawed furiously, even after I had gotten a downward thrust on the spear-head and was literally driving the point into the ground.

I do not know how long this last furious phase of the fight lasted. Perhaps it was only a few seconds. Suddenly I realized that I was grinding the life out of a dead cat. Assassino had gone limp and the great, slashing claws that had ripped the life out of perhaps three or four hundred cattle—and had destroyed all of my hunting dogs except Tupi —were numbed forever.

For a minute I rested on my spear, too exhausted to draw it out of the bloody chest. Tupi, who had retired to the edge of the clearing while the battle raged, now came dancing madly about, as if to claim the kill—an honor I was quite glad to concede. I do not think I have ever been closer to death from a *tigre* than I was during those few seconds before Tupi arrived on the scene.

Later, after I had taken the mangled remains of Jose Ramos to his *rancho* and arranged for the grief-stricken Maria to be taken with her child to the big Fazenda Descalvados, I returned to the scene of the battle. Assassino's carcass was mostly eaten away, but I salvaged the head as a trophy. I measured the torn carcass, and it was a hundred and twelve inches from nose to tail tip—almost ten feet! I could only estimate its weight, but it must have been close to four hundred pounds.

Chapter 24

The spear-fight with Assassino in a sense marked the end of a period in my life in the jungle. During the three years since Apparicio had left, except for the months I was away at São Paulo and in Germany, I was a lone hunter. The feeling that my life might be snuffed out without a trace, which I have described, had become more than merely a solemn and depressing thought during this period. It was on the verge of becoming an obsession.

The fight with Assassino punctuated my thoughts in this regard, as nothing else had. Whether or not it was Tupi who saved my life I will never know, since I have no way of knowing how Assassino would have attacked me. Perhaps I would have killed the *tigre* anyway; or it would have killed me. If I had been killed, it would have been days, perhaps weeks before anyone would have discovered what was left of me. If Maria Ramos should not have survived the ravages of Assassino, no one might have learned of my fate.

The killing of Assassino was in many ways my toughest spear-fight; and it was my last as a lone hunter. I have fought many *tigres* singlehanded since then; but there has always been at least a camp helper, if not a hunting companion, who could report the whereabouts of whatever the *tigre* might have left of me.

It was only a few weeks after the Assassino hunt that the party of amateur adventurers—Urriolagoitia, Duguid and Bee-Mason—came by my camp; and I actually welcomed their suggestion that I join them. They intended to travel from the border of Brazil across the Bolivian Gran Chaco to the foot of the Andes—a five-hundred-mile journey through one of the most dangerous jungle regions in the world, following a route which Nuflo de Chavez, a Spanish Conquistador, had taken four hundred years before. Most of the party, consisting of Spanish soldiers, Jesuit priests and a few ladies, had been killed and quite a few eaten by Indians on the way; and there was very little about the country that was changed since then.

I agreed to meet the party at Lake Gaiba, and we set out from there, on what was unquestionably the most dangerous and probably the most foolhardy trip I had ever undertaken.

It was a party of varying personalities, as interesting in their way as the trip they were taking. Mamerto Urriolagoitia, or "Urrio," as we called him, was a diplomat; Duguid was a young English writer with a thirst for high adventure; and Bee-Mason was a photographer whose bald head and studious countenance belied one of the most adventurous spirits I have known.

We had travelled perhaps a third of the way—pushing ahead on our horses while a wagon brought our equipment and supplies—when we struck a long stretch of almost waterless country, and nearly died of thirst; and a hundred miles beyond this was the northern rim of the Gran Chaco, where we knew our greatest danger lay in the savage Yanaygua Indians.

We got our first advance sketch of this danger from an old Indian postman whom we met on the trail near San Jose de Chiquitos. The old fellow seemed to be cheerfully philosophical about it as he leaned against the wooden saddle of his mule, his sun-withered face wreathed in a grin and a corn-husk cigarette dangling from his broad mouth, and said:

"Good-by, senhors! I will not see you again because you will probably be dead."

As a matter of fact, we did not see him again, and for all I know, he may be dead. He travelled the post trail from San Jose to Santa Cruz de la Sierra, which was our ultimate goal; and in spite of his grin, he was giving us good advice.

We had been told at Lake Gaiba that our chance of getting through was no better than one in ten.

The old postman had told of an experience with the fierce Yanaygua Indians, the most primitive and savage Indians of the Chaco. These bloodthirsty and merciless killers had been driven into the northern Chaco by the war between Paraguay and Bolivia, and while they probably did not understand what the fighting was about, they had been driven from their tribal homes by the soldiers and bore a hatred for all white men.

The old fellow said he had been riding along the trail to Santa Cruz, when he found a large green wigwam, apparently newly built, just off the trail. He stopped to investigate, and almost immediately was surrounded by a mass of naked, dancing figures, brandishing clubs.

"They had some fun with me," the old fellow said, his cigarette dangling from his grinning mouth. "*Dios,* how I sweated! But they were only having a joke, and the women jabbered even more than the men. At last they tore open my pouch and scattered the letters, and I thought I was ready for the pot. But soon they ran away like monkeys."

The Yanayguas are of low mentality, haunting the path of travellers and flitting silently through the trees, invisible to the untrained eye. They will suddenly swarm out upon the unwary victim, jabbering insanely and waving their clubs in an effort to terrify him. As a final touch, they are not only head-hunters but cannibals, and often do not even go through the formality of dispatching their victims before they begin to hack off choice morsels for the pot.

Our plan had been to strike across the jungle, and let our wagon follow more slowly along the Santa Cruz road. However, the postman's story of the Yanayguas indicated that small parties were far more vulnerable than we had thought. So we continued to travel by easy stages, making a rendezvous each night with the wagon, driven by our muleteer, Adolfo, and his helper. Shortly before we reached the stretch where the old Indian postman had found the wigwam, we overtook a two-wagon caravan, led by an eight-bullock team driven by a vigorous old lady, who cracked the bull-whip like a veteran muleteer.

She was taking a load of woolen goods and other material to Cochabamba, southwest of Santa Cruz; and she had two fatherless children with her, a son of about seventeen and another of nine. We camped with the caravan that night, and another travelling east toward Corumbá; and the next morning before dawn they were off again, with a great cracking of whips and snapping of harness.

We followed the post trail west, and perhaps a half-day's ride from the place where we camped, I saw Indian footprints in the sand of a small creekbed. We were riding at distances of a quarter of a mile from each other, and I quickly whistled a sharp blast—a signal we had agreed upon—and waited for the others to ride up.

We were in a long glade, with a line of jungle on each side so dense that it looked like a solid wall; and I realized that the stalking savages might very well be at the edge of the forest, watching us. I also knew the Indians would not attack immediately. They are not cowards, but they are fearful of the strange powers of white men, and would require time to work themselves up to a frenzy.

We rode on, and about two hours before sundown reached an open area with a green wigwam off the trail. I recognized it as the place where the old postman said the Yanayguas "had some fun" with him. The wigwam was made of green poles, slanted together at the top and laced with palm leaves. There were six in our party—Urrio, the two Englishmen, two carriers and myself. One of the carriers jumped off his horse and started toward the wigwam, when I called him back.

Duguid suddenly uttered a small cry, and pointed up the trail. A brown figure flashed from a tree into the depth of the jungle and was immediately swallowed in the darkness.

"My God!" Duguid exclaimed. "It was a woman!"

I saw another brown figure and then a third flash into the forest; and I realized that possibly a dozen or more had been watching us approach the wigwam. The ones we had seen were too far away to get a close look at them, but I doubted if any of them were women.

I called the party together.

"We do not know what the Indians are planning," I said. "They will not attack us at present, and perhaps if we remain together they will not bother us at all. But no one under any circumstances is to go into the forest alone."

We rode on more slowly for perhaps a half-hour, and then I saw a dark spot ahead, lying near the trail. As we approached the place, a lumbering shape detached itself and flopped off, soaring suddenly against the wall of trees and into the blue haze of the sky. Duguid and I spurred forward, and other black shapes flopped away. The *urubú*, as usual, were first on the scene.

The spot turned out to be two oxen. For several seconds not a word was spoken as we looked at the carcasses. It was one of the most horrifying sights I have ever witnessed. They were still warm, and lay in a welter of their own blood. Great strips of skin had been ripped from their backs, apparently while they were still alive from the amount of blood smeared over the hides. The belly of one had been slashed, apparently with jagged stones; the horns had been splintered with rocks that lay near the carcass; and splintered sticks had been thrust into the open stomach. The face of the ox was horribly battered, apparently with rocks, and both hind legs had been broken. It was one of the most savage examples of sheer brutality I have seen, and I felt sick at the agony the animals must have suffered before they died.

I turned to the others. We needed no words to make plain what was in each man's mind. Our fate, in case we were attacked and beaten, would not be much different.

We were able to trace the story of what happened from the tracks around the oxen. They were a few feet from the marks of wagon wheels, and it was apparent the Indians had suddenly attacked the wagon, probably detached the pair from the team while the muleteer was whipping the beasts into a run. The wagon seemed to have gotten away, because the tracks continued beyond the footprints of the savages. The

Yanayguas had then beaten the oxen to death with stones, mutilating them horribly either in sheer fiendish brutality, or in reprisal for the escape of the rest of the ox-team and the wagon.

We held a council of war, and decided to turn back. We had been travelling since noon, but if we headed back at a fairly rapid pace, we might meet our wagon and driver.

Almost at the moment we made our decision, a sudden ripple of noise rose in the jungle. It was not easy to locate or define it. The noise started like a low, muttering whisper, gradually increasing in volume but not in pitch. It was worse on our nerves than screams would have been, like a wave of ghostly small-talk running through the jungle.

I looked at Urrio, and he grinned. It is easy to grin under normal circumstances, but under such conditions it was heroic.

"What do you think of your political future now?" I asked him. He looked at me shrewdly, and his grin broadened.

It was obvious that we would be no match for the Indians if they should attack in numbers. Our chief advantage would be in our wits, not in our guns. An Indian, particularly of the more primitive types, becomes quickly confused by something he does not understand, and unless he is maddened beyond any restraint, he will call off an attack if he is surprised.

We rode on, keeping our horses at a steady pace; and all the while the strange chatter in the jungle continued louder and louder, although still in a guttural pitch.

As we rode down the narrow defile we saw footprints of the Indians, pointing in the direction from which we had been coming; and I realized that we had been riding through a gradually closing trap, sliding silently along the jungle walls, and growing narrower with each mile. The tension was intense, and there must have been an almost uncontrollable desire to whip up our horses and run for it. But this would have been disastrous, since it would have indicated to the Indians exactly what they were looking for: that we were terrified.

"Keep close together," I whispered back to Urrio, who

was riding behind me. "Don't shoot unless they attack. Then shoot as fast as you can."

I glanced back along the trail. Duguid was riding stiffly upright, his usually beaming face now tense, but he managed to nod and smile. Bee-Mason was glancing to one side and the other with his unquenchable curiosity. Urrio's face was set, but calm. I had no fear of the caliber of any of these men.

Without turning my head, I said to Urrio:

"I think they will try to stop us at the end of this glade. We can't stop them all with our guns, so we will stop here to give our horses a rest, and I will tell you what to do."

Urrio passed the word back, and in a few seconds we came to a halt, almost together. If the Indians were ready to attack, they might have struck then; but their psychology, I knew, would be such that unless their own battle frenzy had been reached, they would merely wait.

The sound in the jungle had increased until it was a steady jumble, like a constant overtone of frog-croaking. I knew that perhaps two or three hundred naked savages were trotting through the jungle within a few feet of us, yet there was not a sign of motion. As we drew up our horses, a strange thing happened. The forest suddenly became silent.

"Listen to me carefully," I said, as quietly as I could. "If they are going to attack, they will do it now. Don't fire until I do, and when I fire, shoot at their stomachs. You can stop more of them that way."

Urrio, crouching over the horn of his saddle, looked at me gravely. I don't think he had much confidence in any tactics at this time; but he was a soldier, and he calmly accepted the orders. Bee-Mason was fiddling with a leather thong, and Duguid, sitting upright in his saddle, stared at me.

I nodded toward the narrowing place at the end of the glade, and said:

"They will probably come out there."

As if in response, about a dozen Indians jumped from the trees into the narrow point, perhaps two hundred yards ahead of us. At the same time the chattering was resumed, on a higher key. Some of the sounds became screams, and within a few seconds the noise was deafening. The forest had become a shrill organ of discordant sound, louder than any chorus of howler monkeys I had ever heard.

Suddenly I had an inspiration. I knew that the psychology of the Indians could not stand up against a major surprise. The noise in the woods had levelled off, and I rose in my stirrups and let loose the most piercing jungle call I could summon. I am used to hollering in the forest for my dogs, and to signal others of my party, and my lungs are fairly good.

For a few seconds the noise in the woods wavered, then it stopped. I cut loose with another bellow that rang against the wall of trees. Then I turned to the others and shouted:

"Sing! Sing anything—and make it loud!"

We all began to sing. It was the most tuneless, discordant chorus I have ever heard, Duguid singing "Onward Christian Soldiers," Urrio some Latin love song, and Bee-Mason a robust bar-room ditty, the name and contents of which I have fortunately forgotten.

The group of Indians at the end of the glade seemed to be standing in a huddle, undecided as to what this new activity meant. I raised my rifle and fired into the group. One of the Indians seemed to spurt out of the huddle and pitch to the ground. He lay there, one leg at an angle, and I decided I had hit him in the hip.

Suddenly the others scooped him from the ground and carried him into the forest. The chorus of chattering slowed down and finally stopped. There was not a sound in the jungle around us.

I turned to the others, who had stopped singing, and said:

"Keep on singing! Don't hurry too much—just ride."

We started forward in single file. Urrio's pealing Latin arias soared against the sky, and Bee-Mason continued to batter the jungle walls with an apparently unlimited store of barrack-room ballads. Duguid bellowed "Onward Christian Soldiers" and I sang Russian folk songs.

We continued this weird jungle concert for the better

part of an hour, until we reached the wigwam. There was not an Indian in sight. We rejoined our wagon a few miles beyond, and this closed possibly the most fantastic episode of our trip. We did not see a Yanaygua for the rest of our journey, and ten days later we rode across a muddy Rio Grande river into Santa Cruz.

Chapter 25

It had taken less than two months to cross the Gran Chaco to the Andes; but it was more than a year before I returned to the camp on Ilho do Cara Cara. My first dreams of a motion picture of the Matto Grosso had expanded by this time, and when I returned it was at the head of an "expedition to the Matto Grosso."

This rather ill-fated venture, which I had hoped might miraculously transfer the Matto Grosso to film, was the result of a trip to New York—my first visit to the United States since I left on a freighter bound for Buenos Aires nearly twenty years before.

I had believed that North Americans would be eager to learn of this little-known empire in the heart of Brazil—not a country where white-helmeted hunters travelled on *safari* with squads of native porters and armies of spearmen, but a wilderness of marshlands and jungle, spread over an area as big as the eastern half of the United States, where strange and magnificent animals and brilliantly colored birds lived as they had lived a million years ago.

In the end I realized that I was a jungle hunter, and not a Tarzan; and it was difficult to translate the jungle cunning of Joaquim Guató or the majestic dignity of a *tigre* into cinematic fare for millions of American theatergoers. So I quickly folded my "expedition to the Matto Grosso" and went back to my camp at Ilho do Cara Cara.

I was back in the Xarayes marshes once more, where I remained—except for one small interlude—for nearly ten years. The "small interlude" occurred while I was in Monte-

252

video, awaiting the arrival of camera equipment for the "expedition." I decided on a sudden impulse to visit Buenos Aires and my old shop, *Caras y Caretas*. Actually, I was curious about Elsa. She was the last remaining vestige of my old life, the single memory of the past that remained unfulfilled. Except for Dom Carlos, there was no one else left in my life. How often, during the starry nights when I sat before the fire with my dogs on the jungle trails, had I wondered what had happened to her . . . what she looked like, and above all, whether she still thought of me. Men carry memories, like keepsakes, long after their meaning has died.

I found Hans' address, in a suburb of Buenos Aires known as Quilmes; and when I rang the doorbell, a shy little woman opened the door. She was gray-haired, plump and pleasant; and at first I hardly recognized her. But one thing had not changed: that was her eyes. They were still the same deep blue, shining like stars in the morning sky.

"Yes, what is it?" she asked in a voice in which there were still traces of a German accent.

Then she stared at me an instant, and said: "*Gott*— Alex!"

I smiled and we shook hands. It was a strange meeting, after seventeen years. In a short while Hans came in, and greeted me with his usual heartiness. He was older and had grown heavy; otherwise he was unchanged. We talked awkwardly at first, then some of the stiffness disappeared, and Elsa laughed merrily when I told her of the time I shot a *coati* and thought I had killed twenty with a single bullet.

After I left, and was on my way back into town, I thought of Dom Carlos' rather grim advice: "Go back and die with your animals . . ."

As I have said, I am not given to brooding or melancholy thinking. A man cannot live actively and think morbidly. But I wondered if something had not been left out of my life . . . something I should have. Ernst had gone, and although he was not close to me when he died, there had been a bond between us . . . Apparicio had left; and Joaquim, and Valente . . . and now Elsa was no longer even a memory for me. I thought it would have been better if I had not gone to see her . . .

It was seven years later, in February of 1938, that I lectured in Philadelphia one night. It was a good crowd, and I showed them my film: "Getting the Killer." It was my own story of *tigre* killing—not a sport, but a necessary job, to rid cattle ranchers of the Matto Grosso of their worst enemies, the jungle prowlers which sometimes destroy many thousands of cattle a year on a single ranch.

I had explained how I killed these marauders. In the tall marsh grass, a rifle is useless because the target cannot be seen. Only a hunter who can kill with the *zagaya*, or with a bow and arrow, can track them and destroy them. I showed pictures of my dogs—Vinte and Pardo from the old pack; another Tupi—not the one Senhor Oliveira had given me; Raivoso, Amigo and Leon; and I told how we tracked the *tigre*.

After the lecture I was introduced by Pleny Hartenstein, the manager of the University Club of Philadelphia, to his wife, a charming, brunette girl; and to a young girl with them, Edith Bray. She was twenty, and had finished school only the year before.

"It was splendid, Mr. Siemel," she said, regarding me with deep brown eyes, in which there was the faint suggestion of a smile. "We are quite gullible here in Philadelphia, you know—we are quite glad to believe anything."

"Edith!" Mrs. Hartenstein exclaimed. I found out later that Edith Bray was her sister, although I did not know it at the time.

I was amused; and I asked the young lady how she had become such an expert on *tigre* fighting.

"Obviously you have killed these jaguars, Mr. Siemel," she said. "But killing them with a spear—when you could use a rifle—is a little fanciful, don't you think?"

I was surprised, and a little annoyed, at her skeptical attitude. She was a straight, sturdy girl, and probably used to a certain amount of outdoor life; but I doubted if she had hunted anything. I asked her if she had.

254

"Of course not," she said. "I don't like to kill animals."

I explained to Miss Bray that I also did not like to kill animals; and that my hunting was to destroy a kind of animal murderer, in the same way a policeman might shoot a human killer. She agreed with this, although I was sure she did not understand it; and for perhaps an hour we sat in the club and talked. Finally, she said:

"Mr. Siemel, do you ever have women at your hunting camp?"

For several years I had conducted hunting parties in the Matto Grosso; and as a matter of fact, on two occasions there were women in the hunting parties whom I would have gladly exchanged for a *tigre* as a hunting companion. But these are things a professional hunter cannot talk about; he must accept the "sporting spirit" of his client at face value, and hope for the best.

"Are you thinking of going to the Matto Grosso to hunt?" I asked, with some amusement.

"Yes," she replied, seriously. "I am."

I thought little more of what the girl said, until the following week, when I received a telephone call in New York. It was Miss Bray, and she asked if I could arrange with another woman hunter to make up a party on the Rio Miranda, where I then had my camp.

I was surprised at the request; and I still did not take the young lady seriously. But I immediately telephoned an old friend of mine, Helen Post, who had done some publicity work for me, and asked her if she would like to satisfy a long-suppressed desire to come down to the Matto Grosso. I gave her Miss Bray's address and thought no more about it.

I left for Brazil in May; and it was two months later that I got a message one day from the captain of the little mail launch from Corumbá. Edith Bray and Helen Post were in Rio awaiting my instructions for getting to the camp.

A week later I met them at Miranda, on the São Paulo railroad, and brought them by ox-cart to my camp at Aquiduana. I had been looking forward with a kind of suppressed horror to the next few weeks. Two women in a hunter's camp would be bad enough; but in Edith Bray I expected a woman who would challenge every decision I made, argue with my boys, Lauro and Rosenda, and probably sue me when it was over for failing to lead a *tigre* into camp so she could shoot it from her hammock.

I was not quite certain what to expect, but I intended to find out without delay how Miss Bray reacted to camp life. So I arranged a hunting party the second day after their arrival. We were to start at four o'clock in the morning.

Both girls were awake at three. I had told Lauro to prepare a hot breakfast at three-thirty and both girls ate ravenously. We started with three dogs, and an hour before dawn the dogs crossed a puma track. Mutuca, the leader, broke into an excited bark; and I signalled with my flashlight for the girls to keep close to me to avoid getting lost in the shadow light of early morning.

The puma had taken to a tree, and within a few seconds the dogs were circling around the tree—a low, branching *piuva*. I pulled up within fifty feet of the place. Edith Bray had brought her camera, and she whispered to me that she wanted to take a picture. This meant at least a half-hour wait until it was light enough, so we settled ourselves.

When the sun's rays were slanting through the trees, catching the little cat in a blaze of gold, I motioned to the girl to take her picture. She did; and then I passed my Winchester across to her. She shook her head.

"I don't want to shoot him—he looks so beautiful."

From somewhere behind I heard a low chuckle from Helen Post. I explained quietly, and with as much courtesy as I could muster, that the puma was a destroyer of stock, and one of the rare beasts of the jungle who kill merely for the sake of killing. In Patagonia, I told her, a puma—or mountain lion, as it is known in North America—was known to have killed eighty sheep in a single night.

"They are cowards," I whispered. "They run away from human beings."

"All right," she said. "If that's the sort of fellow he is, I'll shoot."

256

She raised the gun and while I was preparing to advise her just what spot to aim at, she fired. The puma rolled off the limb and tumbled to the ground in a lifeless heap.

Without glancing at me—or apparently even worrying whether the shot had taken effect—the girl reloaded the gun. Then she handed it to me and turned and walked back to her horse.

I followed, after directing Lauro to bring the kill into camp. As I mounted my horse, I could not miss Helen Post's grin.

Chapter 26

The first days at Aquiduana became a kind of mild purgatory. Edith Bray baffled me. She was a scant twenty; but she had a certain sureness that was surprising, and frequently annoying. The girls I had seen in the Matto Grosso were sloe-eyed and docile; they lived by the whims of men, and they obeyed the orders of their men without a murmur of protest.

This slender, sober-eyed girl was different; but I was not certain in exactly what way she was different.

She asked me many questions about the animals—how they lived, which ones were fiercest, and which could be domesticated or trained. She wanted to know a great deal about wild life, including the birds and plants. I could not decide whether she wished to learn of these things, or merely had an insatiable curiosity.

One day we caught a tiny puma cub, and Edith brought it into camp.

"I will keep it for a pet!" she announced. "It is so soft and cuddly—I'm sure it will make a darling pet."

I explained with patience that the little cub had thousands of generations of ancestors who had killed for food and killed to survive; and it would take more than one generation of human love to change this instinct.

"You have hunted too long," she said tartly. "You are callous. You have no feeling for the animals."

I said nothing in reply; but I was thoroughly angry. In all my hunting, I have never killed an animal unnecessarily; and I have followed the trail of a wounded swamp deer for miles to put it out of its misery rather than leave it a helpless prey for beasts who could kill it. This strip of a girl had the effrontery to tell me I was "callous."

Helen Post observed the development of this mild feud with keen amusement.

"Don't make up your mind too quickly about Edith," she said to me one night when we were sitting alone. "I travelled with her for three weeks coming down here. She likes wild life, and I think she can take it. But she really hates to kill things."

Our camp, which we called "Toro Morto" (dead bull) was set in a grove of *acuri* palms overlooking the Miranda. The dark, turgid surface wound like a coiled snake through the flat marshlands and jungle; and from a huge wild fig tree that rose from the bank of the river, we could survey hundreds of square miles of green jungle roof. One evening I walked over to where Edith was standing, gazing at this enormous expanse, her brown eyes glowing in the fading light of the sun.

"How would you like to go out for a *tigre?*" I asked.

Her face lighted up.

"Of course! Can I take my camera?"

"It will be a day's ride from here," I told her. "You are a good rider—I have seen that. If we leave at daybreak tomorrow, we can be at the hunting place near São Ignacio by nightfall."

Both girls were eager for the hunt. Lauro had brought me word from a *vaquero* of the Estancia Miranda, the big cattle ranch for which I worked as a hunter when there were no "customers" in camp, that a big cat had been spotted in that area.

We left at daylight, Edith and Helen riding two excellent horses that Lauro had brought from the *fazenda* for them; and Lauro and I on our mounts, with camp equipment which included mosquito nets and hammocks. We made camp late in the afternoon, and prepared to start before daybreak the next day.

Mutuca was my master-dog. The name in Portuguese means "horse fly"; and the dog was called Mutuca in tribute to its courage, because a horse fly will bite anything. There were three other dogs in the pack; and as we set out on horseback, the four dogs started swiftly as if they had already picked up the scent.

Edith was a good horsewoman; she knew how to ride and how to save her mount. Helen was also experienced, and I had little difficulty directing them; so I let the dogs out and we covered several miles in the first hour. Finally I realized from the worried barking of the dogs that they had crossed the scent in some way, and I rode ahead to cut them off. They had lost the *tigre* and were now trailing a swamp deer.

Mutuca looked at me guiltily, and I cuffed him slightly, admonishing him a bit. He cocked his head as if to say "We all make mistakes, master—just give me another chance!"

I glanced up and saw Edith looking down at me, laughing.

"He looks as if he could talk," she said.

"He can," I replied rather drily, remounting. "But a man has to understand his language."

She looked at me, as if she were not quite sure whether to be angry or amused. We started off again at a slower pace, and in a few minutes Mutuca's steady bay informed me he was on the track again. The brush was thick in the high ground, clawing at our clothes as we rode through; but soon the trail descended to a low, swampy area, where there were fewer thickets and more grass.

"Keep close to me!" I called to Edith. "You will have to shoot your picture quickly if we come up to the cat. I can't risk my dogs."

We rode through a clearing, with little brush on the ground, but covered by low, overhanging branches. Suddenly I spotted the dogs ahead, snarling at the base of a *piuva* tree. An instant later I saw the cat, crouched in the fork of one of the heavy branches, about twenty feet off the ground.

"You haven't time for the camera," I whispered sharply to Edith. "Get your gun ready—it will be your first shot."

She looked at me with startled eyes.

"Can't I have the picture?" she asked.

"No—the cat is ready to move now."

My voice was probably sharp, because I was afraid for the dogs. If the *tigre* came off the branch it might take one or more of the dogs with a sweep of its razor-sharp claws. I was quickly unstrapping my spear.

"Make it a good shot!" Possibly I spoke with more than necessary rudeness. Edith had tucked her camera away and already had her rifle out. I glanced at her, and her mouth was drawn in a tight line. I realized, with some surprise, that she was not at all frightened; she was mad.

"Take your damned picture!" I whispered across the few feet separating us. "I'll try to make him come at me if he jumps."

At that instant the *tigre* launched itself in a perfect arc, but in a direction away from us. It was a magnificent sight, and I saw Edith drop the point of her gun and stare at the great spotted beast as it loped off toward a heavy bank of marsh grass, perhaps two hundred yards away.

I had no time for further instructions. I waved to the girl to follow me and started across the clearing. If the *tigre* should turn into the swamp, we would lose it. But it leaped into another tree at the rim of the swamp, and turned to regard us balefully, its tail swishing slowly back and forth. Its round eyes seemed to be studying us, with more curiosity than malice.

"Shoot now—and for heaven's sake shoot straight!" I called to Edith. I could hear the slap of her boots behind me; and I knew Lauro and Helen were too far to one side to be of any use at the moment. I snatched my pistol from my holster as I ran, and was holding both the pistol and the spear, one in each hand. We were perhaps fifty feet from the branch where the big cat crouched, dividing his attention between the dogs and ourselves, when I signalled with my hand for Edith to take her shot.

I quickly leveled my pistol, and had the *tigre* in my sights, when I heard the crash of Edith's rifle. The *tigre* began to topple from the branch, and from the way it fell, landing on its feet, I realized it was wounded but not dying.

I did something then that in more than a quarter of a century of hunting I have never done before or since. Possibly the exchange of rather sharp words between Edith and myself during the excitement of bringing the cat to bay had jarred my normal thinking habits. Whatever the reason, I shoved my cocked pistol back into the holster and snatched my spear and started forward.

Something snagged my side—probably the branch of a tree—and the next instant I heard a sharp report at my side and felt as if someone had smashed me across my lower leg with a club. I almost pitched forward from the effects of the blow, going all the way to my knees; but I managed to pick myself up and kept on toward the *tigre*, which was now back on its haunches, slapping its great spiked claw at the dogs. At that instant, I realized I had shot myself through the leg with my pistol.

I can remember thinking: "I can still run—so the leg cannot be broken."

The *tigre* was badly wounded, but still had a good deal of fight; and I knew that in a matter of seconds one of those flailing paws would catch one of the snarling dogs, jumping closer and closer to the hurt animal. The *tigre* made a last desperate effort to come off the ground at me, and I drove the spear through its throat. Fortunately, there was little fight left in the cat. Within a few seconds it was all over. The *tigre* made one twisting slap at the spear and then relaxed. And so did I.

The next thing I saw was Edith's face in a receding haze above me. She was mopping my forehead with a wet handkerchief while Helen and Lauro were cutting away the high leather top of my right boot.

I was able to get on my horse, and we started back for the camp. Edith rode on one side and Helen on the other; and I remember noticing that Edith hardly spoke as we rode, but watched me intently, probably to detect any signs that I might pass out again and perhaps fall off the horse. Meanwhile Helen told me that the bullet had gone clear through my leg—and from the fact that I had been able to leap toward the cat with my spear, I knew it could not have shattered the bone.

The two-hour ride to the camp became an increasing inferno of pain and shock. I felt at times as if I were slipping from reality, and had to clutch the pommel of my saddle to keep from falling off. In my hazy thoughts, I had only one fixed idea: I, the great hunter, had been floored by a stupid blunder for which I would have discharged one of my camp helpers. I had shoved a cocked revolver into my holster.

The galling knowledge of my own stupidity was only exceeded in the pain of my recollections by the fact that this strip of a girl had been a witness to the event.

In my half-delirious thoughts, as I bounced and joggled over the trail, I tried to find some semblance of excuse for what had happened. She had been pestering me about her camera . . . the dogs were in danger . . . her first shot had not killed the cat. But it was no use. Her shot had been fired just before I had shoved the loaded and cocked pistol into my holster. I had no possible excuse.

By the time we reached camp I was only half-conscious, due to the pain in my wounded leg; and if I had been given any choice in the matter, I would have rendered myself totally unconscious to avoid the humiliating realization that was coursing through my mind. For the first time in my life I felt like a fool in front of a woman.

We remained at São Ignacio overnight. I was becoming slightly delirious from the increasing heat of the wound and the loss of blood. Helen later told me the blood had been bubbling from my boot top when I toppled over, almost on top of the dying *tigre*; and Edith had ripped off her shirt sleeve and made a tourniquet as soon as they had cut away the leather legging.

The next day was another jolting horror, this time on an ox-cart, in which they had strung a hammock. The girls rode beside the cart at first; and then they tied their horses' lead ropes to the cart and climbed in beside me, each holding one side of the hammock to keep my body from bumping against the walls of the cart. We were riding over ant-hill country, and the broad wheels of the heavy cart rumbled over these mounds without particular regard for my comfort.

We reached Toro Morto by mid-afternoon, and after that I remember very little until I opened my eyes—apparently a couple of days later—and thought I was seeing a ghost. Apparicio stood beside my bed, his thin features wrinkled in a smile.

"You are alive again, eh, Senhor Alexandre?" He laid his brown hand across my forehead, and nodded. "You had a bad fever, but now it is gone."

Later I learned that Apparicio had heard the report of my wound at a ranch some miles upriver, and had ridden immediately to the Miranda Estancia and then to Toro Morto.

When I had recovered sufficiently to use my legs, I walked with Apparicio down to the edge of the river, and we both looked in silence across the jungle we knew so well. Finally he told me about Mariinha. They had been married, and had three children; but finally the closed life of a cowman had eaten into his spirit, and he had left her and the children on a big *fazenda* where they could have a home.

Edith was coming down the pathway from the camp to warn me against over-taxing my bad leg.

She reached down, unceremoniously hauled up the leg of my trousers and examined the bandage. Then she laid the back of her hand against my forehead. She glanced at Apparicio, and actually winked.

"Don't let him have your gun, Mr. Pinheiro," she said. "He might get careless and shoot himself in the other leg— and he's such a bear about it, I don't think we could stand it."

Apparicio laughed; and after Edith had gone back up the hill, he turned to me and said gravely:

"Now it is I who am coming back to ride over our trails through the forest again, Senhor Alexandre. But I think perhaps I will ride alone, eh?"

Epilogue

It was four years later—in September of 1942—that I made my last base camp in the Matto Grosso. We had brought our houseboat up the Rio Miranda, and had moored it below a magnificent bank of purple and scarlet and varying shades of green, that hung like an immense drapery along the steep bank of the river. This was Barranco Vermelho—the "Red Cliffs"; and it was alive with an orgy of color, from the scorched rust-colored soil at the base of the river bank to the great purple crown of *piuva*, rising above us on the rim of the embankment.

Edith was with me. We had been married in Rio in January of 1940, during her second trip to the Matto Grosso. We had brought our floating house downriver from Descalvados, with our two children—Sandra and Dora; and three years later our third "jungle baby," Sashino, was to be born at Barranco Vermelho.

As we moored *Siemel's Ark* at the foot of the cliffs, and I climbed the bank to survey our new home, I thought of the old one-eyed thief-taker of Passo Fundo, when he had looked at me with that solitary and seemingly omniscient eye, and said:

"Go with God, my son—and perhaps he will find some new kind of brute for you to challenge. Perhaps a woman, eh? . . . who will be as good a hunter as you are! Only she will use different weapons."

I glanced down at the slender figure in bluejeans and khaki shirt, her hair bound in a crimson kerchief that made her look like a river pirate, as she bustled the children off the barge—and while the word "brute" was not quite the word I would have used (not to Edith's face, at least) I marvelled at the uncanny prescience of old Dom Carlos.

And I could not help looking southward in the direction of the Rio Grande do Sul, more than a thousand miles away, and wondering if the white-haired old man was still sitting in his *patio*, rubbing his dog's neck . . . and I silently thanked him for having guided me at last to my jungle home.